BORN INTO FIRE

THE AUTOBIOGRAPHY OF
MICK HAINES

authorHOUSE®

AuthorHouse™ UK Ltd.
500 Avebury Boulevard
Central Milton Keynes, MK9 2BE
www.authorhouse.co.uk
Phone: 08001974150

First published by AuthorHouse 7/30/2010

ISBN: 978-1-4520-4628-0 (sc)

This book is printed on acid-free paper.

Cover photograph: Anne Parker.
www.anneparkerphotography.co.uk

ACKNOWLEDGEMENTS

My thanks to those of you who have assisted me in my life story that has resulted in this book. There is no order of priority that I have put the acknowledgements, just to all that I felt deserved one. To Janice for her memory capability about all the times we were together. Tracy for our happy years and her assistance. Particularly for Austin and Steve for what they did that night when we where at the Borough. To all my family for their help and their useful input. Tony for all you have done for my Ma and me. Anne for her help with the photographs. To Poppy for putting up with the long, book-bound silences when I was upstairs in the office. Simon and Alison for their friendship and also their memory which assisted me. Nicola for getting back in touch after all those years. Most of all to Ma who has helped me through many difficult times.

PREFACE

This book is not just a story about my time in the Fire Service, although a lot of that is obviously included. It is the story of my life and tells how my time in the military and the Fire Service affected it. I would just like to say here that in the book I have said Fireman throughout and not Firefighter. The reason for this is just that when I joined the Fire Service there were only Firemen and not any female Firefighters. This is because things have changed a lot since I joined the Fire Service, and it is in no way disrespectful or derogatory to anyone who was in, or is in the Fire Service. It was just for consistency throughout the book. Thank you for buying this book. A good book tells the truth about the hero, but a bad book tells the truth about its author. Not that I think I am a hero of any shape or form! I am just a normal chap who was in the Fire Service, so I hope you enjoy reading it as much as I enjoyed writing it.

CONTENTS

CHAPTER ONE

EARLY DAYS

I was born on the forth of April 1962, and it may well have been the circumstances of my arrival that influenced my mind as to the career path that I would take later in life. I arrived in the back of an ambulance on the way to Wokingham general Hospital and perhaps it was the flashing blue lights at the time that were firmly printed on my mind that influenced me to make me choose my calling. I was the last of five children born to Ma and though I hate to say it, not one of the planned ones! She told me later on when I was somewhat older that after the forth baby she said that she would have no more. Perhaps that is what influenced her in someway and why I was loved by my mother. Or, perhaps it was the fact that she lost one of her offspring even before I was born, baby Paul who died aged two, and maybe I was looked upon as the unexpected replacement for the loss. I experienced sudden and unexpected fame at my untimely arrival while in transit in the ambulance and the local press reported the story accordingly. The greatest pleasure in life is doing things that people say you cannot do, so I decided to arrive anyway! The paper cutting from the Bracknell Mirror reads as follows:

BRACKNELL MIRROR
APRIL 5TH 1962

BABY BORN IN AMBULANCE

A Bracknell man and his wife delivered their baby boy yesterday (Wednesday) – as an ambulance driver, rushing them to hospital, shouted

instructions through the cab window. And after the drama which started at 1.30 yesterday morning, 30-year-old Mrs. Shirley Haines, of Basemoors, Bullbrook, and the baby were doing fine. Mr. Alan Haines, 29-years-old machine tool worker at Sperry's told the *Mirror* yesterday of the ambulance dash and of the "anxious moments" he and his wife spent in the back of the ambulance. "The driver shouted to me through the window and told me where the emergency kit was and how to use it." said Mr Haines, "but I didn't do anything really." The *Mirror* understands that no nurse accompanied Mrs Haines in order to save time. The baby was born between Bracknell and Wokingham. "We were going to a hospital at Reading," said Mr Haines, "but when it got rather urgent the driver decided to stop at Wokingham Maternity Hospital." Mrs Haines was brought home by her husband yesterday because of the shortage of beds at the Wokingham Hospital. The couple have three other children. They were staying with friends.

So there we are! Having spoken to Ma about this, she informed me that it was in front of The Three Frogs pubic house I arrived. How she knows that I do not know. At the time of writing this by doing a little research I found out that the Three Frogs is on the London Road Wokingham.

The place that I was to spend the early years of my life was on an estate in the town of Bracknell Berkshire. The lovely council estate was called Basemoors. I do not have any bad memories of this place apart from the time that my older brother Conrad, the eldest of the four, broke his arm while trying to show off on my much loved red tricycle. Conrad took it to the top of the hill and was spinning down trying to show off to all the other estate kids. "Look I am steering with my feet!" The bike swerved into the curb and threw my brother over the handlebars. Serves him right! It was my bike!

In the summer weekends and holiday times we as a group of kids used to go to a place not far from the estate which was known to us as Franties Wood. Having done some research into this in modern times, I can find no reference to a place anywhere near Basemoors that is known as Franties Wood. It could be that the original place known to us in the mid to late sixties could have been Lilly Hill Park. That is a place that would be about right geographically from Basemoors. Perhaps I shall never know....

Another thing we used to do when I was very young, about three years old, was that the whole family would go swimming in an old quarry called Binfield Brickworks. Ma would pack up some picnic lunch and we would get on the bikes and off we would go. My elder brother and sisters, Conrad, Sarah and

Valerie would ride their own bikes and me, being so young could not ride a two wheeled bike would be transported in a wooden box on the back of Ma's bike. We would spend the whole day at the disused brickworks playing in and around the water. At the time of writing this I was reliably informed by Ma that the brickworks no longer exists and had now been built on to make a housing estate. What a shame!

Here are us four kids left to right; Conrad, me, Valerie and Sarah

Another memory that seems to stick in my mind from those early days in Bracknell was the time that a pidgin with a broken wing was adopted and lived in our shed for a long time. Well, it seemed like a long time to me, but perhaps it was just that I was only about four or five then, and when you are young, time passes slowly. Where the pidgin came from I do not know, perhaps it crash landed in the garden, or was struck by a speeding Tonibell ice-cream van. What I do know is that for a period of time it was in the shed and that someone used to feed it and make sure that it had some water.

When I went into the shed the pidgin used to panic, and flap about a lot, but never actually got airborne! I grew much attached to that pidgin and then one day suddenly it was gone. I was devastated! I never actually found out what happened to the pidgin. I like to think that the poor bird recovered from its injuries and was released to flap away into the blue sky and freedom to continue a long existence. However, realistically the chances are it either died through natural causes, or was topped off, and ended up in the kitchen pot. Money was tight for a family of six living off one income in the sixties.

After leaving Sperry's my father worked for an ice cream firm which was called Tonibell. He was not one of the vendors from the back of the vans, but one of the refrigeration engineers at the plant which was somewhere in the Bracknell area. The reason that I can remember this from such and early age is that my father Alan used to come home from work often carrying small gifts for the children, picture cards and other things that were used for promotion of the Tonibell products.

My grandmother and grandfather on my mother's side lived at the other end of the county in a small and picturesque village called Sparsholt. My grandfather used to drive over from Sparsholt to Bracknell to pick up the children that were coming to stay with him and my grandmother for a period of time during the school holidays. Although of course I was not attending school at that time being too young. As I remember grandfather drove a Morris Minor, and for us children it was a real treat to travel across the county in the car, something that did not happen on a frequent basis. Back in those times to ride in a car was like being a prince. The cottage that they lived in was a lovely place, an old fashioned black and white cottage that had a thatched roof, uneven floors and a circular stair case. The cottage is located in a lane called Watery Lane. The lane is a quiet and peaceful road which terminated in open fields, so obviously there was not a lot of traffic passing by! We loved it there.

The house that they lived in had a large garden that gradually sloped up in a gentle rise to terminate backing onto open fields. The garden was extremely well looked after by my grandparents there were lots of fruit trees of different types, and in the summer months the garden would be full of vegetables and also a large variety of different flowers. At the top of the garden was a large deciduous tree that my older brother Conrad would like to climb. Of course I worshiped my older brother and anything that he could do, I could do. Or thought so! There were a number of occasions I climbed that tree, but unfortunately I would lose my courage when up high in the tree and freeze there and be unable to climb down. At times like that Con would have to climb up and help me down which I found most embarrassing!

When I was four years old I went out to play with Con. Now, Con was not too happy about the fact that I used to come out to play with him, the reason being that he is seven years older that me and he at eleven years old was not keen on the idea of a four year old 'tagging along'. However, he was told that he had to let me tag and long and to keep and eye out for me.

On one occasion we met up with some of the boys who lived further up Watery Lane. We all ended up in a barn at the rear of the Post Office shop in the village. The barn was about half full of bales of straw and there was a wooden beam that stretched across above the bails. They all thought that it was great fun to climb up the bails to the beam and then to dive off the beam, do a somersault onto your back into the straw strewn on the floor of the barn. If my big brother could do that, so could I, right? We spent some time somersaulting off the beam and landing on our backs in the straw. Strangely enough the next day I had a terrible back ache and could not go out. Ma was there with us on at that occasion at our grandparent's house and asked me what I had been doing yesterday and I told her about our activity in the barn and she was furious. Waving her finger at me she said "You are lucky that you had not broken your neck! Don't you ever do that again!"

When we were back at Bracknell it was in 1966 that Con went off to live with his Father and step Mother and left us all at Basemoors. My mother had stopped it happening earlier because she said that he had to stay at the school

5

he was at until he had done his eleven plus exam and was ready for secondary school. Being so young then I was devastated, I couldn't understand why my brother Con had gone away and why he wasn't coming back. Ma felt at the time that it was not correct to tell a young boy about these things that go on, so I didn't find out until later. Con never came back to live with us and I missed my big brother Con terribly.

At the times when I was very young and staying with my grandparents, my inventor grandfather made us a go-cart out of wood. It was like a box on wheels with and extension to the front with which you could steer it with a piece of rope. We loved the go-cart and used to take it to the top of Watery Lane and then run down the lane in our beloved blue go-cart and here it is.

Can you spot me? I am the one sitting in the box of the go-cart.

In 1968 when I was six my family moved away from Bracknell to Childrey, another village which is only a mile from Sparsholt where our grandparent's house was. The only member of the family not to move there was my brother Con obviously because he had already gone to live with his father from Ma's first marriage. The first house at Childrey that the family lived in was called Chapel House and was located in the middle of the village near to the village duck pond.

I remember the duck pond very well due to the fact that I seemed to possess a unique tendency or practice of falling into the pond on a regular basis. Village ponds are a magnet for attracting young boys who love to go and play near, or in my case 'in' the pond. During the warmer weather we liked to play 'ships' with bits of wood and during cold weather in winter if the duck pond was frozen, which it did quite often in the winter months we would go and skate. However, quite often the ice was not thick enough in all places to hold the weight of the skater and again this often resulted in a ducking for the person concerned. The pond was not particularly deep therefore not really a danger of drowning to the unexpected swimmer, but it was rather muddy on the bottom and it did Pen and Ink! (Stink.) This was probably due to all the duck poo. Ma later told me that on one occasion after a ducking I returned home and she told me to strip off all my clothes outside the back door, which I did. I then said to my mother "look Ma it was a good job I had my clothes on because they have kept my skin clean!" Never the less I was still dumped straight in the bath.

Another funny thing that happened at this time was when I first learned to ride a two wheeled bicycle. (I don't know what happened to my red tricycle?) Ma and grandma took me up the bridle-path and Ma said "If you don't learn to ride that thing today I am going to throw it out!" (I think she was fed up with having to push it for me!) So I put a big effort in to learn to ride it. On the way back down the bridle-path Ma tells me that wobbling around somewhat on the bike, I disappeared into the distance. Ma said to her mother "Well he must be getting on alright with it." They walked down the path a bit further wondering where I had gone to, and then suddenly I sprang out of a ditch from under a bush waving my arms and shouting "I CAN RIDE MY BIKE! I CAN RIDE MY BIKE!" I was obviously overjoyed at my achievement. There was no sign of the bicycle itself, and I was informed by Ma at the time of writing this that it was lying in the ditch with the front wheel caved in! I obviously couldn't ride it very well.

When we were living at Chapel House in Childrey Sarah who was twelve at the time left us, as had Con, and went to live with her father. Again I was not very happy about this either, and that meant that just Valerie and I were left living at Chapel House with Ma and our father. My father Alan was not very impressed that Sarah had gone to live with her father as my father was very fond of Sarah and would rather have had it that she stayed with us.

There was one time that he went to see them and did so without telling Ma and she only found out later. Sarah and Conrad's father did not have a telephone in those days so that's why my father went to see them. Their father told them not to open the door to Alan, so he had to speak to them through the letter box. My father told them that if they ever wanted to come back and live with us they were free to do so.

About this time Ma went to see a solicitor about the situation, as she too wanted Conrad and Sarah to come back and live with all of us as we all did. The solicitor seemed like a smart cookie because he told Ma to play it cool. Don't go creating waves as this could make the situation worse. Well, it transpired that he was right later on, but more about that at the appropriate time.

We didn't live long at Chapel House only for about a year. It was a change in circumstances that made us move into another house which was only about three doors away. Ma had taken a job with a company located in the village called Turner and Price. T. & P.'s we called them. I think it was because they were a tea import business 'Tea' and Peas, and mother worked for them as the company secretary. The house that we moved into was owned by the company and provided much cheaper accommodation for the family, so we moved into Findon Cottage.

It was about this time that I started my formal education at the primary school in the village. The school had its own open air swimming pool which was something of a rarity back in those days. It was in this school pool that I learned how to swim something other than doggy paddle in the village pond. Whilst attending the village school I met my first friend. He was a lad who was attending the school whose name was Jimmy. Jimmy was one of a large family that lived in a house in Sparsholt which was not far from my Grandparent's house. Jimmy and I were inseparable. We did everything together both in school time and out of school time. During weekends and holidays I would be either staying with my Grandparent's and spending the days playing with Jimmy or, I would cycle the mile from Childrey to Sparsholt to play with Jimmy.

Strangely enough our favourite pastime was to play Robin Hood and his merry men, as I am sure a lot of young boys did back then. I would be Robin and he would be Little John or vice versa. This of course involved the making of lots of bows and arrows and this pastime was very time consuming as it is quite hard to make a good bow and arrow with only the use of a penknife as a tool. One time at the end of one of the long hot summers probably when we were eight or nine, Jimmy and I were scrumping apples from an orchard which is located at the top of Watery lane. (Scrumping is a colloquial term for stealing fruit.) A man appeared and shouting up at us as we were up in the tree he said "What do you lads think you are doing here and who are you?" I called back to him "I am Robin Hood and he is Little John!" Then as fast as we possibly could, we jumped out of the tree, and carrying our hand made weaponry and some nice fresh apples we disappeared faster than a puff of smoke.

Life in the holidays at the Grandparent's house was good. Jimmy and I would go wandering off all over the surrounding countryside and return home only at meal times. How we knew that it was meal time is a mystery to me. We did not possess a watch between us, but somehow we always managed to arrive home at the correct time for dinner and tea. My Grandmother would cook the most delicious meal for us that kept us strong, fit and healthy. The one desert that particularly sticks out in my mind is the syrup pudding and custard. Absolutely delicious!

Another game we used to play at the end of the summer was stubble fights. When all the corn and wheat had been cut down in the fields by the Combine Harvesters and bailed up. We would build forts out of the bails and then make 'bombs' by pulling up the stubble and forming it into a grenade by squeezing the mud into a lump. Then with our 'ammo' we would attack each others fort and throw the stubble at each other. There was never any winner or loser, it was just good fun which us young lads enjoyed.

Within the mile long push bike ride from Childrey to Sparsholt was a short, but steep hill that we knew to be called Sneed's hill. At the time the bike that I possessed was a small twenty inch wheel bike which had no rear brake. (I CAN RIDE MY BIKE!) On one occasion Valerie and I were cycling to our Grandparent's house and a decision was made that we would spin down the hill and there would be no stopping or braking on the way down. After gathering quite a lot of speed, about half way down the hill my courage failed me and panicking I jammed on the one and only front brake. The result was that I flew over the handle bars and knocked myself senseless on the tarmac. I don't know how long I was out for the count. Possibly for some time. The lesson to learn there is not to have a push bike that does not have a rear brake!

Down at Sparsholt when I was there some interesting things went on. Well they were interesting to a young boy like me! My inventor Grandfather worked under contract for a firm the name of which escapes me. While not at work, he would carry on working on his projects in the workshop that was next to the house. I used to go in there to see my Grandfather on some occasions to see what he was doing. I have no idea what most of the projects were that he worked on in there, but one of the most well known things that my Grandfather came up with is the one thing that anyone would see if they were to go into a public house or perhaps a restaurant. That is the device that is fitted to a bottle and measures one sixth of a gill of any spirit on sale in the premises. It is unfortunate that my Grandfather worked under contract for the company at the time, as it would have made a large difference to the family income if he had benefited from the patent of the device himself!

Life was good in the days of living at Childrey, apart from the occasional ducking in Childrey village duck pond. Obviously I missed my brother Con and sister Sarah, but other than that things were pretty good. On a weekday, once school had finished, Valerie and I would go and see Ma in the office at T. & P.'s and she would give us a thrupenny bit each, or sixpence to share and we would go to the one and only village shop located next to Chapel House and buy some sweets.

As I grew up there and got a bit older, another activity that we kids would like to get involved in was visits to the Holloway. The Holloway is located on the approach road into the village. It was a popular place for youngsters to play when they were not attending school. The Holloway was a wooded area that steeply banked down to the road, and an excellent place for making rope swings and playing kiss chase with the local girls! There was many a happy after school hour spent performing on the rope swing to impress the girls and then chasing the one that particularly took your fancy in kiss chase. I won't embarrass the girls concerned by mentioning any names here, but if they were to read this book I think they would know who they are, because I can certainly still remember!

Due to a change of circumstances of which in my memory escapes me, in 1972 when I was ten years old we as a family now of four were to move out of Findon Cottage at Childrey and go to live in a house about two miles away near the town of Wantage. The house was one of two called Ham Cottages. The house was on the land of the local gentry called Lord Norry who rented the houses out to families. I don't think that I ever met the Lord myself, but he did allow us to come onto the land surrounding his large house and play. This was generous and kind of Lord Norry to allow us to do this.

One thing that I particularly remember about those times, was that at night in the evenings, Ma used to play our piano when Valerie and I had gone to bed. I loved to lay in bed in the dark and listen to Ma play. She would play all classical music, reading the music from the sheets as she played. To this day I still have all that classical music which she gave to me much later in life when her eyesight was failing and she could no longer see it well enough to read it. I also have a piano, but couldn't even attempt to play the music. The music is in a leather satchel which has S. P. imprinted on the front. S. P. Shirley Price. (Her maiden name being Price.) The satchel contains music such as Minuet in G by Beethoven, Solfeggietto by Bach, Golden Hours with the Great Masters, price one shilling net, Mozart piano sonatas, Liszt Ungarische Rhapsodie Nr.2 the list goes on and on. It was a wonderful thing to be able to listen to the beautiful piano music coming up through the floor as you drifted off to sleep.

When we were at Ham Cottages we had a ginger cat called Jimbo who was a bit of a prawn fanatic. At that time my father was working for the same refrigeration company and would often bring prawns home for the cat after accidentally dropping a bag of frozen prawns on the floor where it had split open, making the prawns unfit for sale. Totally by accident of course! He was a card my father. Jimbo would sit on the gate post with his internal prawn clock telling him that it was time that my father came home with the prawns.

One day father came in from work carrying a dead cat, a ginger tom that had been run over. He said "Look Shirley, Jimbo has been run over and killed!" Somewhat upset my mother replied "You had better get out in the garden quick and bury the poor thing Alan. Valerie loves that cat and she will be distraught with grief when we tell her!" My dad nipped out into the garden and quickly buried poor Jimbo. After a short while Valerie came down from her bedroom and taking her in her arms, Ma said "Brace yourself love, we have got some bad news for you. Jimbo has been run over and killed." Taking one step backwards, Valerie looked at her blankly and said "What are you talking about? He is upstairs on my bed asleep!" It had not been Jimbo at all, but someone else's cat that just happened to be a ginger tom! Jimbo was having a prawn watch day off!

We were not there long at Ham Cottages because due to another change in circumstances we were uprooted and moved AGAIN! This time to another house in a village called Stanford-in-the-vale it being in the Vale of the Uffington White Horse. The house was 21 Manor Crescent, Stanford-in-the-Vale. For a period of time I still attended the same school at Childrey, as my mother still worked for T. & P.'s so she would run me to school and then go to work. However, this arrangement did not last long as she then changed jobs and no longer worked in Childrey. Therefore I had to attend the primary school in Stanford. I did not settle in at that school. I don't know why, but for some reason I just did not settle in there. I think that it was maybe because that I thought that Stanford was a village with no character. Whereas Sparsholt and Childrey villages where older villages and they had bags of character.

Another thing that happened that sticks in my memory when we were living at Manor Crescent was the 'dramatic' return of my sister Sarah. One evening and it could not have been that late, because I was still out of bed. The door bell rang and Ma and I went to see who it was. On opening the door standing there was Sarah! In floods of tears she explained to our Ma that she had run away from her father. She was very upset and distraught and at fourteen to run away must have been a very brave and upsetting thing to do. To try and calm her down I said to her "I'll go and get you something to drink." She probably thought I was going to get a cup of tea, but I brought back a glass of cider! She was only fourteen, bless her. I have to say that although she is my half sister, this made no difference to me what so ever, and I just thought of her and Conrad as my blood kin and I was 'made up' that Sarah had returned to the fold.

At that time my father still used to take me fishing on a regular basis and we would go to the river which was up a dirt track to pick a good place to fish. Once we were off the road and on the track, for amusement as we were no threat to other vehicle users, my father would let go of the steering wheel and I would have to grab it and try to keep the van in a straight line. He used to like to lark about a lot did my father. When on the fishing trips, he would always catch more fish than me, and I would soon get bored and wander off. There is a fine line (About 6lbs breaking strain.) between fishing and just standing on the bank like an idiot! At that age, I had a bad habit of seeking bird's eggs for my collection.

One time when I went wandering away, I saw a nest in a tree, but I had no way of climbing up there to see if there were any eggs in the nest. So, I decided that my plan was to find a large stone to throw up into the tree and dislodge the nest and it would fall down for me to catch. Bad mistake! I found the stone, and threw it into the tree a number of times, missing the nest. Then on the last occasion I threw it into the tree and hearing the stone bouncing down off the branches I looked down and the stone struck me straight on top of the head! Serves me right! The falling stone split my scalp open and the blood was flowing like the water in the nearby river! I am told that scalp wounds bleed prolifically. I staggered back and found my father and he quickly bundled me into the van and gave me a handkerchief to stem the flow of blood. It took a number of stitches to seal the injury. My father laughed and said "Never take life too seriously son, nobody gets out alive anyway." Like I said, he larked about a lot and I think that I behave a lot like my father at times, as I like to lark about should the opportunity arise. Strangely enough I have never looked for bird eggs since.

Shortly after this event things in my life where to change yet AGAIN and I was to be on the move to a completely different part of the country. I was not displeased about this because I didn't like the school at Stanford and I don't know why, but as I said, I never really settled in at Stanford-in-the-Vale.

So arrangements were made for Sarah to stay on at the school she was attending because at this time she was approaching her exam time and so she stayed at our Grandparent's house at Sparsholt. She would still come and visit us in our new house when school time allowed it. Which of course I was pleased about.

CHAPTER 2

GROWING UP

When my parents decided that they would move from Berkshire down to Devon to live near to my fathers parents who lived in Torquay. They brought a house near to the town of Newton Abbott in a little village called Abbotskerswell. So, number 1 Sunny Bank became my new home.

I loved it at number 1 Sunny bank! The bedroom I was given was a loft bedroom and spanned the whole area of the house itself. This gave me lots of room to play and set up my train set without having to take it apart. It was at this time that I came across my first fire escape. In my loft bedroom bolted to the floor under the window, at the wall forming the end of the roof, was a steel box. In the steel box was a rope ladder that in the event of a fire in the house you could open the window and throw out the rope ladder to climb down to the ground. At the time of writing this I have to say that that was a blinding idea for a domestic house in the 1970's to have a means of escape fitted. (Blinding meaning 'good' where I come from. Blinding like a flash of brilliance so bright that would blind you.) The previous owner of 1 Sunny Bank must have been thinking 'out of the box'. Well it was literally out of a box!

As I remember it was quite a large house with a reasonable sized garden and my father put up a chicken run at the top of the garden. I liked the chickens, they would provide lots of eggs, and when money got tight, they would provide meat also! At the rear of the house in the garden there was a well and my sister Valerie insisted on using the well water, and also Sarah when she visited, to wash their hair because it gave their hair good condition and a healthy shine. I didn't bother with all that business! I just used to wash my hair in the bath.

There was a pub at the far end of the village that my parents used to visit, called the Butchers Arms. There were two dogs at the pub, a Jack Russell bitch and the male Collie. The bitch had a litter consisting only of male pups and the landlady of the pub would go out and call the pups at meal times by referring to them as the 'boys'. "Boys, Come on you boys, dinner time boys". Homes were being found for the pups to go to. Although we already had a dog called Suzie, my parents knew that I would like to have a dog of my own, so they took one of the pups from the pub for me. Well, I was over the moon to have a dog of my own. Being a Jack Russell crossed with a Collie dog. He looked like a large brown Jack Russell. I was trying to come up for a name for my dog and after much trial and error found out that the only name the animal would respond to was Boys! So therefore I had little choice but to name him Boysie. At meal times I would call him "Boysie, come on Boysie, dinner time Boysie." I loved that little dog more than life itself.

It was during this time at Sunny bank that I had a bit of a medical scare. Normally as a lad I was fit and healthy but one day I developed a terrible stomach ache. I went to Ma and told her. Ma looked at me sceptically and said "go to the loo." I said "I have been to the loo, but I still have a terrible pain in my stomach." Ma could see that I was in fact in agony and decided to call an ambulance. It was a Sunday morning and I was rushed to hospital at Torbay. It was appendicitis and I was delirious before we got there. I was rushed into the operating theatre and the appendix was quickly whipped out before the condition could worsen. I still have the scars on my lower right hand side abdomen. Back in those days they really did open you up! These days it's all done through keyhole surgery and it virtually leaves no mark at all.

When I was in recovery in the hospital bed, the nurse used to come and bathe the wound. I liked the nurse she seemed very kind and considerate to me. I had a little tube sticking out just below the wound which obviously had been stitched up. The tube was there to allow the wound to vent and drain. One morning the nurse said "Hmmm, I think we will take out the drain tube today." I was expecting it to be about half an inch long, but she pulled on the tube and as it started to come out it seemed to go on for ever and ever! I nearly fainted!

After I left Hospital I had to go through a period of recuperation before I was allowed to return to school. Shame, I liked the school at Abbotskerswell. During my time of recovery Ma used to take me out in our old blue Ford Anglia that we owned at the time. She decided one afternoon that we would take the Anglia through the automatic car wash at Newton Abbott. I was over the moon as I had never sat in a car and gone through an automatic car wash before, how exciting! Normally we would wash the Anglia with a bucket and a sponge. Ma paid the fee and lined the car up with the machine. The machine started up and we were off. The machine sprayed gallons and gallons of water at the car from every conceivable direction. Obviously Ma had not though about this too much as the old Ford Anglia leaked like a kitchen colander and we both got absolutely soaked!

It was a shame, but we were not to live in Abbotskerswell for long. Ma and my comical father at this time of life parted company, and the remainder of the family moved house to Newton Abbott. Which was not far away, and this would be where I was to go to school for my secondary education.

The houses were called Summerland Cottages and I still had my beloved dog Boysie, and our other dog Susie who came to live with us in Newton Abbott.

When I started attending the Newton Abbott boy's school it was then that my education really took off! At the age of eleven in a boy's only school a boy could really concentrate on his learning and with no girls for distraction I benefited. I loved going to school there and was very enthusiastic about it.

It was when we were living in Summerland Cottages that for the first time I saw a dead human being. My brother Con was in the Royal Air Force by now and had come home on leave and came to visit us at Summerland Cottages. I was of course pleased about this as it was great to have Con around again.

He and I decided to go for a walk with the two dogs Suzie and my Boysie. We went to the woods where there was a river running through the trees and to our surprise there was a large amount of police personnel milling around. It became apparent that there was a body of a man in the water and Conrad turned me around to try and prevent his little baby brother at a tender age of eleven from seeing the dead man. Of course baby brother wanted to see the dead man and managed to get a quick look before being ushered away.

The next few years were fairly uneventful and I just concentrated on my education. I liked it at the boy's school and can remember some of my teachers there with gratitude. Particularly Mister Kimble my mathematics teacher, and an old guy called Pop who would teach English language and literature. They were both good teachers and I enjoyed my lessons with them. Mister Kimble knew that I was an enthusiastic pupil and we got on well. Mister Kimble owned a car which was a Morris Traveller, a Morris estate with decorative wood around the bodywork. On one occasion I was walking through the school grounds with Mister Kimble and where all the cars were parked I asked him which one was his car. He pointed out his Morris Traveller and said "It's that one over there." Looking at it I said. "Ah I see, the one with the wooden framework holding it all together." Mister Kimble thought that was hilarious!

I did very well at maths and English. 'Good things happen when you pay attention.' (John F Smith.)

I still used to like to take my loved dog Boysie walking and we spent many happy hours out in the woods and fields walking and playing together. There is one occasion that particularly springs to mind. One of the activities that I used to like to do was throw a stick for Boysie which he would go and retrieve for me, but I would throw it for him and when he was not looking, I would run in the opposite direction and then hide in the bushes just to watch him come running back with the stick in his mouth and go speeding past me. I thought that was very amusing.

I would allow him to go about twenty or so yards in the opposite direction and then call him back. "Boysie, here Boysie!" He would spin around and then come running back. On one occasion I let him go too far, and when I called him he just kept running away into the woods. I had lost my beloved dog! I searched for him for what seemed like hours, calling his name over and over. Still no Boysie. I was distraught! Crying like a baby I searched and searched the woods until eventually he came running out of the bushes. I was so relieved. I picked him up and hugged him, crying all the time. I loved that dog more than life itself.

About this stage of my early teenage years I joined the Y.M.C.A in Newton Abbot. The Y.M.C.A. provided good indoors sporting facilities for teenaged lads in the form of table tennis and snooker and other activities such as chess and board games. I liked it at the Y.M.C.A. and used to go there most evenings, and during the day at weekends. My table tennis became pretty good with me and my mate Andy smashing the ball back and forth between us.

Then after a year or so I started to play snooker. I loved snooker almost immediately and the table tennis took a back seat and I concentrated on my snooker ability. There was an old geezer that used to run the Y.M.C.A. at Newton Abbott and everyone used to call him Mr P. Why he was Mr P. is a mystery to me, but that's what we called him. He was a proper English gentleman and always dressed in a shirt, tie and tweed jacket. Mr P also had a tuck shop where us boys, or perhaps I should say young men, could get some drinks and sweets.

It seems at the time of writing this that it was archaic as to how the club was run. After all it was only in the mid 1970's. How things have changed since those days. I gradually became better and better at snooker and soon started to win frames, then after a time I won a number of competitions.

I would imagine that at the time of writing this that Mr P is long gone. If he were still alive he would be about a hundred years old by now. However he was a good and straightforward gentleman who ran the Y.M.C.A. well, and kept us lads in order. I remember Mr P with affection.

Unfortunately I did not have a lot in the way of pocket money at that time, so I needed another way of getting some income. That is when I set up my first business. I created a paper round, which is just a way of delivering news papers to peoples houses. There was a local news paper that was in demand at the time and I would collect the papers from the local press, charge the customers for the price of the paper and also add a delivery charge onto the bill. I collected the money from them at the end of the week. Then, I would pay the news paper producer for the price of the papers that were outstanding on my account, and make my wages from the delivery charge. I would be making five or six pounds sterling a week. Back then in the mid-seventies that was a good wage for a young news paper delivery boy to be making. Bizarre I know by modern standards. These days you wouldn't even get out of bed for five pounds an hour.

In 1975 the family moved again to another house in Newton Abbott at Netley Road. Netley road was a Cull-de-Sac and the house as about halfway along and near to both the boy's school and the girl's school. At that time I used to read a lot when I was in bed. I read a book which had a title of 'As I walked out one midsummer morning.' This was written by the author Laurie Lee. This was a book that was to influence me later in life and still does to this day.

Unfortunately, after the third year of my secondary education in 1976, it was that the government decided that they would do away with boy's and girl's schools and make them all comprehensive. Geographically the boy's school and the girl's school were near to each other, and we had to be mixed together. What a disaster! To mix educated boy's aged fourteen with girls of the same age would not provide any chance for improving their education. I do not feel that it was a disaster for me, because in the mathematics class there was the most beautiful girl that I had ever seen sitting in front of me. How did I concentrate on my mathematics after that?.... Very little! Her name was Jacque and I loved her. Throughout the lessons, I would be cracking jokes and making Jacque laugh. It was the first time in my life that I had been in love with a woman apart from Ma and my sisters, but that is a very different type of love.

My sister Sarah and her long term boyfriend John were to be married and we were to attend the wedding. I was transported up from Devon to do so. This happened about a year before I was to leave Devon and join the Army. My brother Con had had a motorbike accident about then and I knew that his leg was in a bad way. Poor Con could not walk at the time without the use of crutches. He had to leave the Air force because his leg was in such a bad state. We all had to pull together to sort it out. Which all of us did. I was upset at the time about the condition of my brother's leg, but accidents happen, and I would find that out later in life during my time in the Fire Service.

In my younger years I used to build lots of model aircraft from balsa wood and take them flying. They were all rubber band powered and usually crashed and were destroyed and I had to start all over again. I was not bothered by this at all, as building the thing was as much a pleasure as taking it out for a test flight! One time I build a very large aircraft. I brought the plans from a model shop and then all the necessary materials to build it. When it was finished I took it with me on one occasion when we went to visit Sarah and John at Childrey.

The plane was a good model and flew very steadily and landed well. John, with his mate Wiggy and I decided that we would take it to Crockle which is a large valley near White Horse Hill. I flew the plane on a several occasions, but without winding the rubber band up too far. The aircraft has a specialist multi banded power source which would cause the propeller to slowly tick over and keep the plane airborne for a long period. Wiggy said that he wanted to wind the power source right up to see how far the plane would go. I said "Well o.k. but if you want to wind it up, you can go and get it!" He agreed. After winding it up to its full extent Wiggy launched the plane and off it went flying down the valley of Crockle. Wiggy went running after it and I clearly remember the plane sailing away into the distance. It must have landed eventually because after about twenty minutes he returned with my plane, and he looked absolutely knackered! Well that will teach him won't it!

It was about this time that we were to move home again and moved to a house at the top of the hill at Netley Road which was a 1930's semi-detached house and very nice too.

School life carried on and after a time Jacque had to choose between her current boyfriend and that other chap who sat behind her in the mathematics class, which she did and I started to go out on dates with her. I was introduced to her mother and her sister. The father of the family lived a long way away as he was the Governor of a prison near Manchester which was know as Strangeways. In 1978 we decided that Jacque and I would go and visit her father and we did so in March of that year a week before my sixteenth birthday, and a week after her sixteenth birthday, that's why I remember when it was so easily. As you can imagine it was with some trepidation that I went on the trip. I was thinking that any man who could be the Governor of a major prison would be some form of ogre, a heinous monster with a mean streak a mile wide! Anyway, we took the train up to Manchester where her father met us off the train.

On the way to his place of residence he said that he needed to stop off at the supermarket to buy some food supplies. He parked the car and the three of us went into the store. There was some recorded music playing for the customers at the time and the Swedish group Abba started to play Dancing Queen. Her father exclaimed loudly "It's Abba! I just love Abba!" He grabbed his daughter and started to dance with her in the middle of the shop, waltzing her up and down with all the other customers watching. Singing "Dancing Queen, young and sweet only seventeen!" You could have knocked me down with a feather! I was thinking this bloke is bonkers! This is that terrible man? The nasty ogre, who is the Governor of the prison with the terrible reputation? I was flabbergasted. After that, things went very well and we got on like a house on fire.

It was about this time that I again went to visit my sister Sarah and her husband John and the family in Childrey where I had lived in my primary school days. John worked in the garage owned by his father that was at the bottom of the lane that they lived up, by the public house The Hatchet. John had been working on a project for a while which was the building of a buggy which he would race. Somewhere along the line this involved an old Mini. John's friend Wiggy and he decided that they had finished with the Mini and that as it was of little value they would set it up to do a spectacular crash and film it with the camera.

They took the Mini out of the village and went to a good location and set it up to crash into a tree. They tied off the steering wheel with a length of rope with it pointing at the selected tree. They put a crash helmet on top of a box on the seat to make it look like there was someone driving. Starting the engine and putting it in gear they set the thing off. Away it went zooming across the field towards the tree. Unfortunately it missed the tree and carried on zooming across the fields and crashing through the fences with no one at the wheel! With John and Wiggy chasing after it.

After a mile or so the mini reached a road and leapt over the sunken lane and carried on across the fields. Eventually there was an old railway sleeper that someone had used as a good strong fence post and the mini crashed into it and stopped with the front of the engine smashed! Wow thank God for that!

Things went on pretty much the same for the rest of my education. Then when school leaving time arrived I had to make a choice about what I would do for a profession for the foreseeable future. I had no real idea about what I wanted to do, or which direction to go in. Someone made a suggestion about a military post which I thought was a good idea. So, I went to the Army recruitment office to see what was on offer.

At the recruitment office I was informed that I would have to attend an army career selection for two days at a military base at Sutton Coldfield near Birmingham. So arrangements were made and off I went. Having done the selection process, during which I was shown lots of films about various careers in the army. I was given many different tests to see which of the careers I would be suitable for. After which I was informed that there were many options open to me. Did I fancy the artillery? Did I fancy the tank corps? Did I like the idea of the electrical and mechanical engineers? How about being in the signals? The options were endless. No, like a fool I decided that I would like the infantry.

My job started in September 1978 at the tender age of sixteen. Why I had I decided to leave my beloved Jacque? I do not understand to this day. The strange things that you do when you are a young man!

CHAPTER 3

INFANTRY JUNIOR LEADERS BATTALION.

The barracks where I was to live for the next year of training was at Shorncliff barracks near Folkestone in Kent. The army sent me the necessary travelling documents and I arrived at the barracks on the 12ᵗʰ of September. The barracks were those of the Infantry Junior Leaders Battalion. Or the I.J.L.B. as it was known. The idea of the I.J.L.B. was that the recruits who would attend there would have potential to be developed into Non-Commissioned Officers.

There were many other raw recruits there when I arrived and the sergeant lined us all up. For a recruit he was a rather intimidating character because sergeants like to bawl at you a lot. He said to us "What have we got here then? We have got some drop outs, some tramps, and some hippies who need a hair cut!" Then looking at me in my combat jacket which I had brought from a second hand shop he said "Jesus Christ! We have even got some mercenaries!" We were informed as to which block we would be sleeping in and packed of to the accommodation.

I was put in Peninsular Company with all the others who would be in the Prince of Wales division. Most of the chaps that I was to live with for the next year were from Wales, because the Welsh regiment's of the Royal Welsh Fusiliers and The Royal Regiment of Wales are in that division. I was to be in the Duke of Edinburgh's Royal Regiment, or the Derrs as they affectionately known.

The expression of Derrs was used to let a member of that regiment know what a member of another regiment thought of them by saying "Derrrrrr" to indicate stupidity. This did in no way affect how I felt about the being in the Derrrrrrrs! I was extremely proud of my regiment and its history! I was later to find out from another instructor that some of them refer to my regiment as the Duke of any Buggers Royal Regiment because it would appear that due to reorganization of the army the regiment was a dumping place for all the people who wanted to join the army but their own regional regiment was not recruiting at that time, so they were put in the Derrrrrrrs. However, this still did not detract from my pride in my regiment and I would fight anyone who tried to tell me otherwise. Oh, the gullibility of youth! That is army life for you. Off the battlefield and in barracks life, competition and friction is fierce between regiments, but on the battle field we are all one big happy family, united in a cause against a common enemy. As I was to find out later when having completed my year of training when I left the Infantry Junior Leaders Battalion to join my Regiment.

Training at the I.J.L.B. was tough and demanding, but very rewarding. An average day would consist of breakfast at the cookhouse. Then go on parade for formal inspection. Then perhaps a two or three hours on the square, (Square bashing.) marching and doing rifle drills. The foot drills and turns all consisted of the same timing of ONE, two three, ONE, two three, ONE!

There springs to mind one time when our company sergeant had us stood to attention and bawled at on chap who was trying to sneakily look at his watch. Standing right in front of him with his face about six inches from the soldier concerned, He shouted "WHAT DO YOU THINK YOU ARE DOING LADDIE!" to which the soldier replied in a meek voice, "I was just looking at my watch to see the time sergeant." The sergeant went red in the face and shouted, "THE ONLY TIME YOU NEED TO KNOW IS ONE, TWO THREE, ONE, TWO THREE, ONE!" We all chuckled including the sergeant.

After that we all liked our drill sergeant, even though he did bawl at us a lot because we all knew that really he did have a sense of humour and that he was in fact after all a human being and not actually some sadistic monster. Also that he was just training us to be the best soldiers that he could. This was for our own protection. Discipline and obeying instructions when under pressure will be the one thing that could save your life in a combat situation.

Then perhaps in the afternoon, after a good feed up at the cookhouse we would do some navigational training learning how to use a map and compass to understand where you were, and how to navigate to get to where you wanted to go. In addition to this we may have some lessons on military tactics and weaponry.

We were taught some handy sayings to help us remember things. One of the things that still makes me chuckle today is the four S's Shape, Shine, Shadow and Silhouette. These are things that you needed know and to avoid to remain unseen by the enemy. Later in my army time when I joined 19 platoon, we used to make up our own sayings to tell a mate what we were doing. So if someone was on his way to the ablutions and someone asked him "Where are you going mate?" He would just say the four S's "Shit, Shave, Shower and Shampoo!"

During my time at I.J.L.B. there was to be a boxing championship with boxers fighting for their own allocated company. This would produce an overall champion at whatever weight the boxer was fighting at. In the first week of my year there, there was a milling contest to identify which soldiers had any boxing skills and ability, or any who had any potential which could be developed.

For those who don't know, the definition of the word 'mill' is to beat, strike, or fight. Every soldier would be put in the ring for a three minute mill. This was not at all, or in any way optional. Every trainee would go in the ring for a three minute mill. It was visually estimated as to what weight each soldier would fight at and they were then put into groups accordingly.

Now, I may have joined the army, and gone into the infantry, but I was and still am not naturally a violent man and I had certainly never been in a boxing match or for that matter even in a boxing ring before. So it was something that was somewhat alien to me.

Float like a butterfly, sting like a bee. (Muhammad Ali.)

My turn came up and the Company Sergeant gave me a few tips while he was fitting me with the gloves before I got in the ring. Speaking quietly he said "Keep up your guard, tuck your chin into your left shoulder and jab twice with your left, and then throw a right as hard as you can!" It was with much trepidation that I stepped into the ring.

The bell went 'DING DING' and the fight started. My opponent, who at that time looked a lot bigger than me, came at me swinging his fists like a whirling windmill. So, I took my sergeants advice and with my chin tucked in jabbed twice with my left and then threw my right. To my amazement he went down on the canvas! He was not hurt, just stung by an annoying small wasp. He jumped straight up and came at me again swinging away with his seemingly large fists. So dancing around like a true ballerina. (Float like a butterfly.) I did the same again, jab, jab, and throw. Dodge about a bit. Shuffle my feet and circle around. Jab, jab, and throw, jab, jab, and throw. Down he went again! (Sting like a bee.) Yet again he did not seem physically hurt.

There was nothing but his pride that I had damaged, but by now he was really ANGRY! The man certainly did not lack courage. He just wanted to squash the annoying wasp that was buzzing around him. He flew at me and I though bugger this! I ducked by bending at the waist and he went straight over my back and landed on the canvas for the third time.

At that stage to my good fortune the bell went 'DING DING' and the three minute fight was over. 'Phew.' I was the winner! I don't think that he had actually struck me once! The combatants of the milling contest were put into two groups, the winners and the losers. Private Haines the winner! (Hooray!) I was asked if I would like to join the company boxing team, but I declined the kind offer. Boxing was not really my cup of tea.

One of the things that the I.J.L.B. used to do is to get all the trainee soldiers to a fitness level at which they would be fit enough to be suitable for combat. There is an expression in the army which makes good sense and that is 'Sweat saves Blood!' To achieve this there were several methods. One was to instil discipline and strength in the soldiers by giving any small misdemeanour punishment with press ups. Depending on the misdemeanour would result in the amount of press ups given. So, a minor thing such as putting your hands in your pockets would result in "Drop and give me twenty". Or a more serious thing such spitting on the tarmac (Not that I did this of course! Vulgar habit.) would be "Drop and give me fifty". Et cetera et cetera.

Another was the Saturday morning routine. This comprised of a few rigorous hours on the drill square doing a bit of square 'bashing' which was followed by the cross country run. Once the young men were at a suitable level of fitness and discipline there would be a Battle Fitness Test or B.F.T. as it was know.

The B.F.T. would consist of a mile and a half run as a group followed by a mile and half run independently. The three miles had to be completed within the time allowed. As the young men grew stronger and fitter, the competition between them grew stronger. Each recruit wanted to show that he was fitter and stronger than his competitors and could complete the run the fastest.

Also there was a thing that we had to do which was to complete a Combat Fitness Test or C.F.T. This was a demanding thing to achieve. It consisted of an eight mile march and jog or 'bash' as we referred to it.

The 'bash' had to be completed as a platoon within an hour and a half, carrying full battle equipment, weapons and ammunition. Followed by a full assault course of numerous obstacles and terminating in a shooting range where a soldier had to hit the target to achieve a certain score.

This was an extremely demanding event and a soldier would be so exhausted at the end of the 'bash' that when trying to hit the target his arms would be shaking with the effort of just holding the rifle.

Obviously some of the soldiers were fitter and stronger than others and during the C.F.T. the stronger ones would be allowed to try and help their mates along the 'bash' by carrying their kit and weapons. There was no point in reaching the battle ground with half your platoon missing. The object of the exercise was to build strength, combat fitness, and companionship. I know it may seem like a strange thing to say, but I liked doing the C.F.T in my infantry years with my army buddies. At the end you had a real sense of achievement.

There were many things that I did during my time at the I.J.L.B. In fact so many of them that some of them escape my memory. One thing that sticks in my mind is the time that we were taken to somewhere up country to test our navigational skills and also to see if we were suitable to be infantry soldiers. It was in the middle of winter and we were taken to a lake where a man in a canoe was in a stationary position in the middle of the lake. We were told to strip off and individually swim out to the canoe and to dive under it, then to dive back under it and swim back to the bank.

I was somewhat worried about the temperature of the water at that time, but when my turn came I jumped in the river and started to swim. I considered myself a good steady, but not particularly fast swimmer, as I used to go to the swimming pool at Newton Abbott regularly during the summer months with my sister Valerie and swim often.

However the lake water was so cold that before I was half way to the canoe I could feel my strength just sapping away! I kept swimming and eventually reached the canoe and dived under it and taking a breath dived back under it again. Then swimming back to the bank I was getting to the point where I started to think that I was not going to make it! I kept swimming and swimming, but the bank did not seem to be getting any nearer. Eventually I made it and learnt a valuable lesson that day. If you are in a combat situation, don't go into icy cold water unless you absolutely need to!

I managed to get though all the tests of military knowledge, courage and fitness that were thrown at me during my training year at I.J.L.B. and reached the point of taking part in a passing out parade. The passing out parade involved in much marching and saluting with lots of pomp and circumstance going on. All my family from Berkshire where present at that time and I was extremely proud to be a confirmed as a trained infantry soldier in the British army!

CHAPTER FOUR

THE ARMY.

After my year of training at the I.J.L.B. I was posted to my regiment in the summer of 1979 and so the next spell of my army career began. The Duke of Edinburgh's Royal Regiment was based at a town in Germany. Osnabruck, which at that time was the largest collection of military bases in West Germany. When I joined my regiment the majority of the soldiers were in Northern Ireland on a tour of duty in Belfast. They had been there for a number of months and were due to return back to the barracks in a month or so. Therefore I was told that I would become part of the rear guard.

The barracks that we occupied was not only the accommodation for my regiment, but divided into two and also provided a barracks for an Irish tank regiment of the Enniskillen Dragoon Guards. We had the upper part of the barracks and they had the lower. Germany was a totally new experience for me as I had never been to Germany previously. As you can imagine, speaking to the natives was somewhat of a challenge at first, but fortunately a lot of the German people could speak some English and we managed to get by. I was put into D company and nineteen platoon which consisted of approximately thirty soldiers. When the remainder of the regiment returned from Belfast about a month later, barracks life resumed as normal.

Being new to the regiment, I was not sure of how I would get on with the rest of the soldiers in my platoon, but they just treated me like the 'sprog' that I was at seventeen. (A 'sprog' being the new boy in the group.) I soon learnt that there were some 'Characters' within nineteen platoon. However, we were all soldiers, and had to learn how to get along with each other which happened most of the time.

Occasionally tempers would flare and fights would break out amongst the men. Usually in the NAAFI bar when alcohol had been consumed. NAAFI being the abbreviation of Navy, Army, and Air Force Institution. When you went into the NAAFI bar on a Saturday night, you could guarantee that there would be a fight at sometime. It was as sure as the turning of the earth! Plastic chairs and tables where the order of the day.

On one occasion I remember that there was a fight between a mate of mine called Pete and one of the Regimental Police Officers who was off duty. Now, my mate Pete was a not a large man, as I am not. Pete was only about five foot six or seven and the R.P. was a very large man who had a reputation of being a bit of a scrapper. Personally I think 'bully' would be a better word to describe him. However he was very drunk and Pete was not. He picked on Pete thinking that he would be an easy target to give a good looking bloke a good thrashing and re-arrange his appearance somewhat. How wrong was he! Pete danced around his attacker and avoided all his slow and swinging large fists and did the same thing that I had been taught in my training days. Jab, jab, and throw, jab, jab, and throw. It was a wonderful moment to see Pete make a fool of this big 'bully' man who thought that just because he was an R.P. he could take out his personal aggression on anyone at any time. Being a soldier is not about beating up someone smaller than yourself just because you have a need to release your aggressive feelings. Being a soldier is about serving your Queen and country and protecting the ones that you love back home.

There were a lot of things that I would learn when serving in Osnabruck about military life and one of them was that most soldiers, or most people that become infantry soldiers like to fight. As I said, Osnabruck was the largest conglomeration of British Army bases at that time, and naturally there was a certain feeling of competition between the different regiments based there.

Sometimes when we were off duty we would go into the town to blow off steam and chat up the local ladies and have a good time. There were certain bars in the town that the soldiers would attend, and sometimes things went well and you would meet some of the guys from another regiment that you got along with and that was not an issue. However, on most weekend nights there would be a fight break out like a brawl in a western film.

In my platoon there were a couple of soldiers that when they had had a drink they just wanted to fight. So I thought about it and came up with a way to get around this. After some quiet consultation my colleagues who I knew were of a less violent nature, a small group of us formed a gang that would not go into Osnabruck for recreation.

We found another place about fifteen miles away called Furstenau. Furstenau was a nice little town where the ladies were unused to British soldiers. One of the soldiers would drive the car and the rest of them would blow off steam by drinking Pernod and Coke. We got on well with the local girls, who liked a change of company and seemed to like the English. After chatting with the local ladies and having been in Germany a while now our 'pidgin' German was improving.

None of the more aggressive soldiers would bother going to Furstenau and we were happy about that. On our trips, the nominated driver would not be drinking alcohol, which worked successfully most of the time. We had a philosophy about death in our gang. We remembered a certain expression which was, "I want to go peacefully like my Grandfather did in his sleep, not screaming in like the passengers in his car!"

I have fond memories of our visits to Furstenau. There were never any fights and as I said, we got on well with the local ladies. In fact one of my buddies fell in love with one of the girls from that small town and married the girl. Some of the things we used to do there were crazy! It was the time that the group Madness had produced a number of records. When 'Welcome to the house of fun' was played in the Disco, we all used to line up and do a comical dance in the style of Madness. Mad! All of us were as mad as trees!

There was one time that we went to Furstenau for a night out and my mate Chalky and I somehow got separated from the rest of the gang of about ten. How it happened I don't recall. Anyway Chalky and I ended up having to walk the fifteen miles back to Osnabruck in the middle of the night. Fortunately it was in the summer time and it was not very cold, even at two in the morning. Back then the prospect of a fifteen mile hike held no fear for us super fit infantry men, so we just got on with it.

On the way back to the barracks we came across a place where there were some road works going on. Well, I don't know if they still do this in Germany because it has been a long time since I have been there, but in those days they always supplied the workmen with a small metal hut.

The small metal hut provided somewhere where the workmen could go at break time to get out of the weather to eat their sandwiches. For some reason, I don't know why, perhaps we needed a rest, Chalky and I tried the door of the hut expecting it to be locked. To our surprise it was in fact open so we went in. We were not intending to steal anything, just to sit down for a while.

In the hut on the floor were some crates of bottled beer. For those of you who are unaware, in Germany workmen drink beer like workmen in England drink tea. The temptation was too great for us to resist, and we were quite thirsty anyway, so we took a bottle each, knocked of the tops and drank the beer. NAUGHTY BOYS! Robin Hood and his merry thieves. We then continued our journey and got back to barracks about six in the morning. So, belated apologies to those German workmen for stealing their beer, I suspect they did not even notice the two missing bottles as there were crates of the stuff there anyway.

Another thing that happens when you are in the infantry is that you are trained to treat your rifle like someone that you love and you would be given a particular weapon from the armoury that would be allocated specifically to you. This weapon needed to be 'zeroed in' to the soldier that would be firing it.

To achieve this you had to go to the firing range. As infantry soldiers we went to the range on a regular basis for practice. We would go to the firing point and our colleagues at the 'butts' would raise the targets for us to shoot at. Following the training that we had been given we tried to be as good as possible at hitting the target. You get your rifle firmly into your shoulder, control your breathing and when you had a 'bead' on the target, you hold your breath and gently squeeze the trigger. The distances that we were from the target varied and could be as little as one hundred metres or as far as six hundred metres. Trying to hit a target at nearly half a mile away was like trying to shoot a fly off a cow's backside!

Obviously the aim is to hit the target in the most obvious place, in the heart. The bullet holes in the target would hopefully form a 'group' where the rounds (An infantry man calls a bullet a round) had passed through the target and would indicate how the sights on your rifle could be zeroed in. Then the armourer would alter the sights on your rifle accordingly and you would fire again. The idea is that this time the 'group' of your rounds would be gathered near the heart of the target and so on. This process continued until such time as the soldier concerned would be hitting the target with a kill shot on most occasions. Your rifle has then been zeroed into your own personal style of shooting.

A soldier that gets a score of 60 plus when doing the A.P.W.T. (Annual Personal Weapons Test.) would be called a Marksman and get given a badge of crossed rifles to sew onto his uniform. Which is something that the soldier would be proud of. Unfortunately I never quite managed to get this score. I would always get 59, 58, 59, but never 60! Grrrrrr.

Another thing that you had to do as an infantry man was to keep your weapon available for use at all times and this was drummed into us when we used to go on exercise at an area near to Soltau in north Germany. You treated your rifle like it was a woman or your wife, you slept with it. Literally slept with it inside your sleeping bag. The army then issued good sleeping bags to the soldiers as there was no point in a soldier freezing at night and not being able to get up and fight, should the need arise. And there was no point in his weapon not being able to function in a combat situation because it was frozen.

So we slept with our beloved rifles in our bags with us. This was not a problem and did not stop us sleeping because we were so bloody tired that we could have slept on a washing line! I loved my allocated Belgian F.N. or S.L.R. (Self Loading Rifle) as we called them and would have liked to taken it with me when I left the army, but no way are they going to allow that!

At the time of writing this a thought occurred to me that even after all these years I can still remember the number of that rifle, 147 which is something that I had not thought about for donkey's years!

One of the things that happened to me during my time in Germany was an unusual friendship with a musician and bandsman within the regiment. For a private infantry soldier and a member of the band to form a friendship is virtually unknown in the infantry. The bandsmen were the ones which provided the music for the drill square and the marching parades. Also they would double up as the medics and stretcher bearers in a combat situation. So, most of the soldiers had little respect for the bandsmen. They regarded them as whimps or cowards. Of course this was a load of bollocks and not true, and I never thought that it was, but in general most of the bandsmen used to keep themselves to themselves. Probably because they new the truth, and that was that most infantry men where as thick as pig shit!

Luke and I had both lived in Devon, so perhaps that's how we got chatting. I was interested in music and Luke had an amazing ability to play any musical instrument. He took me to the band block where no infantry man would normally dream of going! When we were there I asked him, "So, what instrument do you play Luke?" He said "Any one you like, just take your pick." Of course I thought he was joking. Surely no one could play them all. He picked up the nearest instrument to hand and started to play, and then he played the piano, then the trombone, then all the other instruments that were there. Wow! This guy really could play anything. Luke really could play just about any musical instrument! Why he had ended up in the army I do not know. I was amazed at his musical ability.

Luke owned a nice guitar that he said I could buy from him, and never having been given an education at guitar playing I said "Will you teach me?" He replied "Yes, of course!" So, I brought the guitar from him for 500 marks. It was a beautiful guitar, which I still own to this day. There have been many times, when I had been short of cash that I have considered selling the instrument, but I would never do that now as I do still play occasionally and love the guitar anyway. Luke and I became good friends and there were many times that we would go out for a drink together when we were not on duty.

I am sure that most people know that back in the years that I served in Germany from 1979 to 1982, Germany was still divided into East and West by the Iron Curtain until the collapse of the wall and the iron curtain in 1989. One of the duties that we as soldiers were required to do was what was known as site guard.

All that we knew was that no one was allowed to enter the site and that there were eastern Germans on the other side of the curtain. I think that most people would be able to hazard a guess as to what it was that we were guarding. It was a boring duty to do, the only good thing that we got out of the experience was the trading that we did with the American soldiers that were also there. We used to swap military clothing with them so that they could go home with some examples of British army clothes and vice versa.

One funny thing that happened to me when I was doing site guard was that at one time there, one of the large twin bladed Chinook helicopters was coming in to land and I was stood in the landing Zone. As the chopper came lower the phenomenal downdraft from the twin rotor blades was so strong that it tore off my steel helmet and sent it bowling away like it was made of paper with me scurrying after it!

When I was in Germany for those three years, during the winter months the Regiment would organize a ski trip for the soldiers that wanted to go. As I mentioned earlier I had a mate in my platoon know as Chalky. Chalky was a bit of a boxer and fought for the company boxing team, but he was not a violent bloke really and I have never know Chalky to get involved in a fight outside of the ring, and I had great respect for him. We got on really well together. Chalky and I jumped at the chance to go on a ski trip as neither of us had been ski-ing before.

It was treated as a military exercise and not a ski-ing holiday for the troops. However it was purely voluntary unlike normal military exercises. The trips were two weeks long. The troops that wanted to go had to pay some of the cost of the trip out of their wages. It was not a lot of money, I think it was about forty quid, so it was sort of halfway between a holiday and an exercise. The trip was known as Exercise Snow Queen.

Why the Army organised these things for the soldier's is a bit of a mystery, as they had no military reason to do so. It is not something that I thought about at the time I just got on with it. In retrospect, I think it may have been a twofold reason. One, it would give the soldiers another opportunity to keep fit and strong. Two, it would be good for relations between the English and the Germans.

We would go down to the south of Germany on a coach to a town called Sonthofen where we would be transferred to a four ton Bedford army truck and continue to a small town in the Bavarian Alps and stay in a Guesthouse in the region near to a mountain called the Grunten which is where we would ski. The Guesthouse was run by a traditional old style German Bavarian couple called Tia and Ernst. Tia and Ernst wore traditional style Bavarian clothing with Tia wearing a full dress and a white apron and bib and Ernst would be wearing leather shorts and bib. Real knee slapping style clothing!

The food that we had during the visit was made mainly from army combat rations which was a little strange, but again, this kept the costs of the trip to a minimum.

After a nights rest we were loaded onto the four toner carrying the skis and boots that we had been given and drove the fifteen minute ride to the foot of the mountain. Once there we were given some fundamental instruction on how to fit our skis and poles and then taken up the mountain on the lift. Once at the top of the nursery slope we pointed the skis downhill and off we went.

It was hilarious because most of the guys had never skied before and no idea about how to stop to a controlled halt. There were bodies scattered all over the mountain side with all the people in wide and varied positions of entanglement with their equipment and in some cases each other!

The thing about it was that back then the equipment was somewhat different from the modern equipment available now. The skis had no automatic brakes incorporated into the binding so the only way to stop a lost ski from flying off down the mountain and decapitating someone should it come off the foot, was that the ski was tied to the leg of the skier with a piece of strong ribbon and a clip. So, when the skier took a tumble and the binding released as it should, to stop it from breaking the leg of the skier, as the skier slid down the mountain side he would have the ski whirling around his head like a helicopter blade. I know that downhill ski-ing is an activity during which there are a high percentage of injuries, but I am amazed that we as a group only had a few split heads, twisted thumbs and pulled muscles and no broken legs!

Part of our equipment we were issued with was an orange canvas cagoule which would provide some protection from dampness, but did nothing to keep the wearer warm! Tumbles were a very regular thing amongst our group. After some time on the mountain side trying to learn how to get from the top of the mountain to the bottom without taking several tumbles we found out that we had built up a bit of a reputation with the local Germans who also skied on the Grunten. They referred to us as "Zee mad English in zee orange cagoules!"

For those who are not familiar with downhill ski-ing, when the skier wishes to have a rest and take some refreshment there are usually several restaurants on the mountain side. What the skiers do is take their skis off and then plunge them into the snow so they will not be a trip hazard to others and they can see them when they come out of the restaurant, even if it is snowing heavily.

On one occasion some of my colleagues where in the restaurant and so I decided that I would ski down the piste (the slope) and join them for a coffee. There were many skis sticking up out of the snow outside of the restaurant. As I skied down unfortunately I lost control, and flew down much faster than I had intended to. Just before the up ended skis was a slight rise and zooming over this I flew up into the air and on landing, both ski bindings operated as they should and the skis pinged off. Falling flat on my stomach and still sliding down with the skis lashed to my legs trailing behind me, I crashed into all the skis poked into the snow and they all went flying it was a miracle that I was only winded with a slightly twisted ankle!

I stood up and dusted myself off, then I picked up some of the skis that I had sent flying and stuck them back in the snow, not necessarily in the pairs that they should have been. Then trying to show no pain I limped into the restaurant. One of the local chaps sat outside nearby looked at me and shaking his head said "Zee mad English in zee orange cagoules!" So, the moral of the story is, if your partner wants to learn to ski, don't stand in his or her way!

Back at the guesthouse we would service our skis by waxing them and sharpening the edges if this was required, then we would have some dinner cooked by the lovely Tia. We would eat our meals in the bar area which doubled up as the family dining room as is the case in most Guesthouses in Bavaria.

It was the largest room in the house. The bar had several small tables and also the Stammtisch which was the family table or Head Table and the largest table in the room. You did not sit at the Stammtisch unless you were invited! This was made plain before we even got there "Don't sit at the Stammtisch unless you are invited, they will be deeply offended if you do!" That applied to all people in the bar, German of English. It was the tradition of the Guesthouses of Bavaria.

All the washing up was done by us the squaddie 'guests'. This was done in turns on a rotary basis. Then in the evening we would go out to the local Disco for a knees up. Anyone who came back to the guest house after midnight got extra duties doing the washing up. Strangely enough Chalky and I did a lot of washing up! We had a great time on the ski trips during our three years in Germany. Chalky and I went every year and on the third year we stayed for four weeks. By the time we returned to England we were both accomplished skiers.

At the time of writing this book downhill ski-ing had changed somewhat since the days that I learned to ski. When we used to ski on the Grunten Mountain. They did not piste the slopes into oblivion with pisten bullies. They would allow some of the slopes to develop into mogul fields.

This presented a real challenge to the skier. A mogul field is like a downhill slope that the snow is formed into heaps by the action of the skiers. So, there would be bumps and humps and dips everywhere. If you allowed gravity to take over and fly down the mountain side the moguls will throw you into the air and you will almost definitely 'wipe out'. To ski a mogul field was one of the biggest challenges to take on, and I liked to be able to ski down a mogul field.

You needed a certain different technique to take on moguls than you did for powder or piste.

With moguls, you need to sit back a little and use your poles to get a good early plant, to initiate your turn before the next mogul. The idea was, that you kept your ski in touch with the snow as much as possible and provide you with the control required. It is not something that is easy to do, and in the early days would generally result in a wipe out! When you ski a steep mogul field, you do not have time to think. You just have to go with the snow and use your gut rhythm. That's why Chalky and I loved the mogul fields. We would watch each other ski down and keep fingers crossed that our mate would make it to the bottom without a serious wipe out! Great fun!

These days, they do not allow mogul fields to develop on mountain sides, as they want to attract as many tourists as possible to the resort and the thinking is that mogul fields will put skiers off coming. They worry about all that (poofty) 'carving' ski-ing. So, they just Pisten Bully the moguls to oblivion. This is such a shame. If there was a resort in Europe that had some moguls, I would definitely book a holiday there! I don't know that I would be able to cope at the time of writing this, as I am some twenty odd years older and certainly not as fit! Yeah, I could do it. I could get fit in a month or two to take on the moguls!

During our visits there as our German improved, Chalky and I had got to know Tia and Ernst better. Tia thought about Chalky and I in a strange way which at that time, we didn't understand. "Wir haben nicht verstehen!" "We did not understand!" She would do our laundry for us and behaved like she was our mother. Cooking for us and washing our clothes for us. Which of course we thought was very nice.

On the last time of going and staying in Tia and Ernst's Guesthouse and on the last night we were there, Chalky and I were invited by Tia and Ernst to come and sit at the Stammtisch with them. We both felt that this was a great honour bestowed upon us. Of course we went and sat with them and it became apparent that over the three years that we had been going there, we had gradually got to know them and we had become more than just guests. We were now viewed as family friends.

I think that Tia almost looked upon us two as her two adopted sons. I find it very moving at the time of writing this that she felt like that. And that is why she had been doing all those things for us. The washing and cleaning and cooking for the two of us wild English boys! God bless her. I will never forget what that Bavarian woman did for us. As I said, it was a great honour for both of us to be invited to go and sit at the Stammtisch with Tia and Ernst. "Vielen dank meinen Freunden."

Another thing that happened to me when in Germany regarding ski-ing, is that I went on a cross country ski-ing course in the Harz Mountains near to the Iron Curtain. Cross country ski-ing is a different ball game from the downhill in the fact that we called it 'Skinny Ski-ing.' Skinny Ski-ing was a very popular thing in the rural areas of Germany and still is to this day. At the time of writing this I was watching the 2010 winter Olympics and one of the final events was the fifty kilometre cross country ski-ing race. A tough and demanding event by anyone's standards and the German competitors managed to win a silver medal by Axel Teichmann and a forth placing by Tobias Angera. This just goes to show how important cross country ski-ing is in Germany.

Why was it that the Army sent me on this course? To be honest I can't really remember. Perhaps it was to be able to be mobile in a winter combat situation. I enjoyed the course immensely. It was great to get out there in the Harz Mountains and learn how to get about in the woods and forests when there was so much snow around.

Our instructor on the course was an old German guy called Hans. To us young men of about late teens or early twenties he seemed about as old as the Harz Mountains themselves! Hans had obviously been at this for a long time, because he really knew his onions when it came to getting around in the mountains in winter. At the time, our German was not good, and Hans did not speak much English, but somehow we managed to communicate. Mainly by Hans demonstrating to us as to how to fit the equipment and also how to use the correct rhythms of bodily movement to provide the necessary forward motion depending on the gradient of the terrain.

The equipment that we used was somewhat different from what I had initially learned to downhill ski with. For a starter, there was no rear binding on the ski and the ski boot or shoe was only attached at the front end. Also, the ski poles where much longer than the downhill ski poles, and there was a reason for this. The poles would provide much of the propulsion to provide the forward motion required. In addition to this it was very important as to what wax you would apply to the middle section of the ski, depending on the temperature of the snow.

The front and back third of the ski was waxed with gliding wax, which would allow you to slide when required. The middle third of the ski was waxed with the appropriate wax to give you the propulsion when you put your weight on the ski and flattened it out and this would grip on the snow and apply the power that you supplied. What wax you applied to the middle section of the ski was the most important factor.

If you put on the wrong type of wax, the ski would not grip on the snow and provide no transmission of power from your muscles to the snow, and you would just slide backwards when trying to go uphill. Or, if you put on another type of wax, the snow would just stick to the ski and stop you from gliding when you needed to. The waxes were all coloured depending on what type and temperature of snow that you wanted to travel across. I cannot remember what colour of wax was applied to the middle section of the ski to enable you to get around in the mountains, but I think that these days the skis are manufactured with a fish scale effect on the middle of the 'Skinny Ski' that removes the need to wax the middle section of the ski. However, Hans showed us the way, and that it was great that we had the opportunity to be able to move around the trails of the Herz Mountains under the old German man Hans's guidance. I wish I had had a camera with me back in those years all that time ago to take some pictures that I could have put in this book.

Moving on. When based at the barracks at Osnabruck we were a mechanized infantry battalion and had vehicles called A.P.C.'s Armoured Personnel Carriers. We had some hangers at the barracks where the vehicles where kept. They were tracked vehicles, a bit like a tank, and Sergeant Trench was the man responsible for making sure that we looked after them. Each platoon would have three of these vehicles to mobilize them into the battlefield and to attack enemy positions. Each vehicle would carry soldiers consisting of the corporal, a driver, a turret man for the machine gun, and six to eight men.

To practice all the aspects of combat we would go on exercise in an area at Saltau as I mentioned earlier. This could be at any time of year and would involve going a long way up the Autobahn (Motorway) to reach the exercise area. The vehicles had no heating and this was fine during the warmer months. The A.P.C.'s did have a number of small periscopes for use when the hatches were battened down in battle, but this was not adequate vision when on the Autobahn. So in winter it could be a bit of a nightmare as the corporal and the driver had to ride with the hatches open as they had to have all round vision when on a public road. This would mean that everyone in the vehicle would be exposed to the elements, and North Germany can get extremely cold in winter!

The army relaxed the rules somewhat during these times, and the guys driving and navigating the A.P.C.'s up the Autobahn where allowed to improvise as to what clothing they wore. Wrapping up in as much warm clothing they could lay their hands on!

Whilst on exercise at Saltau we would practice all the aspects of modern warfare as far as the infantry were concerned. This would be attack role, defence role, patrolling, ambush, and camouflage, which involved the four S's Shape, Shine, Shadow and Silhouette. (The four S's Shit, Shave, Shower and Shampoo!)

When going into the attack of an enemy defensive position the driver would take the vehicle in at full speed and then when the corporal shouted "DEEEEBUUSSS!" The driver would screech the vehicle to a halt and the crew would open the rear door and leap out and go into the attack. We would of course only be firing blanks, but it gave the soldier a good idea as to what it would be like in real combat.

Some of the soldiers that I served with at that time were bloody good at their job. There was one guy that I particularly remember, but his name escapes me at the moment. He was the driver of our wagon and if our A.P.C. threw a track in the deep mud, he would be able to manoeuvre the vehicle about in the mud to get the track back onto the rollers. To get us back in motion. If this failed, we would have to split the track by removing a track pin, and do this manually. Which was messy, and hard graft! We got so covered in mud that our D.P.M. (Distributive pattern material.) became so muddy, that we just looked like brown men. That was fine for the landscape that we were dealing with. We just melted into the landscape and became invisible.

On another occasion we had the opportunity to go on exercise where we would be firing live ammunition. This was, and still is, at a place called British Army Training Unit Suffield or B.A.T.U.S. The training area is located in Canada in the southern part of Alberta near to the Canadian/American border. I don't know what the situation was at the time that I went to the training area back in the early eighties, but the organization I now know has a Web site and you can see what they are all about now by visiting their Web site.

The whole trip to B.A.T.U.S. is something that I remember with affection. It was a great trip and I remember one time when we were lying in our tents at night out on the huge and seemingly endless prairie, I heard some commotion outside and one of the chaps in my platoon saying "My god, look, it's the northern lights!" I climbed out of my sleeping bag and got out of the tent and sure enough, there, shimmering in the sky above the prairie was the northern lights. I had never seen such a beautiful thing in the sky in all my life and it is a moment I shall never forget. The whole time that we were out on the prairie was a great deal of fun and I have to say very exciting for a young soldier who had never been to a live firing exercise before.

We would go into attack mode with the hatches battened down and just looking through the periscopes of our Armoured Personnel Carriers. I at that time was the turret man who could see the explosions of the artillery being fired over our heads landing on the impact zone of the position that we were attacking. It was pretty exciting stuff! We had to spend a long time living in a tent during our time over there, but who cares!

After our military manoeuvres were over we were allowed four days and nights R and R, Rest and Recuperation. The soldiers were offered a number of activities that had been organized by the 'good ole' British Army. One of them was to go to Great Falls Montana of U.S. of A. and stay in a hotel there. Well, never having been to the U.S. before, our little band of 'Furstenau' rag tags decided that we would like to go to Great Falls and stay in the Hotel.

Transport had been laid on, so off we went to the Holiday Inn in Great Falls. America was a new experience for me and my mates and we were very surprised and pleased at how friendly they were to us British squaddies. That would probably not have been the case if we had gone to somewhere like New York, but Great Falls Montana is a country town and the locals seemed very friendly.

When we emerged from the hotel the next day for a look around the town, a large American car, with the hood down, pulled up with a squeal of tyres with three girls sitting on the bench like front seat. One of them said in her broad American accent "Hey, are you guy's brits?" Putting on my best 'posh' English accent I said "Yes we are Madame, and we are very pleased to make your acquaintance." After a brief conversation of introductions, the driver of the car said "Hop in and we'll show you the town." Obviously being extremely pleased with our introduction to America we 'hopped' and off we all went.

After a tour of the town we all had a good night out and take-away pizzas were purchased on the way back to the hotel. The pizzas where about the size of a flying saucer so we only managed to eat about half of it and the remainder ended up in the corner of the hotel room with all the boxes and wrapping that they had come in.

All in all we were very pleased with our choice of location for our R and R. We did attend a lot of the nightlife spots, but we were absolutely flabbergasted that all the establishments we attended had both types of music, Country and Western! Not a single disco in the whole town! Not that we were bothered we only wanted to go and ogle all the lovely young ladies that were there. The young ladies were extremely friendly and everyone that I spoke to invited me to "Come out and see the ranch sometime." Where there ranches were, and how to get there, we did not know! But we were very pleased with the invite. What we found interesting was that every one of them in the clubs was wearing a Stetson hat of some form. Even when they were indoors they did not take off their Stetson hats. Amazing! I think that because we didn't have Stetson's on that they immediately guessed that we were 'Brits'. Especially when they heard our strong British accents. Talk about cultural clash!

On the last night of the trip we returned to the hotel and had an attack of the 'Munchies'. This is one of the squaddie expressions that we used and it means to suddenly feel hungry. So, when we had our attack of the 'Munchies' we dug out the pizzas that we had discarded into the corner of the hotel room on the first night and finished them off! We were lucky not to get food poisoning! But a British squaddie is a tough sort with a cast iron constitution.

When the trip had drawn to an end we were all loaded back onto the airplane and flew back to our barracks in Germany and life resumed as normal. Well as normal as a soldiers life can be.

When in the army an infantry soldier does a lot of marching and drilling on the square. Square 'bashing' as we would call it. The Regiment would do a full and formal parade on the square on the 21st of December for remembrance of our Battle Honour of the Battle of Ferozeshah during the First Sikh War on that day in 1845. We would be out there continuously bashing away for about two weeks before hand to make sure that it all went as planned on the day.

At the time of writing this it seems strange to me how things can change over the years as person gets older. Back then, when I used to do the parade during my army years, I could feel nothing but pride for what my Regimental predecessors had done back then in 1845. That they had knocked ten buckets of shit out of those guys. However, being that much older, I cannot think about what happened back then without feeling anything but just sadness. Anyway, back to the story.

Often at that time of year the drill square would be covered in ice and frost and on the about turn some of the guys would take a tumble with their weapons clattering over the square. The drill sergeant would give them a damn good bollicking and shout "DIG YA HEELS IN AND YA WONT FALL OVER!" How rubber heels were meant to cut through solid ice and frozen tarmac escapes me! We did the practice drills with bayonets fixed as they would be on parade day. One time we were all stood to attention and the soldier next to me fainted and the bayonet of another soldier went straight through his jacket and out again, but amazingly and fortunately for him it never pierced the skin.

Another experience I had when on parade that I particularly remember was the one occasion that we went down to the other drill square in the bottom half of the barracks where the Enniskillen Dragoon Guards were based. This was to do a parade on Remembrance Sunday. We were marched about for a while and then after being brought to a stand still told to present arms for the 3 minutes silence. "PRESENT…..ARMS!" ONE, two three, ONE, two three, ONE! Crash, Crash, CRASH!

Then after the 3 minutes silence, in the distance a bag piper could be heard. He slow marched from behind us in the ranks, and obviously we were not allowed to move. He was playing the bag pipes with a slow, beautiful and extremely harrowing tune. Taking some time, he slow marched between all the ranks of the soldiers who were at the present. Then he slow marched off the square and into the distance until we could no longer hear the pipes. It was a moment that really touched me and I have to admit that being there at the present for such a long time was extremely hard, but even harder still, was not to let the tears come to my eyes, and show that I found it incredibly moving. It even brings tears to my eyes at the time of writing this and it was a moment I shall never forget. It was done in respect of all our fallen comrades in the past and how we should remember them all.

While in the army in Germany we would take our leave in England and be given all the documents we needed to return there. I had a good mate who was called Chang. All us chaps in the platoon called him Chang, but he was in no way Chinese he was an English guy from Torquay in Devon. We did come up with some bizarre nick names for each other in the mob. But strangely enough they never came up with a nick name for me, I am pleased to say.

Chang and I used to take our leave together so that we could stay at his mother's house there. Torquay was a good place for a young man to go for a holiday as there was plenty to do. We both liked snooker and there was a snooker club, and plenty of discos where we would go at night. To get to Torquay involved taking the boat train across Germany and Holland to the docks and then the overnight ferry to Harwich. Once in Harwich, we would have to get the necessary train connections to Torquay in Devon.

One time Chang and I went on leave and I had made up my mind that I was going to go AWOL! Absent With Out Leave. Why did I want to do this? Well being the keen young soldier that I was, I had been told by someone that a soldier would never be a good soldier unless he had done sometime in the guardhouse. So, to me it was the best way to get myself locked up! I overstayed my leave period for two days and then walked into the local police station one night and said "I'm handing myself in." The police officer on duty looked at me sideways and a bit strange and said "for what?" I said "I am absent without leave from the army." So, they simply just locked me up in a cell for the night and the next day let me out and sent me back to the regiment in Germany where I happily went!

I was put back on duty as normal and a few days later I was marched into the office of the company commander. I was given a punishment of twelve days in the guardhouse. Great! Whilst in the guardhouse there was another soldier from my platoon also serving twelve days. I won't mention his name as he maybe offended if someone were to find out, whereas I don't care because I had done it deliberately and this was a long time ago and young men sometimes do some stupid things that they regret. However, he was a mate of mine and a very funny bloke. So my days in the regimental jail flew by as my mate used to keep us amused.

We had a lot of our kit with us in the guardhouse and we had to iron it and press it and then fold it all into a perfect nine inch by nine inch square. Shine up our mess tins until they gleamed and 'bull' our boots until you could see your face in them. Occasionally the Regimental Police would come into the communal large cell where our beds were and all our kit was laid out nice and neatly on the bed. They would pick up some of our kit and exclaiming 'THIS IS MINGING!' They throw it across the room. (Minging being British Infantry speak for dirty.) Of course it wasn't 'minging' at all, but we had to start all over again!

At meal times the Regimental Police used to march us over the square to the cookhouse for our meals at double time. So it would be "Left right left right left right left right Mark time!" (Mark time is to march on the spot raising your knees to waist height.) The Regimental Police would just stroll along casually behind us. When they had caught us up it would be "Quick march, left right left right left right left right left right Mark time!" This process carried on until such time as we reached the cookhouse somewhat puffed out. We would then have our meal, which we had to throw down our throats as quickly as possible, and then be marched back to the jail at double time again. As you can imagine, it was not the best way of getting sustenance for the digestive system.

After about ten days of this, my mate that was in for his twelve day stretch lost his rag. He went to his bed where all his kit was laid out and grabbing the edge of the blanket, he whipped it up in the air throwing all his perfectly arranged kit all over the communal cell shouting "IT'S MINGING, IT'S MINGING, IT'S ALL BLOODY WELL BLOODY MINGING!" The frustration had got too much for him and he had 'lost the plot' for a moment! After he had calmed down and I had helped him rearrange all his kit, we both had a bloody good laugh about it.

After my stretch came to an end and I was let out, I felt that now I am a proper soldier. Which in fact it is of course a myth, you don't need to get locked up to be a good soldier. What a load of bollocks! The stupid things you do when you are a young man.

In 1983 the regiment was posted out of Germany and back to Britain to a barracks at Canterbury in Kent. I had never been to Canterbury before and I have to say that it is a beautiful city. It was to be a place, in or around, where I would spend the next 17 years of my life.

CHAPTER FIVE

South Armagh

After a short time based at Canterbury the regiment was sent on a four month tour of duty to Northern Ireland this was during the summer months. We were posted to a base in South Armagh near the border between southern and northern Ireland. The base that we were at was in fact the busiest heliport in the world, with choppers coming in and going out every few minutes. We rarely walked out to go on patrol. Normally we would go out in a chopper, do the patrol and then be picked up by a chopper and flew back in.

During my time there, there was a car bomb in the town and the bonnet of the vehicle we found four streets away. I was amazed at how far the bonnet of a car could fly! There was not much left of the car itself, just a burnt out twisted pile of metal.

Einstein said; "The world is a dangerous place, not because of those who do evil, but because of those who look on and do nothing." How right was he?

We as soldiers were not allowed to go off barracks unless it was for a patrol. So things got a bit boring at times. I wrote a letter to Ma and requested that she would send me something that I could use to start learning Spanish. For some reason having read 'As I walked out one midsummer morning,' I was still interested in learning to speak Spanish. She sent me some tapes and a book which were called Breakthrough Spanish, which I used to pass the time when not on patrol. There was also a gym within the barracks building which we used to use regularly. (Sweat saves Blood!)

During patrol, we were put into something called a brick. This was a division of a section of eight soldiers into two groups of four, and we used to patrol the open country of South Armagh near the border. We were given a bag of rations that normally consisted of two cheese sandwiches, a bag of crisps and an apple. Good healthy diet! If we were on patrol at night we would come back to the base sometimes in the wee small hours and the cookhouse would be open and a chef would be on duty most of the time. If not, there would be some bread and eggs available and a hot plate turned on. We would cook and live on fried egg sandwiches or 'egg banjos' as we called them. I know that the tour of Armagh was a dangerous time, but I loved it there! The countryside of that part of Ireland is beautiful in the summer months and it was a good summer in 1983.

When we were on patrol at about grub time the patrol commander would find somewhere where there were a lot of ferns growing, and a lot of ferns grow in that part of Ireland. He would put his hand on top of his head, which is the sign for 'on me' which means gather around. We would hunker down in the ferns and have our grub. Strangely enough, I was never scared when serving my four month tour. I don't know why today, being so much older perhaps I feel more mortal?

On patrol we would wear an amoeba jacket under our combat jacket to protect us from blast and gun shot. The jacket consisted of a blast proof jacket and a bullet proof plate over the heart front and back. They were damn heavy things! It was like wearing a suit of armour. As well as all the other things we had to carry. In a strange sort of way, we grew to love our amoeba jackets. We knew that they would protect us and possibly save our lives. To put them on we would throw them in the air shouting "ARRIBA, ARRIBA!" Which is Spanish for "ABOVE, ABOVE!" then we would get under them and let them fall onto our bodies and fasten them up. We shouted arriba because it sounded similar to amoeba. The mad things you do when in the infantry!

During that four month tour in the summer of 1983, there are three things that happened there that particularly stick out in my memory. These are written here in this book.

Firstly, we were choppered out on patrol one night and did our patrol in the rural areas and went to the R.V. point where we would be picked up by the chopper and flown back to base. We had to hand in all our ammunition and rifles to the armoury on return from patrol. (S.L.R. 147) Before handing in my weapon, I realized that I had lost a magazine of twenty rounds! My god when had that happened! To lose one single round of ammunition was a court martial offence in the British Army. Let alone twenty rounds! The only thing that I could think of was that it must have been when I was laying in the long grass waiting for the chopper to land. It must have slipped out of my pouch! Now, I am not knocking the army, but the webbing that I was wearing and had been issued with, was not of the greatest standard and sometimes a closed pouch could sometimes still let a magazine slip out with the soldier concerned being unaware.

At the time I had a platoon commander for whom I had the greatest respect for. Farren was my platoon commander. So I thought the only and best thing that I could do was to go to him and confess. I went to him and spoke to Farren saying "Sir, I appear to have lost a magazine of ammo, but Sir, I am really sure I know where the magazine will be Sir." I couldn't think of any where else in the whole patrol that it could be! He said "Give me a moment to work this out." After a short time, Farren came back to me and he said that we were all going back out there!

The whole patrol was loaded back into the chopper and flown out to our pick up point. I debussed from the chopper and went to the place on the ground that I had been laying in. I could see exactly where I had laid, because of the flattened long grass, even at night in the dark I could see, as it was a moonlit clear night. And laying there was that BLOODY magazine and the BLOODY twenty rounds of ammunition! Exactly where it had slipped out of my pouch. PHEWW! SAVED!

The second thing that happened that I remember about my commanding officer for in that in that blisteringly hot summer of 83, when we were always confined to barracks except patrol time, was when he arranged for our platoon to go to the beach for the day. It was in August of that year. We as his platoon were unaware of what was going on.

We got on a four ton truck, with full ammo and weapons, webbing gear, and our beloved amoeba jackets, and thought that we were going on an unexpected patrol. We were driven out across county and got to a nice beach. We piled off the Four Tonner, thinking whats going on? Farren just said "Go for a swim boys!" It was a boiling hot day that day and we all stripped off and ran into the sea, clothing, weapons and webbing all forgotten. Our platoon commander had even arranged for some grub for us to eat. We spent all day in the hot sun with no sun block available!

49

When the day drew to an end we would be returning to barracks and then had to put all our gear back on for the trip back. We all looked as red as lobsters and with the four ton truck bouncing around, and all our heavy kit and weapons it was fairly uncomfortable I can tell you! However, it was a marvellous day out and I have a great photograph which Farren took to remember it. What an officer! If all the officers in the British Army were like that, the British Army would be invincible!

Can you see me in the picture? I am the one at the back posing. And that is my ski mate Chalky next to me and my new buddy Lloydie third from the left.

Lastly, as I mentioned, during my time there in Armagh I was to meet a guy who was to be a good friend later in life. He was new to the army, so, just a sprog. He was put in my brick and his name was Lloydie, well that's what I called him. He asked me to nurture him in N.I. which I did. Later in life Lloydie and I were to take different paths, but we did remain good friends.

At the end of the summer of 1983 we returned to the barracks at Canterbury where we did a parade during which we were presented with the Queens Medal for Campaign Service, which I am extremely proud of. I know that a medal from the Queen is just a piece of metal and a ribbon, but they are from the Queen and I am very proud of my medals. To be honest as you read this book, you will find out that I also got two more medals from the Queen and I find it hard to explain why they mean so much to me! I think that it maybe that it was because the things that I did were not for the money, but for the protection of the country, but I have to say, I don't really know for sure!

It was not long after this that I decided that I would leave the army, as the prospect of being in the infantry for about the next twenty years did not appeal to me. I think that it may have been the tour of Ireland that influenced my decision, and there was a reason for this.

Something else that had happened when I was out there and when I was on a night patrol. While forming a road block at the border I was in position in a ditch. A car approaching us saw the road block and screeched to a halt, spun around and while wheel spinning sped off in the opposite direction. I had them in my sights and had to make a split second decision as to whether to fire or not.

Our lives where not threatened in any way so I didn't open fire. They were probably not even terrorists. They could have just been smuggling illegal goods over the border. This incident did really bring it home to me that we are not playing at toy soldiers anymore like I had felt when at I.J.L.B. and there maybe one time in the future that I would have to shoot a human being and not just a wooden target. I had grown up a bit since I had joined the army at sixteen and felt that I would like my life to take a different path. So I left the army at that time. I have to say that at the time of writing this, thinking about my time in the military, it does stir up some emotional feelings about all the things that I experienced during those years.

Anyway, perhaps I could find a job that involved saving lives not taking them, a medic or ambulance driver perhaps? Something involving blue flashing lights hmmm. So, leaving the military and with some remorse I had to say goodbye to all my army mates. I kept in touch with my ski-ing buddy Chalky for a while and he had met a young lady that he wanted to marry who was called Sharon. He invited me to their wedding and although I was not a soldier anymore and I attended the wedding gladly as he was still a mate. Chalky looked great in his military number ones for the wedding and I looked like a twat in my 1980's suit, but we all make mistakes.

CHAPTER SIX

MAKING PAPER

During my time in the mob, I had met a local girl who lived at Canterbury and we had formed a relationship. Debbie was her name. She and I used to frequent the night spots with our mates and have a good time. After leaving the army I was at a bit of a loss as to what I would do for work. After all, the things they teach you in the infantry are certainly things that will save your life at the time, but apart from being extremely fit, most of them are not a lot of use in Civvie Street.

I did have some money put by, that I used to rent a room in a house. The house was called Woodbine villa, but the residents referred to it as Fag house because of the cigarettes called Woodbines and in English slang in the south of the country people call cigarettes Fags. Fag house was in a road called Nunnery Fields and was not far from the public house called The Cross Keys that we used to frequent when I was in the mob. So, Debbie and I continued to go to the pub for some social activity with our friends.

The first job that I got was working in a petrol pumping station located on the London to Dover road the A2. My job was to attend the pumps and fill the vehicles with fuel and to sell other goods over the counter. The other guy that worked there was Chris. Chris was a huge guy, very tall and very large, and he had a wicked sense of humour and was always cracking jokes about the customers. It was great fun working there, the wages were not great, but I really liked it, because Chris was such a comedian, and it was such a change from military life, but I was not to be there for long, only eight weeks.

Debbie had a brother who worked at a Wiggins Teape paper mill in a village about five miles out of the City of Canterbury called Chartam. The mill had a reputation as being a good place to work so whilst I was working at the pumping station with my good old mate Chris, Debbie said she would have a talk with her brother and see if he could put in a good word for me at the mill. He managed to get me an interview for a job, which I attended and the result was that I was offered a job at the mill working in the finishing end part of the factory known as the Salle. So, I left the pumping station and my large and funny friend Chris and went to work at the mill.

Being an old mill, the paper making factory was located on the river Stour and the whole site was set out on both sides of the river. There were 3 paper making machines called numbers one, two and three. The paper was made on one side of the river by numbers one and two machines and on the same side of the river as the Salle by the largest and most modern machine number three. Wiggins Teape made top quality tracing paper. After the paper was made the huge paper webs that rolled off the end of the machines were transported by the greenbat to the place I worked in the Salle, where they were put on the reelers and then were cut in various size 'webs' according to the orders received, and then packed. Or the web would be then cut into sheets according to the orders and then packed in the sheet packing room.

The mill operated 24 hours a day seven days a week because it takes a lot of time, effort and cost to shut down, and start up a paper making machine. The shifts that I worked were laid out over a rather odd shift pattern, or so I thought anyway. There would be three shifts. 6 am to 2 pm. 2 pm to 10 pm, and the night shift 10pm to 6 am. Each shift you would work for seven days or nights and finish at 6 am on a Saturday morning when you would have a long weekend. The only drawback was that you were so knackered that you slept most of the weekend!

My job, as I was the new boy was to be the general 'dog's body' in the Salle. This involved shifting the webs around and bailing up the paper off cuts from the reelers into bails by using the bailing machine, and any other tasks that were required. The bailer was in fact an old piece of agricultural machinery which was designed for bailing straw. It was that old I think it must have been made when Moses was a boy! The old bailer used to jam up often and it would be a bugger to sort it out.

Before paper is cut into sheets it is called a Web, because that in effect is what paper is. When the bails of treated wood fibres are put into the pulping machine they are mixed with water and other ingredients to form a pulp. Then as they come out onto the huge and continuously moving felt which revolves around the rollers the water slowly drains off and the fibres settle into a web. This is then put through a series of rollers to squeeze out the remaining water and then the heated rollers to make any remaining moisture evaporate. At the end of the machine the now dry tracing paper is rolled onto a huge roller bar ready to go to the Salle.

For those who worked in the machine house you either had not much to do because once running, the machine was mainly automated. Or they had to go like a bat out of hell, because if the paper web broke at any stage during the process, paper would be spewing out of the machine everywhere over the floor. With all the heated rollers and moisture working in the machine houses was a good place to be working on winter nights, but like HELL on earth on hot summer days.

When I had been working at the paper mill for a while, Debbie and I decided that we would like to live together and we rented a flat at Dover road in Canterbury. So, I left Fag House in Nunnery Fields and moved in with her. The flat was on the second floor of a Victorian building over looking St Lawrence Cricket Ground which is the home of Kent County Cricket Club. In the winter you could see the whole ground from the flat window, and if it had not been for the deciduous trees that were on the other side of the road between the flat and the cricket ground you would have been able to watch cricket matches in the summer free of charge! However, I was not at all bothered by this as I think cricket is about as exciting as watching paint dry! (My apologies to any Cricket fans!) I am not a football fan either, but football has the great advantage over cricket of being finished sooner! (My apologies to any Football fans! And I know there are a lot out there!)

I did not live at the flat with Debbie for long as we soon fell out when living together. Strangely enough that seems to happen a lot with me and my lady friends. Anyone who has never made a mistake has never tried anything new! So I asked the owner of my last accommodation if my old room at Fag house was available. She said no, but there was a small wooden building available at the rear of the bed and breakfast on the opposite side of the road from old Fag house that she said was vacant.

I had a look at it. Hmmm, and although they called it a 'chalet' realistically it was little more than a large hut or shed. It consisted of a small room with a bed and few other features apart from small room with a loo and basin. If I wanted a bath or shower I would have to go to the main house for that. The price for renting the chalet was as cheap as chips, and it was in the summer months and I didn't intend to stay there long so I accepted the accommodation. I called it 'The shed'. It was basic accommodation but being an ex-infantry man I was used to roughing it a little if the price was right. While living there I did get quite attached to 'The shed'. What I liked about it was there were no other inhabitants, so it was the first time that I had ever lived alone in a building.

I moved out of the shed in 1984 as I had met another young lady at the Cross Keys who was called Nicola. She used to lurk by the bar with a good looking friend of hers called Jerry. I used to play pool nearby to the bar and we got chatting and then dating. I called her Nick. She was a lovely girl and we decided that we would rent a house in Dover Street not far from the city wall. The place was a bit of a dump, but in a good location as it was near to the Cross Keys, a good French restaurant, a Chinese take away and another good pub The Flying Horse. Or The Flying Divorce as we used to refer to it.

Here is a picture of Nick and me at her cousins wedding reception.

Nick worked as a secretary and was a good typist, it was then in the mid 80's that I had the inspirational idea that computers and word processing would be a thing of the future, so I asked if Nick would teach me how to type. She of course agreed. I brought an old second hand manual typewriter and started to learn how all the fingers could be used to create text faster than writing it by hand. After a while I started to get the hang of it and brought a new electronic type writer which had a crystal display screen. There is a well known excellent university in Canterbury where certain students must hand in their thesis in type text. So, I put an advert out that I could convert their written thesis and dissertations into type for a certain price. There was some response so I made some money on the side by typing their thesis and dissertations up for them.

My time at the paper mill was good enough, they had a good canteen where you could get a cheap dinner and desert before starting the 2 to 10 shift, and as time wore on, and as I worked there, I started to get trained in other aspects of the job. Packing the cut webs was one of them, and working in the sheet packing room another. Working in the sheet packing room was quite a laugh sometimes. I had made friends with most of the guys that worked at the finishing end and the main two mates were Guy and Pete. Quite often two of us, or even the three of us would be working in the sheet packing room where it was quiet and cool and you could have a laugh and a chat.

It was never made official between us, a sort of an unspoken agreement, but we would have a competition to see who could pack the most sheets in a shift. Which I am sure the foreman on our shift loved. Guy was about my age, but Pete was about ten years older. He had had the miss-fortune of that his hair had gone completely grey prematurely which made him look somewhat older than his thirty odd years. Not that he cared though. He had a nice wife and some lovely kids. There was a lot of good natured piss taking that went on between us in the sheet packing room and one of the things that Guy and I did was to take the piss out of Pete by singing a song that was in the charts in 1984 by a band called The Bluebells. The song was Young at Heart! Pete didn't mind he just used to have a good laugh about it with us.

It was at about this time that Guy and I decided that we would like to go on a ski-ing holiday together. We wanted to go to a good resort that was not too pricy, had good ski-ing and good night life. I told him I knew just the resort for that. Sol in Austria. As I told you before about my army days I had learnt ski in the army and having been a number of times since I had my own boots and skis so at this stage would considered myself an accomplished skier, well, by British standards anyway.

Guy was not quite so as advanced as me but he told me he was willing to have a go at anything. We booked a holiday for the winter staying at a hotel in Sol with a twin room for two. When the date arrived off we went to the resort. Firstly we arranged some boots, skis and poles for Guy. The next day dawned and when we looked up at the mountain we where somewhat disappointed that there was no snow on the lower slopes. This was not really a problem as there was plenty of snow further up. We gathered our gear together and took the lift up to the upper slopes. We would ski throughout the day with me giving Guy some tips on his technique and then at the end of the day we would take the lift back to the bottom of the mountain.

It was a good week's ski-ing and good entertainment in the bars in the evening so Guy and I had a bloody good wild time! The funniest thing that happened was on the last day. Rather than queue to get down the mountain, I suggested that we ski down instead. Guy looked at me sideways and a bit dubious, he said, "Are you sure about this Mick?" but we decided to ski down. What the hell, it was our last day!

At first the snow was not too bad and we coped alright, then as we got lower the snow became less and less and the ice became more. I said to my good mate Guy. "Let me ski down first, and I will pick the easiest route for you, and when I stop and wave, you follow me down." He agreed. I skied down and having my own skis on with nice very sharp edges they cut the ice like ice skates.

Guy started to follow me down and about half way down, where it got steep he lost his grip on the ice and his rented skies went from under him. He carried on hurtling down, sliding down the mountain side coming head first towards me. As he got near I could see the look of absolute terror on his face, with his eyes like saucers. He zoomed past me and carried on clattering, sliding down until eventually going into the trees he came to a halt, fortunately unharmed. I laughed and laughed. Did Guy laugh? No, he had nearly SHIT himself! I just carried on ski-ing even when the snow and ice ran out I just skied on the wet grass. Guy took off his skis and walked down the rest of the way.

In general it was a great trip apart from that time when Guy saw his life flash before his eyes. We both swore that we would one day return to that same hotel together. We even wrote and hid a little message to us both in the woodwork of the room that we could find later in life. Unfortunately due to a change in circumstances this never happened, but still a trip to remember. So, Guy, if you ever read this, give me a ring and let's go back to Sol and go ski-ing together. Who knows we may even find that hidden message to ourselves from all those years ago!

As I said working at the paper mill was o.k. What I would have liked to do was to get onto operating the reeler as this was a more technical operation and certainly not such hard labour. However, working at Wiggins Teape was dead mans shoes for promotion. You had to wait for someone to die or retire before you can move up the ladder. Perhaps that was another premonition of what was to be in the future for me, the aspect of moving up a ladder.

During my time there I applied to join a working mans club in Canterbury close to where I lived and near to the Cross Keys. I was accepted as a member and started to frequent the place more often in 1986. As a club it was good enough and had two snooker tables and held social functions on a regular basis when a band would come and play for the evening and there would be various entertainment.

It was about this time that I bumped into my old army mate Lloydie. (How strange.) We had lost contact a number of years ago when I left the army after our time in South Armagh. The regiment had moved on from Canterbury and I was not expecting to see any of my old army mates again, but when I was walking through the subway near to my rented house in Dover Street, who should come walking the other way but Lloydie! What a surprise! You could have knocked me down with a feather! "Lloydie, how are you me old mate?" We shook hands and even had a little embrace which we both found a little embarrassing!

I asked Lloydie what he was doing in Canterbury and he told me that he was here to visit his daughter Hannah. Lloydie and his previous, and I must say very beautiful wife Heather who he had met when based at Canterbury in the Army had parted company and he was now serving as a Police Officer in the Metropolitan Police Force. He would come to Canterbury on a regular basis to visit his daughter. After that I saw a lot of Lloydie because he would always stay with me when he came to Canterbury for visits. It was through me that he met his next long term girlfriend, but that is later in the book.

It was at this time in late 1986 that I was starting to get somewhat miffed about my job in the paper making industry. As I said earlier, I didn't want to spend the rest of my life working as the Salle boy. Promotion was dead mans shoes and to work until retirement age as a sheet packer or a reeling machine operator did not appeal. So what was I to do? I had no idea! As and ex-infantry soldier I had no skills in anything that was very useful outside of the army. It was not until the spring of 1987 that I had a stroke of luck that brought it to me. More on that shortly.

It was the Christmas of 1986 that I spent Christmas in the French Alps with my buddy Julian from the Paper Mill and some of his buddies on a ski trip. Why did my then girlfriend Nick not come with us? Well at the time of booking the trip we had had a bit of a fall out and she was not included. We were back together now but it was too late to book her in. Why did my mate Guy from the Paper Mill not come? Because I think that slide down the ice on our last trip to Sol, had put the fear of God into him about going ski-ing with me! So it would just be Me, Julian and his mates who didn't actually work at the mill.

We had booked into a high altitude purpose built resort called Flaine. This was high in the French Alps where snow was guaranteed. I had never been to one of these purpose built places before and was looking forward to it.

As it turned out the resort was fairly characterless, as I should have expected I suppose. But the snow that trip was phenomenal, buckets of the stuff everywhere. Talk about a white Christmas! In the evenings the entertainment was pretty tame. Not really much going on to write home about, unlike the wild times that Guy and I had experienced in Sol.

All in all it was a pretty good ski trip and we had a great time. Powder snow everywhere and I have some good pictures of me ski-ing down through the powder and all you can see is my hands and head above the powder snow. FANTASTIC!

In the spring of 1987 I was at the social club playing snooker with a friend and I started to have a good Darby and Joan (moan) about my current occupation and that I would like to do something else, but didn't know what. He said to me, "What about being a Fireman?" Hmmmm interesting. Hmmmm I had considered a job as an ambulance driver or something that involved blue flashing lights, you would have thought I would have had that idea myself! Perhaps it was my destiny! So, the next day I went to Canterbury Fire Station, knocked on the door and asked. "I would like to know more about being a Fireman, what can you tell me?" The Officer gave me a contact telephone number. I went home and called the number and found out that I could come to Maidstone for some mental and physical tests. The Kent Fire Brigade were recruiting!

On the day specified, I went to the Kent Fire and Rescue Service Training Centre located at Loose Road, Maidstone. I was pretty fit in those days and sailed through the fitness tests with flying colours. Also, the mental tests did not provide much of a barrier.

At that time the Fire Service was recruiting a lot of ex-military people, because they were fit, had discipline and new how to take orders. The only thing that almost stopped me joining was the fact that I am only five foot six and a bit! Things have changed since then, but then, in 1987 a Fireman must be a minimum of five foot six tall. And I just scraped over the bar. I was pleased to hear that the recruit course would start in September the 12th 1987of that year, which strangely enough was the same day of the same month that I started my army training nine years back in 1978.

So, I left the paper making industry and started the next stage of my life. It was a shame that I lost contact with Guy and Pete. (Young at heart.) I did hear later from someone that Guy had got married and was starting a family and the Pete and all his family had moved to Australia. Good luck to them both. Good buddies from the paper making years and I hope they both come across this book one day and read it.

CHAPTER SEVEN

MAIDSTONE

Find a job that you love and you'll never work a day in your life. (Confucius)

The training at the Training Centre where I had been to for my initial tests was to last for a period of three months. Us, the recruits were to be split into two groups Red and Blue. The reason for this naming of the groups was because on the operational side of a Fire Station there are four Watches, red, blue, green and white. There were not a large number of us on the training course, only about twenty men. We were all about the same sort of age, men in their early or mid twenties. Some of them had no background in military or formal training, so I felt that I may have an advantage in that department.

Each Watch had two instructors to educate them during training. A Watch commander is called a Sub Officer and a second in command is called a Leading Fireman. We where to refer to them as Sub and L.F. My Sub was John Bence who was a excellent teacher and a bloody good Sub. Unfortunately John is no longer with us due to his premature demise.

Each Watch had a Fire Engine or Fire Pump, or just the Pump, as it is referred to by members of the service. In those days most people were unaware of the all the equipment that is carried on a Fire Pump, me included! This was because they had never got to look into the lockers on the sides of the Fire Appliances. The only time they would see a Fire Appliance was on the road or at a fire and at times like that they stayed well away. Most people thought that there was little more than some ladders on the roof and hose in the lockers. Things have changed a lot since the eighties and these days part of a Fireman's duties is to attend schools and educate people in Fire Prevention and what equipment they would find on a Fire Appliance and what it would be used for.

The first week of my training course was fairly simple and easy. Firstly we were fitted with our fire kit, which back then was somewhat different from the fire kit that I used to wear just before my retirement. The fire kit consisted of a fire tunic, which was like something made from horse hair! A pair of water proof rubber leggings, a pair of rubber Wellington boots with a steel toecap. And a leather belt and pouch for the fire axe. Underneath this fire kit we would wear our work wear which was a tee shirt and a pair of blue cotton trousers. The idea of a Fireman's fire kit is to protect him from the heat during fighting a fire which worked to a certain extent, but the trouble with the plastic leggings was that they would keep the moisture in just as much as keeping it out. So, as soon as a Fireman started working hard in the heat and humidity and sweating the underclothing he was wearing would be soaked in sweat.

After being issued with our fire kit, we were shown all the equipment that was carried in the six lockers on the sides of the appliance and explained to what it would be used for. The rest of the week was mainly in the class room during which we where shown some pretty horrific films of some of the real fires that were actually caught of film.

One that I particularly remember to this day was of a high rise building where the smoke and flames were moving up through the building and the people trapped on the roof had no way to escape. Things got so desperate that people were flinging themselves off the roof to a certain death below to escape being burnt to death. I think the idea behind being shown this was to put the fear of god into us (Shock tactics.) so that we would give all the lessons our full attention, which worked!

On Friday afternoon of the first week we were taken out into the drill yard where there was a Turntable Ladder parked. We were lined up and the T.L. was extended to its full height of one hundred feet. The head of the ladder was not rested onto the tower, it was just free standing with nothing to support it. We were told that this was another test. We all would have to climb the T.L. to the top.

One volunteer required. I took one step forward and volunteered to be the first to have a go. Lower down things were all right, but as I climbed the ladder it started to sway about, the higher I got, the greater the swaying became. Near the top it was swaying around like a piece of grass in a strong wind. Somewhat worrying! However, I had strength in my convictions, I was sure that it was completely safe or we would not be allowed to do it. Eventually I reached the head of the ladder and climbed down again. Once all the recruits had done this that was the end of our first week of the thirteen weeks that we would have to get through to become Firemen.

The next twelve weeks passed by like a flash. The training was wide and varied and tests were taken throughout the course terminating in exams at the end. One thing that we were not trained on during the course was the wearing of Breathing Apparatus, as this was done separately on another course once the Fireman had passed out. When I say passing out I do not mean that he fainted. That is the expression that is used to say that the trainee had completed the course and become a Fireman. At the end of the course there is a passing out parade which is done in undress uniform with the man's family and friends in attendance.

There was a wide and varied amount of things that the trainee Fireman must learn during his time at the Training Centre. Some of the terminology used may be strange to someone who has not had the experience of being a Fireman. When a man is training to be a Fireman there are a number of books that are available to assist him. These are useful when learning in the class room and on the drill ground. These are called the Manuals of Firemanship. The copies of which I was given I still possess today. These are as follows:

The Manuals of Firemanship

Book 1. Elements of combustion and extinction.
Book 2. Fire brigade equipment.
Book 3. Fire extinguishing equipment.
Book 4. Incidents involving aircraft, shipping and trains.
Book 5. Ladders and appliances.
Book 6. Breathing Apparatus and resuscitation.
Book 7 Hydraulics and water supplies.
Book 8 Building construction and structural fire protection.
Book 9 Fire protection of buildings.
Book 10 Fire Brigade communications
Book 11 Practical firemanship. (Published in 1981)
Book 12 Practical firemanship. (Published in1983)

These books were mainly for use in the class room. In addition to this there was also the Fire Service Drill Book. This was for use in the class room, but also for use out on the drill ground.

Most of the words and expressions used by a Fireman are self explanatory, but there are a number of words and expressions that would sound like another language to a person who was not trained to be in the Fire Service.

Terminology

Get to work.	This is used on the drill ground to put into action men and equipment
Branch.	The nozzle at the end of a line of hose.
Knock off.	Close the branch and put the pump in idle.
Rest.	To make a drill that is going wrong come to a halt.
STILL!	To use in an emergency if an accident is imminent.
Slip.	To remove a ladder from the appliance.
Pitch.	To erect a ladder against a building.
Pawls.	The device that locks an extended ladder in extended position.
Extend to lower.	Raise the ladder a little to disengage the pawls.
Carry down.	When a Fireman puts a person on his shoulder and climbs out of the window and onto the ladder and descends.

For the drill yard there were things such as hydrant and hose drills, appliance drills for 3, 4, and 5 men crews. The laying of the line of hose from a hydrant. Adding one length of hose. Replacing a burst length of hose. Getting a branch to work on a roof or upper floor. Using a dividing breeching to split the line of hose into two streams. Getting a hose reel to work. Soft suction, hard suction, working from open water. The list goes on.

When doing drills out on the drill ground the crews were lined up where they could see the whole drill ground and there would usually about 9 or 10 in Red Watch squad. So if the Sub detailed a drill for perhaps a crew of 4 then the remaining trainees in the squad could watch the drill and benefit from seeing it in action. Obviously when we were early on in the course and new to the drill yard the drills would be to do something quite simple, but as our knowledge and skill improved, the drills would become more and more complex.

As the course developed we all became stronger and fitter. When we got to the point when the Sub thought that we were strong enough he had us do a live carry down from the forth floor of the tower. This was a somewhat nerve searing moment. Not so much for the one actually doing the carry down, as he was holding onto the ladder. It was the one being carried down that had the nervous experience. After all, being on someone's shoulder up a ladder about 40 feet up off the ground would put anyone who even had balls of steel on edge a bit!

Obviously if the casualty is insensible then the crew would have employ the method of evacuation called the 'Picking up drill'. This enables the crew of two to pick up the unconscious casualty. For any one who has never had the misfortune of having to pick up an insensible person, I can tell you that it is not as easy as it sounds. Even if you are a large strong man, and the victim just a small and fairly light little granny. If the person genuinely is insensible they go like a rag doll and it makes things difficult, or if the person is a six foot six tall, and half as wide builder, virtually impossible. If they are completely 'zonked' out it's like trying to pick up a handful of worms!

Anyway the drill goes like this. With the casualty laid on his or her back, Fireman number one places one foot between the legs of the person and kneels down on the other knee. Then Fireman number two places one foot to one side of the head and kneels down on the other knee with the knee on the other side of the head. Then Fireman number one grasps the wrists of the casualty one in each hand. Fireman number two slides his hands under the shoulders of the casualty and they simultaneously lift the casualty into the sitting position.

Fireman number one puts his hands under the shoulders and Fireman number two slides his hands around the chest and links them. Number one says "One, two, three lift" and the casualty is raised to the standing position. Then while number two supports the casualty, number one drops down and passing his right arm between the legs and grasping the wrist in his left hand while simultaneously jamming his shoulder into the groin. He then stands up with the casualty on his shoulders. Then with his right arm still wrapped around the casualties right leg he takes the wrist of the casualty into his right hand. The casualty is now securely on his shoulder and he has his left hand free to use if he has to do a carry down. As you can imagine, not something that is simple and easy to do!

For one Fireman alone to pick up a insensible person on his own is almost mission impossible, But there is a drill for this that we would have to practice. This could be achieved if the person is a small light little granny of perhaps a younger person not fully grown who is quite light.

The Fireman drags the body of the unconscious person over to the nearest wall. Then with the person rolled over onto his or her front, he puts the casualty with the feet up against the wall. He is now ready to go for the pick up routine.

Getting down on one knee he slides his hands under the arms of the casualty and raises the person into the kneeling position. Then squatting down he links his arms under the arms of the casualty, then standing up, raises the casualty to the upright position while pinning him or her against the wall.

Then taking the right wrist in your left hand. Then you step back and bending over allow the body's trunk to fall over your right shoulder. Then resume your upright position and you have the person on your shoulder. You normally have to juggle the body about a bit to get it balanced right, and then make your way out of the building. Like I said, not easy and even more like picking up a large handful of worms than doing it with the assistance of someone else.

Another thing that was incorporated in the course was 'Knots and Lines'. Many of the things that a Fireman has to do when on the drill ground or at an incident is to be able to employ the correct knot for the job. This can involve many different knots and it had to be tied quickly, efficiently and in the dark or smoke which is the circumstances on most occasions. We were shown how to tie all the different knots. These consisted of: Overhand knot, half hitch, reef knot, double sheet bend, clove hitch, rolling hitch pulling to the left or right, round turn and two half hitches, bowline, running bowline, chair knot and sheep shank.

Then we were taught using all our equipment what knot you would use and when. To ensure that we learnt all the knots, we each given a short length of line, (Never say 'ROPE' in the British Fire Service, almost a court martial offence!) which we used to practice all the knots until we could do them with our eyes shut.

Another thing that we needed to know was all the hand signals that we may have to use. A fire ground is, or can be, a very noisy place. Or the occupants of the fire ground maybe so far away from each other that they cannot hear each other shout. In this case only a hand signal will convey your message for you.

There were many activities that we got involved in at the training centre to get up fitness levels for fire fighting. Not only all the charging around the drill yard and doing drills there was also a 5 mile run that we would do on a regular basis. We would run as a squad until we got within a half a mile of the training centre and then we were let off the leash and tore off to see who could get to the drill yard first where the run would finish. Before we were let off the leash we felt like race horses chomping at the bit! (Let me go, let me go, let me GO!)

Another activity that was done in the service was a game of volley ball. We learnt how to play while at the training centre. This was a game that I enjoyed immensely even though I am not a tall guy, and being taller does give you some advantage. We would put the net up in the drill yard and have a game. Unfortunately later in my Fire Service career volley ball was disallowed as it was deemed to have being causing too many injuries among the men. Probably because the Firemen were much too enthusiastic about it!

During my time at the Training Centre we also had to learn how to do the foot drill that is used in the Service. The marching, turning and saluting etc. You would think that as I was an ex-infantry man, I would have no problem with this, but, the British Fire Service is based fundamentally on things that are done in the British Navy and not things that are done in the British Army. Therefore the foot drill was completely different to what I had learnt earlier in life. But I was a man who was used to discipline and orders so I managed to convert fairly easily from British Army Drill to British Navy Drill. ONE, two three, ONE, two three ONE. Not much difference there then in the timing between the army and the navy.

In the lecture rooms we did a lot of learning about all the technical side of fire fighting, having instruction and lectures from the Sub Officers of Red Watch and Blue Watch. As I mentioned earlier we were provided with the Manuals of Firemanship to assist us in our studies. We studied the physical properties of matter, heat and temperature, the triangle of fire that enables combustion to take place, heat, oxygen and fuel. The transmission of heat, the basis of chemistry, fire extinguishing equipment, air Breathing Apparatus, oxygen Breathing Apparatus, the duration of the Breathing Apparatus, operational procedures, first aid and resuscitation, how to gain entry depending on the nature of the building, etc, etc.

The most dreaded subject was the most technical which was hydraulics. I remember when the study of this subject started. Our Sub John Bence walked into the lecture room and said "Today we will start with the study of hydraulics, or hibollicks as it is know in the Fire Service." God bless him.

There was one thing that happened during the time that I was at the Training Centre that was to put my training course of hold for a while. On the night of the 12th of October there was a hurricane in Kent. It was the described in the press as "The storm of the 20th century." Leaving 18 people dead and thousands of trees uprooted. Albeit the fact that we were trainees we were called into service a bit early to help clean up the mess and cut up all the fallen trees of which there where thousands across the county.

Our weeks of training continued and a number of the guys dropped out of the course for various reasons. One day that we were to go on morning parade one of the trainees that was on the course, whose name escapes me decided that he would have a bit of a joke. He got some sunglasses and knocking out the lenses wore them on parade as a pair of glasses like the band from Scotland who were popular at the time, the Proclaimers. He did this just to see if the instructors of the course would notice. Obviously they did and when he was questioned about it on the parade square he started singing "When you go will you send back a letter from America" We all fell about laughing including the instructors.

Another thing that we had to learn at the training centre is about radio procedure. There is a standard of radio procedure that is adopted all across the country and is very similar to the procedure used in the Army, so I was fairly familiar with it already. However I was to find out later that different Brigades vary the radio speak somewhat. The Fire Service uses the same Phonetic Alphabet as what the military do, so I did not need to be taught this because I knew that already. Alpha, Bravo, Charlie, Delta, Echo, Foxtrot, Golf. Etc etc.

A large section of the class room work on the course involved learning about the nature and behaviour of fire which we would find useful when fire fighting. To assist us in studying this we would use the Manual of Firemanship Book One. Elements of combustion and extinction.

Before our passing out day we had a series of competitions between Red Watch and Blue Watch, which where of a physical nature. One of these competitions was a tug of war. During the tug of war even though I was very fit I badly pulled a muscle in my back and collapsed. I was taken to hospital to be checked over. I was given some pain killers and sent back to training centre to do my exams.

While I was trying to answer the exam question papers I was in so much agony that I could hardly write. I tried to answer all the questions, but then I really did pass out! I fainted and collapsed on the floor of the exam room. The service were good to me about that, perhaps they felt that they had some obligation to me, who knows. Anyway, I was allowed a few days to recover from my injury before taking the exam. When I took the exam I passed with flying colours. I was to be a Fireman after all.

I have to say that it was that bad back injury that gave me a bit of jip for about the next year until it finally healed up. But obviously I wasn't going to mention it unless I had too, because I was worried at that time they might boot me out of the Service!

On the day of our passing out we did a demonstration of the fire fighting skills that we had gained on the drill yard and also dressed up in our undress uniform did some marching and a parade for the spectators. Then suddenly that was it! I was a Fireman and my posting was to the Fire Station at Canterbury on Red Watch.

CHAPTER EIGHT

RED WATCH

After leaving the Training Centre with all my fire kit I had a weeks leave before reporting for duty. I reported for duty as required on the specified day at Canterbury Fire Station, and immediately met a guy who was an older Fireman due to retire from the service in few years. His name was Keith and he was a nice guy and a real character and made me feel welcome to the Watch. Keith had a few funny features about him. He was a balding man, but used to hide this with what the other Firemen on Red Watch called the walnut whip. Also he had a false set of teeth, but more about that later.

Keith used to come to work on his black push bike which looked about as old as the hills! He lived up the top of the hill from Canterbury Fire Station at Nunnery Fields, where I lived when at Fag House, and he used to spin down the hill to the side entrance to the drill yard and then banking his bike over, he would put his right foot out, without using the brakes, and with his blakeys skidding, skid across the road to enter the drill yard. It was hilarious to watch old Keith arriving at work as if he was coming in on a fire 'Shout'. I am sure that he used to do that deliberately just to keep us amused! What a character!

At Canterbury there were two Fire Pumps and a number of 'Specials'. A Special is a vehicle that does not have a pump incorporated into it. These can be things like a Turntable Ladder, a Command Unit, etc, etc. Each Watch had eighteen Firemen on the Watch at that time which was considered to be a large Watch by Fire Service standards.

The Watch commander of Red Watch at that time was Eddie, yet another character from the old days that had some funny and strange, but not offensive ways about him. At those times Canterbury was a fairly busy Fire Station and fire calls were frequent. My Watch Sub Eddie knew that I was a new boy to the Watch and thankfully he took it as his duty to protect the new boys, but also to teach them the skills of being an operational Fireman at the same time. As operational Firemen we all knew that it was a hazardous occupation.

Even before my Breathing Apparatus course which was due to go on soon, I entered a building on fire, under the orders of my Sub. At that time in the city there was a pyromaniac going around and setting fire to all the schools of the City. So, my first operational job as a Fireman was to assist in trying to put out a fire in a school at night. Eddie said to me "I want you to go in and ventilate the building."

This did not mean that I had to go near the fire, just crawl under the smoke and through the water that was on the floor and open all the windows. This I did and it ventilated the building. It did let a lot of the smoke out of the building so that the Firemen wearing Breathing Apparatus could achieve their goal and put out the fire. There were many fires in the schools of Canterbury that year. I don't know if the culprit was ever found, but I certainly hope he or she was, the little toe rag!

One unfortunate thing that happened on that incident was that we had to set into the hydrant for a plentiful supply of water for the pumps. The hydrant was up the hill about three lengths of hose from the pumps. From the locker we removed the standpipe key and bar and three lengths of hose from the hose locker. Then running up the hill we set in by removing the pit cover, setting in the standpipe key and bar. We then ran back down the hill while unrolling the hose connecting the lengths together and finally setting in to the pump. I then gave the water on signal to one of the guys standing by the standpipe, he had flushed the hydrant and connected the hose, receiving the signal he then he put the water on. The water on signal being an arm raised in the air.

There was just one snag with this plan. We had not taken the small battery powered yellow flashing lamp with us up to the hydrant and the hydrant was in the middle of the road right on a bend. A motorist came screeching along the road not seeing the standpipe until it was to late he drove straight over it and snapped off the standpipe sending it flying. Of course the hydrant was on full bore and the water was now spurting straight up into the air like a geyser venting off. Bummer, no water supply to the pumps! Drastic action would have to be taken. Someone would have to go and turn off the hydrant and ship another standpipe from the other pump locker. One of the other chaps got this job and you guessed it, he got absolutely soaked and it was in the middle of the night in the middle of winter. Poor chap.

Another incident that we attended that I remember and makes me chuckle was when there was a barn on fire in a remote rural location, but still on the fire ground of E80 Canterbury. It was at night that the incident occurred and we were tipped out of bed to attend it. Barn fires are quite a common occurrence for the Fire Service as this can be caused by something called spontaneous combustion.

Spontaneous ignition temperature is the lowest temperature at which the substance will ignite without the introduction of a flame or source of ignition. Certain materials, especially of an organic nature, can ignite in such a way, which can be the result of the action of bacteria contained within the fuel source which in itself is a good thermal insulator.

My Sub at that time Eddie used to wear his fire axe belt and had attached a lot of other things to the leather belt he wore for fighting fires. He had his axe, torch and a length of line, amongst other things. As he ran towards the fire, with all his regalia flapping around, he did not see the ditch in the darkness and went straight down faster than a roman candle, but to my amazement he bounced out like a rubber ball! And he just kept running towards the fire! I assume that he was hoping no one had seen it at the time. I was impressed. Now that's what I call a good Fireman!

The draw back with spontaneous ignition within a barn is that the ignition can be, and usually is, deep within the hay or straw contained in the barn or hayrick due to the thermal insulation, and this then requires a lot of hard graft from the Firemen to pull it all apart to get to the seat of the fire. Also, as the straw is pulled apart it can flare up as you are actually assisting in completing the triangle of fire by introducing a plentiful source of oxygen to the fire. However, there is no other way of going about it. As I am sure that everyone is aware that straw is pretty good at shedding water, as that is why people used it to thatch the roofs of their houses.

So, the upshot of it is. Is that it is no good just pouring gallons and gallons of water onto a barn fire because all that you will be achieving is wasting a lot of water and diesel fuel! No good what so ever. You have just got to 'bite the bullet' and get in there and pull the thing apart.

On a number of occasions that I have been involved in putting out a barn fire, and there have been plenty of them over the years, we have used any farm machinery available to assist in this task. So, if the farmer happened to have a tractor with or a forklift truck available we would get them to help us complete the task. Either the farmer or farm hand would drive the thing, or on some occasions there were some Firemen who knew how to operate the vehicle, and we would use it to pull the straw or hayrick apart to get to the seat of the fire.

Barn fires, my God there have been a lot of them over the years, and they are just nothing but bloody hard graft. And why is it that they always occur in the middle of winter in the middle of the night? Damn it! If you know the answer to that one, would you please be good enough to tell me. Anyway, moving on.

A few weeks passed and then I was sent back to the Training Centre at Maidstone to do my Breathing Apparatus training or B.A. training as Firemen refer to it. The course was a testing time. It was a two week course and a Fireman had to learn how to wear the B.A. set. Also learn how to do the entry control procedures and to work as a team in heat and dark with their colleagues.

With a mask on, communicating with their mate was a problem. Also at a fire things are usually pretty noisy with the fire crackling and the pumps outside roaring away at full tilt. So we had to learn about communicating through hand signals. We needed to know how to lay a guide line to make sure that we did not get lost when searching in the heat and smoke and for other teams coming in behind us. This enables other Firemen to be able to follow the route that the first team had taken through the smoke and search the building in the darkness. There would also be something called a branch line, which would be tied to the guide line and enable other B.A. teams to search other parts of the building.

The instructors would set light to a real fire of wooden pallets in the Fire House and we had to go in through the smoke, locate the fire and extinguish it. It was incredibly hot in the Fire House. So hot in fact that the heat affected our plastic leggings and the material they were made from would go all wrinkled and change from yellow to brown. The course that I attended was extremely good and the instructors knew what they were doing. At no time did I feel in danger. Perhaps this was because when I was on my recruit course I saw other Firemen being put in the Fire House and no one was in any way burnt or injured. So, after finishing the B.A. course I felt like at last I was a proper Fireman.

On my return to Red Watch at Canterbury things in the service continued as normal for a while. You had to do four years in the service before you became a qualified Fireman. I think that has changed at the time of writing this, but that's the way that it was in the 1980's. In all my time in the service the shift pattern did not change. You did two days of 9.00 a.m. to 6.00 p.m. Then two nights of 6.00 p.m. to 9.00 a.m. then you had four days off. This was a good shift pattern and was still in place when I left the service, but there had been much talk about changing this shift pattern for years.

There was a dormitory at the Fire Station and when we were on night duty we could get our heads down if of course we weren't 'tipped out' to a 'Shout'. To be asleep when the bells went down was like being woke up by someone putting an air horn in your ear and pressing the button! It would immediately set your heart thumping! No surprise there! On the rare occasions that we got two nights sleep without being tipped out, my old mate Keith used to say in the morning, "Fire Brigade two, general public nil." Of course we used to chuckle.

It was about this time that a funny thing happened while on the Red Watch. Firemen like to have a bit of a laugh occasionally and play a joke on each other. No surprise there either! There was one Fireman who lived outside the City in a country hamlet and he had to drive into the City passing through a place where pheasants were bred to provide a bit of sport for people to go on a pheasant hunt. One day as Simon was driving to work two pheasants flew out of nowhere and Simon hit them and killed them both. He thought 'I'll drop them in the boot of the car and the family will have them in the pot tonight.'

Unfortunately for him, Simon made the mistake of telling the guys on Red Watch what had happened. One of the guys on the Watch phoned the Police Station which was just across the road from the Fire Station to ask the Cops if they would help play a joke on Simon, which they were more than willing to do, in fact they were a little over enthusiastic!

They sent two Police Officers over to the Fire Station and they asked if they could see the owner of the vehicle registration number… (I can't remember the number). Simon was brought to the office at the front of the Fire Station and one of the Cops, speaking in his formal police voice said "Is this the registration number of your vehicle Sir?" Simon confirmed that it was. Then the Cop said "I am formally arresting you for the theft of two pheasants stolen from the grounds of Lower Hardres Woods." Simon's jaw hit the floor and then they handcuffed him and marched him off back over to the Police Station. Then after reading him his rights they told him that a solicitor would be summoned and then they threw him into a cell and left him there to stew for about four hours!

Eventually we thought that enough was enough and called the Police Station and asked them to let him out which of course they did. They went to the cell and said to Simon, "It seems that there has been and error sir and the owner of the pheasants will not be pressing charges after all, you are free to go." Simon returned to the Fire Station somewhat flabbergasted and life continued as normal.

At the Fire Station at Canterbury we had something called the Mess Club to provide meals for the on duty Firemen. The Mess Club employed two cooks to cook for the Firemen. The cooks would swap around their hours where on the first week, one of the cooks would cook for the day shift and one to cook supper for the night shift. Then the next week they would swap around and so on and so forth. One of the Firemen was the nominated Mess Manager who would arrange the menu and what meals the Firemen would be having for that 'set'. A 'set' was the word used to describe a period of duty of two days and two nights. The Mess Manager was responsible for collecting the money from the Watch members, and organise the accounts book for the Mess Club.

The cooks would be informed as to what meals would be eaten for dinner and supper during each 'set'. If she was working the day shift she would prepare cheese rolls or cheese and onion rolls for elevenses and cook what was going to be consumed at lunch time at one O'clock. If she was working the evening period she would prepare supper ready for nine O'clock.

Obviously, there where times when we got a 'Shout' at meal times and if this happened the cook would put all the prepared meals in the hot plate to keep the meals warm until the Firemen out on the 'Shout' returned back to the Fire Station. The hot plate, as it was called was little more than a large warm oven with a couple of shelves that the plates of food would be put in. There were some aluminium hoops which could be placed over the plates of food and then they could be stacked up in the hot plate. There was just two drawbacks about this arrangement. One, on return to the Fire Station at the end of the 'Shout' if the meal was partially eaten, you had to try to identify which was your dinner or supper from the hot plate, and two, if it turned into a bit of a long job on the 'Shout' even if you did manage to identify which was your dinner it would be dried out to a crisp!

Then after a few years the Mess Club turned a corner. We got a microwave oven! (Hooray!) Those that were not tipped out on the 'Shout' could write on the side of the plates with the use of his chino graph pencil, the name of the person that had been eating which dinner or supper. Then on his return each Fireman could locate the right meal and bung it in the microwave and reheat it. Marvellous!

Going back to the operational side of the job another funny incident was when we got a 'Shout' was to a cat stuck up a tree. Not funny for the cat obviously! Cat up a tree was something that the service gets called out to on a fairly regular basis a bit like barn fires.

Not having been in the service that long this was my first call to 'cat up a tree'. On arrival at the address of the incident I could see that the cat was a fairly long way up the tree. I asked Eddie as to how we were going to get the cat down. He said "We are going to connect a length of hose to the pump, fit a branch and charge it to about seven bars pressure, and then one of you guys is going to point it at the cat, open the branch, and blast him out of the tree with the jet of water." You could have knocked me down with a feather. The fall alone will definitely kill the poor cat. It was about forty feet up off the ground! He was of course only joking!

We slipped and pitched the one three five ladder to the tree where the cat was. (The one three five ladder is called that because it can go up to 13.5 metres in length.) We took the rescue line off the appliance and took the line out of the bag. Then one of the chaps put the line bag over his shoulder and after putting of some gloves, climbed the ladder to the cat's location. The cat did not seem very pleased about being approached by a hairy arsed Fireman, because as he got further and further up the ladder the cat began to meow and growl more and more.

Eventually the Fireman got within range and seeing that the cat was behaving in a very aggressive manner, with claws and spit flying about, he just bit the bullet and grabbed the cat by the scruff of the neck and stuffed it into the line bag, then pulling the line bag cord tight he had the cat secure. Job done! Putting the line bag on his shoulder he then descended the ladder.

Once safely back on the ground he said "Who wants to let the cat out of the bag?" (Who let the cat out of the bag!) Strangely enough there were no volunteers. The bag was now sitting on the lawn and writhing around like it was a thing possessed. I put on my gloves and standing with the bag opening facing away from me and pointing towards the house I opened the bag. The cat shot out like a cannon ball out of a cannon and disappeared into the house. Job done. Radio message required, "Hello Control 801 now mobile and available 801 over".

It was about this time in 1989 that I split up with my long term girlfriend Nick who was living with me. She wanted to go on holiday with her friend Carol. (I used to call her Barrel because she was very large. Not to her face of course!) Initially I said that it was o.k. for her to go and she booked the holiday. Then later I changed my mind and told her that I didn't want her to go. She went anyway and as I was not amused and that was the end of that. Why I changed my mind I cannot remember, but that is what happened with Nick. Shame.

At the time of writing of this book I made contact with (Nick) Nicola, by searching the internet and trying find out were she was living in 2010. I called her cousin who was the only person with the same Sir name I could get in touch with in Kent in that area. I gave him my name and number and explained why I wanted to talk to her. Just to be able to get all the facts straight in my mind about my past. He said that he had not spoken to his cousin for years, but would, by using family contacts try and get in touch with her and give her my details.

I didn't hear anything from her and assumed that he had lost interest, or failed to get in touch with her, or as time had moved on, she just didn't want to talk to me.

However, about two weeks later the telephone rang. I picked up and said "Hello." A strange voice said "Is that Mick?" I said "Yes, who is that?" She said "It's Nick." GORDON BENNETT! You could have knocked me down with a feather! MY GOD! After all that time I hardly recognised her voice, but we got chatting about things in the past and we had a bloody good laugh. I asked why she had not called me earlier, and she said that she had been plucking up the courage to do so! I am nothing to be afraid of! I am just about the most passive man in the world! How life moves on.

Anyway, during our telephone conversation, Nick told me that she knew in the back of her mind that I would contact her at sometime later in life. SHE KNEW THAT! How did she know that? I don't know. That's spooky! She had almost had a premonition! We had a real good chat about the old days and a bloody good laugh about it. She filled in some gaps for me regarding the past which was really useful.

Anyway, going back to the story, after I had been on Red Watch for a number of years and felt like that I was now well settled in, the then Mess Manager Joey wanted to hand over the Managing to someone else. I volunteered because things were on the change at this time and healthy eating was starting to raise its profile and I thought that the Mess Club would benefit from eating less 'Stodge' and have some healthier meals, such as grilled chicken and salad, pasta and rice etc. So I volunteered to do the job.

On one occasion I remember I told one of the cooks called Anne, who was about sixty years old and had been working at Canterbury Fire Station for just about a dog's age, that I would like her to cook Lasagne and prepare a nice fresh salad for the men. She took a step backwards and looked at me blankly and said in her very squeaky little voice and a tear in her eye "I CAN'T COOK LASAGNE!" Poor Anne, I think that perhaps I might have been asking a little too much of our Station cook! However, I have to say here, thanks for all the time that you cooked for us men Anne. We did appreciate what you did for us.

One golden rule that a Fireman should never break is to enter a building in Breathing Apparatus alone. The Breathing Apparatus crew of two or more must be linked together by a line of 1.2 metres. This can be extended to 6 metres. This will stop the crew from being separated in the smoke and one of them getting lost. You should either be carrying a line of hose or be using a guide line. This will enable you to find your way out of the smoke filled building when required. A compressed air breathing apparatus set has the duration of forty minutes, and a warning whistle will operate after thirty minutes to let the wearer know that he is getting low on air. There was one occasion that I broke this rule, not by my own doing, but by instruction from one of the officers. I still bear the scar to remind me.

Carrying a hose reel my colleague and I entered the building full of smoke and did a search for any persons inside. However we didn't find anybody.

Getting low on air we exited the building to report to the Entry Control Point. After disconnecting our line an officer asked me just to nip back inside for a specific task just inside the door. Not a problem I thought. I cannot remember what it was I had to achieve, probably to isolate the electricity or something, but I don't remember for sure. However I went in and did the task, but when I turned round to exit the building through the door, in the smoke suddenly it had disappeared, and I was lost and alone in the smoke. I searched and searched but could not find my way out and by now my low air warning whistle was sounding.

I hate to admit it but by now I was starting to get a little concerned and agitated. I searched some more and now was totally lost. I knew that I was on the ground floor as I had not been up any stairs. It was then that I came across a window and thought to myself "I'll smash the window and climb out." Using my torch I smashed the window and a shower of glass rained down, one shard of glass penetrated my glove and cut into my right hand. I climbed out of the window and I was free! The cut in my hand was quite small, only about an inch long, but very deep. It required stitches to seal the wound. Who cares!

Following that I had to have a little time off duty to allow the wound to heal and another funny thing happened during this time about that cut. After a few weeks, I had to visit the Nurse at the local medical centre which was not far away from where I lived. Just around the corner to have the wound looked at.

The Nurse said that she would remove the stitches that day. I looked at her sideways and a bit odd and thought are you sure about this? It does not look completely healed to me? Well she was a qualified Nurse and I was a mere Fireman, so I thought I'm sure she knows what she is doing. So, I didn't say anything. She removed the stitches and I went on my merry way.

When I got back home, I realized that I needed the loo, for what we in the south of England call a number 2. I went to the loo, dropped my trousers and sat down. Well, without going into too much detail about a mans ablution habits, It required a little bit of straining, and while I was doing so, suddenly the wound split open again and there was blood everywhere. SHIT! Literally shit, it was all over my backside. What was I going to do now?

I managed to stem the flow of blood with the some of the toilet roll, wipe my bum with the left hand, and get my trousers up. I went back round to the medical centre and the Nurse patched me up with some more stitches. Job done. I had a good laugh about it later.

Another amusing thing that happened while in the early years that I was on Red Watch was the volley ball incident with Keith, who I mentioned at the beginning of the chapter. Keith was a Fireman who was nearing retirement age at that stage and he had false teeth and his walnut whip hairstyle. When we would be tipped out to a 'Shout' at night he would be turned out of bed and had to jump on the fire engine to drive us there faster than he could arrange his walnut whip, so he would keep his Undress Uniform cap in the Fire Engine so that he could put it on fast to hide his encroaching baldness. Not that it bothered anyone except Keith himself!

At weekend days, before the banishing of volley ball in the service, we would be allowed to put the volley ball net up in the drill yard and have a game. There was an address system in the Fire Station and a couple of us would put the net up and then the standard announcement was. "NETS UP!" Then usually most of the Firemen on duty would come down and have a game. We would split into two teams depending on what appliance the men where riding that day. Water Tender verses Water Tender Ladder. Those riding the specials were divided up between the two teams to balance them up.

There was a mate of mine who I had trained with called Darren. He was a tall lad who was very good at volley ball and could spike a ball to the opposing side with a lot of power. On one occasion, he spiked the ball and Keith jumped up to block the ball and it hit him straight in the face. His head flew back and his top set of false teeth went flying one way, and his walnut whip the other. It was something to behold and absolutely hilarious! Who won that game? God knows and who cares. As a note to this, if ever you read this Keith I am sorry about letting others know. You were a good mate and it was an honour to serve with you.

Also during my early days in the operational mode, I attended an incident on the A2 half way between Canterbury and Dover where I saw the first dead person that I had ever seen close up. I was to see plenty more over the years. When there is a Road Traffic Accident it is referred to as an R.T.A. by the Fire Service and on the Fire Appliances they carry equipment that will be used to cut people out of the crushed vehicle and also resuscitation equipment to be used if needed. On this occasion fire pumps 802 and 801 were called out to attend the R.T.A. on the A2 road to Dover. On arrival there was not much that we could do, there was a woman lying on the tarmac who was as dead as a doornail, and there was no one to cover her previous to our arrival. I had never seen a dead body close up until that moment. We made the scene safe and put the woman into a body bag prior to the arrival of the ambulance.

When I had been on Red Watch for a while probably a few years, it was decided that we would take a Watch photograph. We backed the Turntable Ladder out into the yard and the whole Watch assembled out there and climbed onto the T.L. and someone took the picture

Can you spot me? That's me on the right at the top on the T.L.

One incident that we attended about that time was when there was a 'persons reported' and we had to search the building to find the missing person. I cannot remember the name of the hotel concerned but there was one person unaccounted for. On arrival the Officer in Charge had a consultation with the Duty Manager. The Duty Manager had done the correct thing when the fire alarm had gone off and evacuated the hotel taking the register with him. The Officer in Charge was informed that the register indicated that there was a person missing. If there is in any way even the smallest doubt that someone could be missing the O.I.C. will initiate a search.

At a time like this the O.I.C. will assess the situation and if necessary ask for assistance from Control. The O.I.C. told his pump operator to get on the radio to Control and to make pumps six. The standard message being, "Hello Control 801 assistance message, make pumps six 801 over." It was obvious that the hotel was actually on fire and not a false alarm as there was smoke billowing out of the second floor window.

My colleague and I had already donned our B.A. sets on route to the incident and on arrival one of the guys had set up the Entry Control Point. We reported to the Entry Control and donning our masks we started up our sets. After handing in our tallies from our Emergency Distress Units, we entered the building linked together by our lines and carrying the hose reel from the pump.

Searching a hotel can obviously be a problem and what can happen is that fires can affect different people in different ways and can sometimes force people, especially those unfamiliar with the premises, into all sorts of odd corners, such as toilets, storerooms and even lifts, or if they can get there, onto the roof. Children when trapped by fire or smoke can often take refuge in the strangest places such as under beds, in cupboards, under piles of clothes etc. So the search needs to be thorough.

Fortunate for us the hotel was not a large building and we did a thorough search of the premises, but found no one. We were getting low on air and on emerging from the place, we reported to the Entry Control Point, got back our tallies, and shut down our sets. It was at this time that we found out that the person reported had actually left the hotel and gone to the pub over the road to meet a woman, (who was probably not the woman who was his wife I suspect?) and not informed the front desk or handed in his room key! As you can imagine we were absolutely furious! Anyway, the fire was extinguished fairly easily because it was only a small fire, and then we packed up all our gear and went on our merry way. Saying on the radio "Hello Control 801 and 802 now mobile and available 801 over."

While on duty another of our duties as Firemen was to test the hydrants on our fire ground. The fire ground that we covered was a huge area and a large number of hydrants on that ground. The object of testing all the hydrants was two fold. One to make sure that they all worked correctly and two, to make sure that the Firemen would know where they were so that they could locate them in a hurry if required.

To achieve this we had a set of route cards which it was our old buddy, Keith's (Walnut whip.) responsibility to manage. So a crew on one of the pumps would be given the route card and they would go around the route testing all the hydrants using the standpipe, key and bar. Obviously the Fire Appliance would be taken, firstly to get us to the hydrant route as some were in very rural areas, and two, in case there was a fire 'Shout' while out on the route. If the hydrants functioned as they should they would be ticked off the list.

Quite often if the hydrant pit and cover was located in the road it would be clogged up with silt and debris that had got washed in, so we would have to put some gloves on, get down on our hands and knees and dig it out. Not something that you would want to do in the middle of the night in the dark with a nearby building on fire! If there was a fault with the hydrant, this would be reported to my buddy Keith and he would fill in the necessary form and send it to the Water Authority.

The hydrants could be found by those who are not familiar with the location by a nearby yellow plate which had a black **H** on it and two numbers. The numbers mean the width of the water main in inches, and the distance the plate was from the hydrant in feet. You may ask "Why do you need a plate to locate the hydrants if you are familiar with where they are?" To answer that question I would say this "Fire pumps and crews are not always on their home fire ground." Sometimes pumps and crews are moved around the whole county, or even over the border to the next county, to provide cover in unfamiliar areas.

I quite liked doing hydrant routes it would provide a reason to get off station and go for a walk, which was often nice in the rural areas, where you could get to see the nice Kent countryside in the summer, and also nice in the town as you can get to chat up the girls as they were passing by!

Another task that we had to do rather similar to hydrant testing was to test the dry risers on the beautiful Canterbury Cathedral. What is a dry riser? It is just a piece of fixed pipework on a building that will convey the water up to the outlet on each level of the building. There will be a male coupling on the ground floor for delivery hose from the pump to be connected to, and female couplings for delivery hose to be connected to on the upper floors.

The Watch would test the dry risers on an annual basis to ensure that no blockages had occurred. After all we could not risk our extremely beautiful Canterbury Cathedral burning down now could we? Not on our Watch anyway! It was a good opportunity for us to have a good look around the internal stairs and roof spaces of the Cathedral that are out of bounds to members of the public. We would take the Fire Appliances to the inside of the Cathedral precinct and set up the equipment for the test.

The pumps would be connected to the hydrant and most of the crews would go aloft carrying enough hose and branches to do the test. When the crews aloft had set into the dry riser they would use the hand held radio to let the pump operators know that the crews were ready for water on. The pump operators would charge the dry risers. The crew members who were holding the branch were balanced on the parapet of the Cathedral and must be braced and ready, or the jet reaction from the water pressure may bring a member of the crew plunging down the hundred feet of so to the ground.

The jets of water were directed away from the building and into the precinct below. The overall effect of this was to make the Cathedral look like one massive water fountain. When the test was complete and the gear was made up those who wanted to, could continue up inside Bell Harry actually inside the walls of the Cathedral on a spiral staircase, to the very top of the Cathedral where you would have a bird's eye view of the City below.

When the Firemen at Canterbury were off duty, some of them would work doing other jobs to earn some extra cash. We all referred to this as 'fiddle' work. Why we did this I don't know because there is nothing illegal about having two jobs. We all needed the money as a Fireman's wage was not particularly good and also a large portion of his wages would be paid into the pension scheme which of course meant that he had even less disposable income.

I had given up my typing work when I joined the service as this work was only available at certain times of the year. The first fiddle job that I had was running a business cleaning windows on my days off to boost my income. After all a Fireman does not have any concerns about going up and down a ladder! This was fine in the summer months, but in the winter months became a bit of a grind. So in 1990 I looked elsewhere for some fiddle work.

There was a Pub in the city called The Shakespeare's Arms at Rose Lane, near to the Cathedral. The Pub was run by an Irish Couple, Ron and Mary. I applied for doing some bar work there and they gave me a job. I only worked there in lunch times on my days off and I enjoyed it immensely. It was a very busy pub during the lunch times with a lot of business types coming in for some lunch. Ron and Mary's son John and his girlfriend Naomi also worked at the 'Shakey'. That is what we used to call The Shakespeare's Arms, the 'Shakey'.

In addition to me there were a few other non family members who also worked there part time. One of the other part timers was a girl named Julie who was a student at Canterbury University. She was an incredibly attractive girl, well I suppose you would say 'Stunning!' and she and I got on like a house on fire. Which I think is an appropriate expression.

Quite often when we had finished our lunch time shift and the pub went quiet at about three O'clock we would come around to the other side of the bar, get a beer and sit there chatting for hours. I being single at that time had visions of things going a little further between us, but alas, Julie already had a boyfriend, so it was not to be. However neither of us would deny that there was a certain amount of chemistry there to the point that when we were sat together if the atmosphere had got any hotter there would have been spontaneous combustion!

I told Julie about the times that the duty Watch tested the dry risers on the Cathedral and how we went up Bell Harry to the top and she went absolutely green with envy. She said "Oh, I would love to go up Bell Harry!" As it happened, I did have some contacts at the Cathedral and I put a word in, in the right place. I didn't tell her about this, because I wanted it to be a surprise. After our lunch time session next week I took her to the Cathedral and with right permission, and the right keys I took her to the top of Bell Harry, she was over the moon.

While I was working at the Pub on my days off from the Fire Service I met a woman who would be my first wife. Her name was Lorraine and she worked not far from the Pub at a retail outlet called Mothercare. Lorraine and her work mates used to come into the Shakey in their lunch hour to chat me up. I was very complemented that they had even bothered to come and see me when I was there and sure enough after a time, Lorraine and I started dating.

Lorraine was a cute girl and I think looking for a potential father of her children. She had a wicked sense of humour and was cracking jokes about me all the time. Of course, I was not offended by this, because I knew that she knew that I was a Fireman and she liked the idea of a Fireman being the father of her children. After some months of dating, we decided that we would get married.

My best friend and ex-army mate, and now Police Officer buddy Lloydie was who I wanted to be my best man. We had a party in the garden of Lorraine's Mum and Dad's house to celebrate our engagement. We invited all our friends over to the barbecue to make the big announcement. I had invited Lloydie because as I said I wanted to ask him to be my best man. Lloydie turned up 'late' as usual and when the announcement about the planned wedding was made Lloydie went absolutely BERSERK. Bless him. I asked Lloydie if he would be my Best Man and he said that he would be honoured to do so for me.

All the arrangements where made and things set in place, but I have to say that my marriage to Lorraine did not get off to a good start! During the marriage service I have to admit that Lorraine looked absolutely stunning in her wedding dress, and I like to think that I looked pretty handsome in my suit. Nick looked good in his suit apart from his wonky moustache.

During the service I was very choked with emotion and found it hard to utter my vows, Lloydie was stood at my shoulder and was repeating things by muttering in my ear what I should be saying. I turned around and almost shouted "YES I KNOW! SHUT UP AND JUST GIVE ME A MINUTE!" Once I had got a grip on my feelings the service went fine and Lorraine and I walked out of the church as husband and wife.

Lorraine and I signing the register

One of the strangest things that happened to me was when we got outside she turned to me and said "Right, you are now married, there will be no more drinking or smoking, got it?" I was somewhat flabbergasted! This nice woman who had been my lover and friend earlier had turned in a demon possessed! We went on our 'honey moon' at place in Stelling Minnis. Where we spent a weekend and did not do much. This is about six miles from Canterbury, money was short.

When Lorraine and I had got married we had brought a house at a place near to where we had had our honey moon trip. This was called 3 Chequers Cottages and I was to live there for some time. It was the first house that I had owned. I liked 3 Chequers Cottages and I had some good years there.

It was at about this time shortly after getting married that I decided that I would like to get into sailing, so I enlisted on a sailing course at a sailing club on the north Kent coast at Herne Bay. (Hernia Bay we used to call it.) The course was eight weeks long held on Saturday mornings. There was a group of about 15 of us on the course and we would be given instruction by the club instructor.

The craft that we were to learn on was a Topper which is a small yacht on which the sailor sits upon. We had to provide our own buoyancy aid which I brought from one of the local shops in the town selling all the equipment associated with sailing. Initially the students were given instruction upon the sea wall and taught all the true points of the wind and how to run before the wind. Reach across the wind and how to sail into the wind by tacking, or beating into the wind.

At first this was all a mystery to us, but with some practice we learned the points of sailing and after the course, when I knew the fundamentals I joined the club. It was at this time that I brought my first yacht which was a Firefly. An old 1950's yacht that was in some need of renovation. I moved the Firefly to my new wife's parent's property, because they had the room that I needed to do the Firefly up. I spent most of my spare time at their house fixing the yacht up and once this was done, using a road trailer I shipped it to the yacht club at Herne Bay.

Now a Firefly is a particularly unstable craft and requires two people to handle it, a helmsman, and a crew man. At that time I had no one who would crew for me, so I tried to sail the Firefly single handed. Some of the more experienced sailors of the club knew that it would be a disaster. Obviously, with my limited experience and no crew, when I went out to race with the Firefly I would almost definitely end up in the drink! Fortunately the club always had a safety boat available and they would come along and tow me back to the jetty.

After spending a lot of my times of sailing and ending up in the drink, I obtained a second hand Mirror Dingy which is somewhat smaller and more stable than the Firefly. This is best handled by two people, but it is possible for someone who new what they were doing to handle it single handed. This was somewhat more successful than the Firefly and I often used to make it around the course without taking a ducking.

I still used to take out the Firefly on occasion when there was a mate of mine available to crew for me. He was a Fireman at the Herne Bay Fire Station. He was a big lad and also a member of the sailing club. On one occasion we went out and the weather was blowing a gale and the sea was really rough. We took part in the race that day and we were out on the course and on the third and final lap, most of the others had called it a day and gone in.

The bow of the Firefly was cutting through the big waves, so every time we hit a wave about six gallons of water would wash inboard. The automatic self bailer was just about coping with the quantity of water. My mate was crewing and was hiked right out over the side hanging onto the jib sheet and with his feet hooked into the webbing strap. Suddenly the cam cleat on the other side of the dingy which is used to hold the jib sheet sheared off and as he was holding on to the jib sheet he tumbled over the side and into the sea. That was the end of our race that day! I picked him up and we limped back to the jetty.

With regard to my marital status, Lorraine and I were only married for about a year and a half as married life was not as I had expected.

The course of true love never did run smooth. (William Shakespeare.)

Well it appears that it is true what they say about marriage. "Always get married early in the morning. That way, if it doesn't work out, you haven't wasted a whole day!" That is of course not true for everyone, but it seems to be true for me.

CHAPTER NINE

Settled in

It was at about this time that I though I would like to have a central heating system at Chequers Cottage. I had had enough of mucking about with open fires. Although I did like the flames of an open fire! I did a few night school classes on plumbing at Canterbury College and when I thought I knew enough about plumbing I set about putting in my central heating system. My work mate at the Fire Station Simon (the one arrested because of the stolen pheasants.) told me that he had a solid fuel boiler for sale. I went over to his house and had a look at said boiler and I don't recall how much he wanted for it but I bought it off him.

I then set about installing the second hand boiler and the central heating system. The plan was that I would put this boiler in the cellar underneath the fireplace in the front room and then brick up the fire place above the boiler to provide a solid flue for it. At the front of the house was a metal plate which could be lifted to make a chute for the coal delivery to go into the cellar, which of course would double up as a chute for the delivery of anthracite for the boiler. The first hurdle to be crossed was how the hell was I going to get the boiler down into the cellar? The thing was made of solid steel and weighed an absolute ton! I went around the corner and had a word with my other mate Ian.

He came around to the house and between us we managed to get the boiler down in the cellar by tying a rope to the thing, laying it down and with both of us hanging onto the rope we lowered it down the stairs into the cellar. My next task was to get all the pipe work put in and the radiators hung on the walls in the rooms of the house. I had to tear up all the floorboards where I wanted the pipe work to go. Then by working through in a systematic method and by drilling holes in the rafters when needed I fitted all the pipe work, hung the radiators and put the hot water cylinder into the cupboard in my bedroom to make an airing cupboard.

I had to make the loft hatch larger to enable me to get the two water tanks up into the loft. I joined all the lengths of copper pipe together by welding them with a blow torch. I also fitted an electric emersion heater into the hot water cylinder to provide hot water in the house when the central heating system was turned off in the summer months. This all took sometime to complete as I was having to go on duty some of the days.

Eventually the time had come to flood the system and fill it with water. It was with some trepidation that I opened up the water supply stop cock and flooded my central heating system. After a few moments I started to hear lots of strange hissing noises, hissss, hissss, hissss, hissss. It sounded like the house was a nest of vipers! It was water pissing out from a lot of the welded joints I had done on the copper piping! MY GOD! I AM GOING TO FLOOD MY HOUSE! I quickly located the stop cock and isolated the supply. It was fairly obvious that my attempts at welding copper pipes together did not have a very good success rate. I got a garden hose and connected it to the drain point and drained down the system into the garden drain. It was quite apparent as to which joints had been unsuccessful as there were wet patches at each one. Oh well, if at first you don't succeed try, try again!

I had another attempt at trying to weld all the joints that had leaked and when I had done this I said "Right, central heating system by Mick Haines Mark 2." I flooded the system again, and the same results again! hissss, hissss, hissss. I drained it down again. There were not as many leaks as the first time though. I did a bit more welding and said "Right, central heating system by Mick Haines Mark 3." I flooded the system. Hissss, hissss. I then completely lost my rag! Shouting I said "BLOODY HELL AM I EVER GOING TO GET THIS BLOODY SYSTEM BLOODY WELL WATER TIGHT!" I then threw whatever tool I had in my hand at that time at the opposite wall.

After I had a cup of tea and calmed myself down somewhat, I carried on with that process of flooding, draining and welding for a while longer and when I finally got to central heating system by Mick Haines Mark 6, the system was finally water tight. I flooded the system and no leaks. (HOORAY!) Now came the time of the moment of truth. I had to fire up my central heating. I loaded up the boiler with anthracite and fired it up. Slowly and gradually the radiators got warm and then eventually hot. It works! (HURRAH!)

I think the problem I had during the installation of the central heating system was that the little hand held gas torch that I had brought for the installation of the system was not generating enough heat to get the joints to seal. I would have been better off hiring a professional standard torch from the tool rental place in Canterbury. Ho Hum, you live and learn.

It was about this time that I was living alone at Chequers Cottages that I got another dog as I had not had a dog since I had Boysie, with whom I had to part with when going in the Army and since then poor old Boysie had passed away. I was not particularly fussy about which dog to get, although I did rather fancy a Black Labrador. I found a rescue home that was in the area of Tonbridge Wells up county and I went and paid them a visit to see what dogs they had. I had a chat with the owner of the home and she said they only had one dog at that time and she brought the dog out. She was certainly not a Labrador that's for sure. More of a brown and white Spaniel Cross. Hmmm maybe I though. I leaned down to pet the dog and as I did so, taking me by surprise, she jumped up and stuck her tongue straight into my mouth. Yuk! She certainly seemed a very friendly dog! If somewhat older than I was hoping for. However she had kissed me now, so as we had swapped spit, I would have to have her.

I thanked the woman who ran the rescue home and let me have the dog. I made a contribution to the homes funds and then I loaded myself and my new pet into the car and we set off for home. I had to give my new pet a name because the woman at the home said that she did not know the dog's original name as she had come to the home because her previous owner had died. I called her Lucy which was a name that she responded too. Perhaps it was a lucky guess!

Lucy and I got on well enough and she liked to go down the field at the back of the house and play fetch with a stick. Initially she did not seem that mobile when I first got her. Probably because when she lived with the old lady who had passed away she probably didn't get much in the way of exercise. However she soon picked up and got fit again with the walks I took her on and the good diet I gave her. No little treaty tit bits, just a Bonio in the morning for breakfast and a good square meal of meat and biscuits in the evening. After a time her legs got stronger and her walks got longer. You could actually see the difference in her, her eyes where brighter and her coat was shiny. She had certainly lost a few pounds as well!

It was about this time that I nearly burnt my own house down. Something that as a Fireman you don't particularly want to happen! Having plumbed a central heating system into my very wooden house, I would come home from work at Canterbury and smell a distinct smell of electrical burning in the house? Then it would go away. I was somewhat baffled and confused as to why this was happening? How could it be there at one time and not be there the next? Initially, I thought that it was just a figment of my imagination. But as the summer weeks wore on I knew that it was getting more and more real, because the smell was getting stronger and stronger. The last thing that I wanted to happen was to be at work and get a 'Shout' to number 3 Chequers Cottage or to come home at some other time to find the row of wooden cottages burnt down and my dog dead!

Eventually I worked it out. Well, that is not quite true, it worked it out for me! One day I came home from work at about six fifteen in the evening and I could smell the smell of electrical burning really strongly in the house. I went upstairs and there in the airing cupboard was a small fire. The junction box that supplied the power to the hot water cylinder emersion heater was alight! There were flames coming out of it. There was obviously a dodgy connection there, and as the thermostat for the emersion heater asked for power, the electricity was being supplied and then just before it got to the point of ignition, it had shut down. That's why I had smelt the intermittent electrical burning! Eventually it had got to the point of ignition and the junction box had caught alight. I had got home just in time. I shut down the electrics and after replacing the junction box I reconnected the wires as they should have been. PHEEEEWWW. How close was that!

Lloydie still came to visit me when he came to Canterbury to visit his daughter Hannah. He would see Hannah then get a taxi over to Petham and stay a night or two at my house. We would go to the Chequers Inn which was nearby and have a drink or two. At Chequers Inn there was a Welsh girl working there as the assistant manager, her name was Heidi and she and Nick fell deeply in love almost instantly. When they were chatting the atmosphere was almost like my old junction box, electric with the sparks flying between them.

Strangely enough I saw a lot more of Lloydie in the next year or so as visits to my house and the Chequers Inn became very frequent. The manager at the Chequers was a chap called Steve and he also became a good mate to Lloydie and me. We all had some good times together. Unfortunately eventually Steve had to sell on the Chequers Inn and Heidi and Lloydie brought a house together in Essex and from which he would commute to work.

By this time I was now well settled in to my work life on Red Watch at Canterbury and was thinking about promotion. In most cases when a member of the public wishes to speak to the person in charge of the fire pump they approach the drivers window, because they assume that if he is driving he will be in charge, because when they drive their car they are in charge of the vehicle aren't they. Or if there is a H.G.V. vehicle, the driver is the person in charge, right? No, wrong, this in not the case with a fire pump.

The driver will be the person that operates the vehicle, so he drives it to the incident and operates the pump on arrival, well in most cases. The person in charge of the vehicle will be the one sat next to the driver and will be a Leading Fireman or a Sub Officer. Who will be looking at the information available about the incident and monitoring messages on the radio, and also on arrival sending messages for assistance if required in the form of more pumps and specials, and will use the resources at his disposal to achieve a successful conclusion to the incident. We hope!

To get promotion to be a Leading Fireman and then to a Sub Officer in the Fire Service you need to have taken the right exams. To pass these exams you certainly need to do a lot of studying. When I had first joined Red Watch at Canterbury I was given some advice by one of the guys who said "Get studying now if you want promotion later in your career, because a lot of the things you need to know are fresh in your mind from Training Centre" That's what I like about advice, its free, don't cost you a bean and you can take it or leave it. I took his advice and began to study.

There are three exams that you can take in the Service, two of which are split into two parts so, effectively making it five exams. These are Leading Fireman Part One, which is technical, Leading Fireman Part Two which is practical. Sub Officer Part One, which is technical. Sub Officer Part Two, practical. And the Station Officer's exam. If you are a smart cookie, you can pass all of these exams within three years. I however am not such a smart cookie. I am just an ordinary bloke and it took me a lot longer to get my qualification to Sub Officer and I never bothered to take the Station Officers exam because due to the responsibilities of that rank and above it did not appeal to me. I liked being on the Watch with my buddies. Or perhaps I realized my limitations later in my career. A man should realize his limitations in life as it makes things easier! The ranks in the service are as follows:

Fireman
Leading Fireman
Sub Officer
Station Officer
Assistant Divisional Officer
Divisional Officer I, II and III
Senior Divisional Officer
Assistant Chief Officer
Chief Fire Officer

I studied for my first exam of Leading Fireman and to my amazement passed it first time! Then I studied for my second Leading Fireman exam and again passed it first time! Wow things were going well! It was then that things got a little more difficult. I studied for my Sub Officers part one and taking the exam failed. (Bummer) I did a lot more studying next year and passed that one. Then going on to Sub Officers part two the following year I failed, and again the next year. (Double Bummer!) On the third attempt I passed and was over the moon about it, this was much later though in 1999. When I took my Sub Officers practical exam, I was amazed that I passed because a strange thing happened.

What you, as the person trying to pass the exam should do is follow a certain sequence. You have to turn up at the simulated incident being in charge of the two pumps. Then you 'get to work' the Firemen depending on the situation and sort out the fire. When this is achieved you make up all the fire fighting gear and then debrief the crew accordingly. I made a serious error on that day.

Well perhaps in hindsight not so serious. I got to the simulated incident and sorted it out, put out the fire and made any necessary rescues. Then when this was done I lined up the crews on the drill yard and debriefed them on what had gone on. I was going to fall out the crew and it was then the examiner came up from behind me and whispered very quietly in my ear. "Well, aren't you going to get the men to make up the gear?" I had completely forgotten that I had to have all the gear made up!

Flustered, I just shouted as if I knew what I was doing "CREWS MAKE UP!" Those who were the examiners obviously thought that this was not the end of the world, because I still passed the exam anyway! I have to admit that I was somewhat embarrassed by my error! That is truly what actually happened that day at the Maidstone Training Centre, but who cares. I got my Sub Officers qualification!

While based at the Fire Station at Canterbury, I had the experience of being in the Fire Station on New Years Eve, when we have our New Years Eve Party. On these occasions there would be many women who would attend the event having a pre- booked ticket to come in. It was nothing spectacular really. Just a disco in the Fire Appliance bays and all the Appliances would have been parked out the back in the drill yard to make the fire bays available to have a good 'ole' bash.

The on duty Firemen would serve the drinks to the ladies and gentlemen and of course stay sober in case they where tipped out to a 'Shout'. By now as you probably know, Fireman call a fire call a 'Shout'. This is something that stems back to the old days before telephones came along and when there was a fire someone who discovered the fire would run to the Fire Station, shouting "FIRE! FIRE!" so to this day it is still called getting a 'Shout'. If during a bash the bells went down, and the duty crew had to be tipped out that was fine. As the non duty crew would take over the serving. The bashes went well and it was not just at New Year we had a bash, there were usually about three a year.

During my early years at Canterbury I was to get a temporary promotion to go into Fire Safety at the office in Ramsgate. This was to fill a hole because one of the Station Officers there that had gone on long term sick. I was new to doing Fire Safety work, as this is a specialized role for which you had to go on some specialist courses at the Fire Service College.

I however was new to it and only there on a temporary basis. So I had to learn 'on the job' as it were. There were other officers at the rank of Station Officer at the office, who would give me some advice as they were the specialists and experienced. I was given the temporary rank of Leading Fireman. As it happens I was only there about three months and returned to my post at Canterbury after this. I did find my time there interesting and it would be something that I would get involved in much later on during my time in the Service.

It was during 1990 that I did some courses on my own back when I was off duty to improve my typing skills. These were Basic copy typing (February) Pass. Typewriting extension 1 (March) Pass. Typewriting extension 2 (April) Pass.

I did these courses because I had the notion that in the future computers would be the ticket to freedom for everyone and that within ten years there would be a computer in virtually every household in the country. As I said earlier, I could type, but I was not a fast typist and just wanted to get better. Most people could operate a QWERTY keyboard, but to be able to type in a fluid style using every finger and thumb on the two hands is not a skill that everyone possesses. In fact most people who operate their computer in the home type using just the two forefingers on each hand while switching their gaze back and forth from the keyboard to the screen. I wanted to possess the skill to be able to type while looking at the screen to see the text that you are creating.

That is exactly what I was doing when writing this book and if I manage to sell any or enough copies of this book, perhaps doing those courses twenty years back will pay for themselves. So, if you are reading this and have brought a copy of my book please encourage others to buy it. Go on. Do a poor old retired Fireman a favour!

Apart from barn fires, and getting cats out of trees, another type of incident that we used to get a lot of back in those days was attending chimney fires in domestic premises. Back then a lot of people burned wood and coal on their open fires and because they didn't get the chimney swept often enough the soot that was deposited on the internal sides of the chimney would catch alight. A 999 call was received at the Control and 802, which was the pump that I would usually ride, would get tipped out. On arrival we would see copious amounts of smoke and often flames coming out of the top of the chimney.

There was some specialist equipment that we carried on the pump for dealing with this type of fire and this is called the Chimney Kit. We would open the locker and carry the Chimney Kit into the house and make preparations to attempt to extinguish the fire. The Officer in Charge of the crew had no need to tell the Firemen what to do. As they had dealt with enough chimney fires before to be able to go into autopilot!

The Chimney Kit was kept in a steel box in the rear offside locker of the Fire Pump and this Kit contained the following equipment.

Chimney sheets
Stirrup pump, hose and nozzle
Chimney rods in a canvass bag
Dust pan and brush
Steel bucket times two
Thick cloths
Hand held mirror

The crew would try to keep the house as clean as possible and keep mess to a minimum when putting out the chimney fire. They would move any furniture as far as possible out of the way and then spread the chimney sheets over the carpet or floor covering to protect it.

The first job to do was to extinguish the fire in the grate. This would be done by getting one of the buckets full of water and splashing it onto the burning coal or logs. Once out this would be swept up with the dust pan and brush, put into the second bucket and taken outside and dumped in a suitable place in the garden.

Then it would be time for the rodding process to begin. This was done by attaching the hose and nozzle to one of the rods. Then another of the rods, and another of the rods and so on and so forth, while one of the Fireman who had the Stirrup pump plunged into a bucket of water pumped away. This process continued until such time as the fire up the chimney had been extinguished.

We could tell if the seat of the fire up the chimney had been hit because loads of steam would billow out of the top of the chimney. There was also the mirror in the Chimney kit, which was usually a wing mirror from a scrapped car that had been salvaged from the scrap yard, and this was for looking up the chimney to see what was going on up there without having to stick your head in the chimney and risk getting some hot embers or ash falling into your eye and blinding you!

On some occasions the Rodding of the chimney was not effective, because particularly in old houses chimneys can follow a convoluted and tortuous route and we would not be able to get the rods up the chimney and have to come up with an alternative way of extinguishing the fire. This would involve one of us having to go up onto the roof of the building.

A ladder would be slipped and pitched to the eaves of the roof and then a member of the crew would ascend the ladder with a roof ladder on his shoulder. For the benefit of those of you who are unaware a roof ladder is a specialized ladder that has a hook at one end and some small wheels attached to the other side. The Fireman would ascend to the eaves of the roof. Once there he would take a 'leg lock' which will enable him to let go of the ladder with his hands, and then take the roof ladder off of his shoulder and turning it around, roll the ladder using the wheels up to the point where the apex of the roof was near to the chimney. He would then turn the roof ladder over and hook the hook over the ridge or apex of the roof next to the chimney.

The Fireman would then descend and get a hose reel for a water supply from the pump. Then, after putting an overhand knot in the hose reel and putting it on his shoulder, would again ascend and would climb onto the roof ladder. Once there he would ascend the roof ladder to the apex of the roof next to the chimney and opening the branch, spray water down the chimney until the fire was put out. The remainder of the crew below would be able to tell that the fire was out by feeling the temperature of the water that was coming down the chimney.

While dealing with a chimney fire it would be wise for one of the Firemen to go into the loft of the house to have a look up there. Sometimes a fire from a chimney can break out of the flue and into the loft. Particularly with older houses as in the old days they used to incorporate the rafters of the roof into the structure of the chimney itself and sometimes the fire could spread into the loft, or perhaps if one of the bricks may have been dislodged by an over vigorous chimney sweep. Somewhat similar to the sweeps seen in the film Mary Poppins. "Me ol' bamboo, me ol' bamboo, you'd better never bother with me ol' bamboo!" A fine example of vigorous chimney sweeps!

Once we were confident that the fire was out, we would make up all the gear and then have a good clean up around the fire place to the satisfaction of the poor owner of the house. After stowing all our gear back onto the Fire Engine, we would say to the house owner "Don't light another fire until you have had the chimney swept!" We would then say our farewells to the people concerned and be on our way after booking mobile and available by getting on the radio and saying "Hello Control 802 here, stop message for 3 Chequers Cottages 802 now mobile and available 802 over". The reply would be, "Roger 802 Control over and out." They were bloody good at their job those Control girls. The radio procedure was almost like they used in the military during the war, with the girls at Control and the men on the ground using the same radio speak to each other.

CHAPTER TEN

THE CHANNEL TUNNEL

My time at the Channel Tunnel was a strange time of my life. So I have included a history of how the hell it all happened in the first place here.

It was in 1802 that a French mining engineer Albert Mathieu first put forward a plan for the digging of the Channel Tunnel. From 1830, with the invention of steam trains and the construction of the rail network in Britain led to the first proposals for a rail tunnel. By the mid 19th century, French mining engineer, Thomé de Gamond had spent 30 years working on seven different designs.

Then in 1880 the first actual attempt to dig a Channel Tunnel took place with a boring machine digging at both sides of the tunnel, this attempt was however soon abandoned.

It was in 1960 that the Channel Tunnel Study Group proposed a rail tunnel system consisting of two running tunnels and one service tunnel.

Then in 1973 that the then British Prime Minister Edward Heath and the French President George Pompidou officially launched an attempt to dig the Channel Tunnel, this was however again abandoned in 1975 due to the fuel crisis.

It was during 1985 that the British and French governments announced their intention to seek private investment for the construction and operation of a fixed link between the two countries. This would be done without public funding. It was of October of this year that four serious proposals where put forward. Europont, Channel Expressway, Euroroute and Eurotunnel.

In August of 1986 that the Eurotunnel group was formed and the construction contract was signed between Eurotunnel and the Trans Manche Link (T.M.L.). Then in July of 1987 both Prime Minister Margaret Thatcher and President Francois Mitterrand ratified the Treaty of Canterbury paving the way for the construction to begin and in December of this year construction started. It was in December of 1990 that the first historic breakthrough occurred in the service tunnel. Thinking back to it, in hindsight it was incredible what they had done.

The Tunnel was finished in 1992 two years late and way over budget. During the construction phase of the Tunnel the Kent Fire Service was faced with a problem. Hmmm. How would they fight a fire in a long tunnel with only access from one end? The best solution that could be found was to get some Breathing Apparatus sets with a longer duration than the Compressed Air sets that we were using in normal firefighting.

This was done by obtaining some oxygen Breathing Apparatus sets Saber Sefa mark 2 that had duration of two and a half hours compared to the forty minute compressed air sets. They would be charged with 750 litres of compressed oxygen with a flow rate of 5 litres per minute. You planned on wearing the set for two hours with a thirty minute safety margin. As opposed to the ten minute safety margin with a Compressed Air Breathing Apparatus set. Obviously the Firemen that would be wearing these sets needed to have some further training to make sure that they were familiar with the equipment and knew how to use it and what procedures would be adopted.

To do the training a number of Firemen were sent on a course of two weeks which would be done at the firehouse and Training Centre located at the Fire Station at Folkestone. Initially I was over looked with the Long Duration Breathing Apparatus training, but eventually my name came up and I was sent on the course with several other colleagues from Canterbury.

Part of the course was to do something called entrapped procedure. This was done to simulate that there had been a collapse in the tunnel and a number of Firemen where trapped in a hostile environment and what they had to do to survive while awaiting rescue. Although during normal use the oxygen set will only last two and a half hours, when entrapped the wearer of the set would have to extend the time that he could make the oxygen last.

This could be achieved by closing down the valve that allows the oxygen out of the cylinder and just to be breathing off the bag that was incorporated in the set. The drawback with this procedure is that the oxygen gets recycled through the wearers lungs and in that environment, it gets hotter and hotter until such time that it is like breathing oxygen from a hot hair dryer! Not very pleasant.

When the wearer gets to the point that he can no longer stand it, he reaches behind him and opens the valve from the cylinder and flushes the system with fresh oxygen and then he would close the valve down again. By doing this it is said that when a Fireman is entrapped, the set can be made to last up to thirty six hours, even if it is extremely uncomfortable.

When I was on the course doing the entrapped procedure one of the other Firemen, who was a big man about six foot six tall, lost his nerve and ripping the mask from his face raced out of the firehouse and into the open air screaming "I can't stand it, I can't stand it!"

The poor chap obviously had a touch of claustrophobia! Personally, I had no problems with this. I would just stay calm, breath the nice clean pure oxygen, lay still in the dark and heat, and think happy thoughts. I would just pretend that I was in a tent in the mountains and breathing the good air of the hills. Or pretend that I was on the open prairie of Canada looking up at the Northern Lights. It worked for me, because I never got overly stressed by the situation. In addition to this I also knew that it was only a training environment. How I would have done it for real hmmm well who knows.

Also I think that some chaps had a bit of an issue about breathing pure oxygen, saying that it affected them in someway. How this could be the case is beyond me, because when you inhale normal compressed air it is composed of 79% nitrogen, 21% oxygen. When you exhale is 79% nitrogen, 17% oxygen and 4% carbon dioxide. So the only thing that your lungs are actually taking in is the oxygen! So how breathing pure oxygen is going to have a bad affect on you, I am mystified at that one.

The instructor in charge of this course was a Watch Manager and a good instructor. His name was Simon and he was later to become a very good friend of mine. Watch out for his picture in the book. He is in the shots of White Watch later in the book (In both shots he is kneeling down at the front.) and doing the tree hugging on The Ridgeway, but more about that later.

Once the tunnel started operating fully with all three tunnels in use the Sabre Sefa breathing sets where done away with and I am reliably informed at the time of writing this by my ex-instructor, and ex-sub officer, Simon, that the sets were later sold on to a South African mining company, mining for diamonds no doubt. There was a big collapse in the mine and a number of the men working there were entrapped in the mine and trying to make the Sabre Sefa mark 2 sets last as long as possible they finally died before they could be rescued. How sad, what a HELL OF A WAY TO GO! Having said that, they were good Breathing Apparatus sets and I had every confidence in them at the time of the Channel Tunnel construction.

The Tunnel was fully opened in 1994 and there was an official opening ceremony by Queen Elizabeth II and President Francois Mitterand on 6th May. It was it was sometime before this that Kent Fire Service put a full time crew down at the entrance to the service tunnel which would provide. 24 hour fire cover for the tunnels. I applied for and got my first promotion to the rank of Leading Fireman and on 7th June 1993 was posted down the channel site on a permanent basis. I seem to remember we did some tests on a twin cylinder Breathing Apparatus, to find out if the duration of the compressed air Breathing Apparatus could be extended, but this was not successful, as the cylinders on your back would rock about and at times the seal between the cylinder and the set would be broken resulting in the loss of all your air. We needed a bloody good B.A. set that was reliable!

We found such a thing. Although while serving down the tunnel we would be now back on compressed air B.A. and not oxygen, they would in fact be slightly different from the normal B.A. cylinders in our Breathing Apparatus sets, instead of being made of steel, which could not take the pressure required, they were be made of spun carbon fibre. This meant that the cylinders could be charged to a pressure of 306 bar, 4000 pounds per square inch as opposed to the old steel cylinders which could only be charged to 207 bar, 3000 pounds per square inch. This would give us a longer duration than the old steel cylinders.

Why we did not keep our oxygen Sabre Sefa sets, I don't know? That was a choice made by the Upper Echelons of the Kent Fire Service. The reason that I say this is because they were good and reliable Breathing Apparatus sets and I as a Fireman I had complete confidence in them, and I have never had a problem with breathing pure oxygen myself. In fact if I had to make a Breathing Apparatus set last longer, give me that oxygen set any day! I suppose the Service would have been faced with all the additional training and equipment required that keeping the oxygen sets would have generated.

THE TUNNEL SYSTEM.

The tunnel system is three tunnels. There are two running tunnels for the trains and one service tunnel which runs centrally between the running tunnels and there are air locked cross passages every 375 meters, to enable people from the service tunnel to access the running tunnels. To access all the tunnel system we would use the service tunnel as well as all the maintenance crews. The Channel Tunnel is the longest undersea tunnel in the world. The section under the sea is 38km long. The three tunnels, each 50km long, were bored at an average 40m below the sea bed, and link Folkestone in Kent to Coquelles in Pas-de-Calais.

Eurotunnel shuttles, Eurostar and national freight trains run in the two single track and single direction tunnels. As mentioned these are connected to a central service tunnel by cross-passages situated every 375m. The service tunnel allows access to maintenance and emergency rescue teams and serves as a safe haven if passengers need to be evacuated in an incident. The service tunnel is a road tunnel used by electric and diesel-powered vehicles. Air pressure is higher in the service tunnel to prevent the ingress of smoke in case of a fire in one of the rail tunnels.

The two rail tunnels are 7.6m in diameter and 30m apart. Each rail tunnel has a single track. Overhead line equipment (catenary) and two walkways (one for maintenance purposes and the other for use in the event of an emergency evacuation and on the side nearest to the service tunnel). The walkways are also designed to maintain a shuttle upright and in a straight line of travel in the unlikely event of a derailment.

The service tunnel is 4.8m in diameter and lies between the two rail tunnels 15m away from each of them. In normal operations shuttles use the south tunnel in the France to UK direction, and the north tunnel when travelling from the UK to France.

The track in each rail tunnel has two continuously welded rails laid on pre-cast concrete supports embedded in the concrete track bed.

Fixed equipment in the tunnels comes under four categories: electricity and catenary, rail track and signalling, mechanical systems and control and communications.

Cooling pipes, fire mains, signalling equipment and cables are fixed to the sides of the tunnels and are fed by cooling plants at Samphire Hoe in the UK and Sangatte in France.

The overhead catenary supplies traction power to the shuttles as well as to other trains using the Tunnel, e.g. Eurostar and international rail freight trains. The catenary is divided into sections, so that maintenance work can be carried out in stages. Electrical power supplying the tunnels, drainage pumps, lighting and the trains, is provided by substations on each side of the Channel. In the event of loss of power from one side, the entire system can be supplied from the other side.

The tunnel system was accessed by travelling in a specialist vehicles designed for the access through the service tunnel. These vehicles are called the Service Tunnel Transport System, or S. T. T. S. There are a number of these specialist vehicles that are used down in the service tunnel by all the personnel that need to have access to the tunnels. They are coloured accordingly depending on which personnel use them. The S. T. T. S. Fire vehicles are red. The ambulance crew's vehicles are green. The maintenance crew's vehicles are yellow.

The S. T. T. S. vehicles are an extremely long and narrow and because there is no way that it can be turned around once it is in the service tunnel there is a drivers cab at either end to enable it to be driven in and out of the tunnel. When not in the service tunnel the vehicle can be turned around, but this takes up an incredible amount of room because it has got a very large turning circle and consequently this is something that does not happen often.

My time down the tunnel was a strange time for a Fireman, but at least it had provided me with my first promotion. We still worked the same shift system as the rest of the Brigade and would do two days on, two nights on and four days off.

When we where on nights when serving at the tunnel, one of the two crews on the Watches would have to go down the tunnel and spend the night down there. We were provided with some camp beds which we took with us and our sleeping bags, and it was most bizarre to go into one of the cave like rooms off the service tunnel and try to get your head down! To try to sleep down there knowing that you were underneath the English Channel with all that rock and water above you was very strange!

The trouble with a fire down the Channel Tunnel is that it presents a unique set of circumstances for the crews that have to fight the fire. To start with the fire may well be a moving fire! There have been occasions that a vehicle has caught alight while actually being on the back of the freight train moving through the tunnel. The freight carriages are like a cage and this means the Heavy Goods Vehicle is exposed to the air. So when it catches fire on the back of the train the flames of the fire are given a nice plentiful supply of fresh oxygen to fan them as the train moves through the tunnel and a good fire loves to eat oxygen, yum yum!

At the time of writing this there have to my knowledge been many occasions of small fires in the tunnel system, and three major fires since the tunnel opened where temperatures have been know to be in excess of a thousand degrees centigrade.

As I said previously my time down the 'tunnel' was a strange time in a Fireman's career. One of the other odd things that happened is that the junior officers, the Leading Firemen and the Sub Officers were sent on some courses to learn to speak French. If there were to be a big incident down there in the tunnel, there would have to be communication between the Sapper Pompier, (French Firemen.) and the English Firemen. You cannot co-ordinate your fire fighting tactics between you if you cannot communicate!

This took place and I was getting pretty good with my French Language just to the point where I could string a sentence together, and then due to financial restrictions this was suddenly abandoned. BUMMER! We did however visit our French Colleagues in Coquelles in Pas-de-Calais to have a pidgin style French talk to them at one time.

Fairly soon we ran out of things that we could say to each other. This was due to my lack of decent French language, and their lack of decent English. We all thought sod it, and the next thing that happened was the volleyball net went up and we played international volleyball with England Firemen versus French Firemen at volleyball! What a laugh we had that day. There was no bad feeling's between any of us. We were just brothers in arms having a good time together. Who won that day I cannot remember, and who cares!

When my time at the Channel Tunnel came to an end in March of 1995, I was posted back to Canterbury onto Green Watch and life as a Leading Fireman resumed as about as normal as it can be.

At the time of writing this, I have to say, that the Channel Tunnel is just about one of the most amazing feats of engineering that I have ever seen or been involved with. What they did back then at that time was something that is pretty amazing really. Just to think that they dug those tunnels under the English Channel between England and France. Phenomenal! I know that there were a lot of people killed during that project and that the guys that worked down there got paid good money. After all in the construction phase of the tunnels it was an incredibly hazardous thing to be doing. When the freight trains were running the spoil out of the tunnel to the surface, from the boring machines, the trains were running at no more that six inches apart. Ten men were killed during the construction of the tunnels, eight of them British, most by being squashed between the two passing freight trains.

If you go down the M20 to Folkestone in Kent now, you will see one of the boring machines at the side of the motorway with a big 'FOR SALE' sign on the side of it. What about that then? I don't think that it is actually for sale, and who knows if it would even work if you could buy the great hunk of steel, but it does bring it home to you about what was achieved when they dug the Channel Tunnel.

CHAPTER ELEVEN

THE CHALLENGE WALKS

As mentioned it was the nineties that I started to get into doing various challenge walks. These are long distance walks that you do in one day and are usually in the region of about twenty five or twenty six miles. This started off by taking part in events organized by other brigades in the country and a group of us would travel up country on the Friday, do the event on the Saturday and then return back home to Kent on the Sunday.

The Brigade had a mini bus which they would allow us to use for travelling to and from the events and even paid for the fuel for the vehicle which was most generous of our employers to provide this facility. Perhaps it was to encourage their employees to go on these events and encourage them to remain fit and healthy whilst in their employment. After all, a fireman who is on the sick is of no use at all to the Officer in Charge of an incident.

One of the first challenge walks I did was The Hadrian's Hike organized by the Tyne and Wear Fire and Rescue Service. This was a circular walk of 26 miles. It was earlier in 1993 that I first took part in this event. I booked the mini bus well in advance and a group of us met at the Fire Station on the Friday morning, loaded in all our gear and we set off up the A2 to the outskirts of Newcastle upon Tyne to the service Training Centre and Fire Station there.

I had advertised the event in the Brigade Bulletin and had received a good response. On arrival at the Training Centre we were shown to the gym where we would sleep on the floor. We had brought with us all the gear necessary, sleeping bags, roll mats etc. That evening we went out to a restaurant to get a meal and then returned to the gym and got our heads down for a night's kip.

In the morning once we were up and about Tyne and Wear Fire and Rescue Service provided us with a good cooked breakfast and we all jumped in the mini bus and headed off for the point where the walk would start. The event kicked off at 08.00 a.m. and off we went armed with our maps and compasses. Earlier on in the event navigation was fairly easy, just a matter of following the people in front, but as the day wore on and everyone had their own pace the field became more strung out and accurate navigation became essential. Thanks to my army training this was not a problem.

The Service had volunteers along the way who would man the various check points along the route to ensure that no one took some 'short cuts!' It was a great day out and the weather was good. Our little band of wanderers stayed together along the route. The section of the walk along Hadrian's Wall was the best part. This incorporated a part of the Pennine Way and unknown to me at that time, I would be walking along there again in the future in 1996 when walking the Pennine Way itself.

We completed the Challenge Walk in just over eight hours. Some people did it a lot quicker than that, but my philosophy when doing a challenge walk is that the challenge is just to complete the walk and enjoy the day out. Not to put your head down and rush round in the fastest possible time and miss all the good scenery. Especially as you have come a long way from Kent to see it!

When doing this event after the day out you would then have a good night out in Newcastle, if of course you still had the energy! What sticks in my mind most of all about Newcastle is the young ladies that I met there. They would come out in the town looking like they were in somewhere hot like Spain, wearing little more than a skimpy top and a mini skirt! They were sight to see, God bless 'em'! I remember one year that strangely enough there were a couple of Cops from London who had somehow come up to do the Challenge Walk. How they had heard about it I don't know, and who cares!

We went out into the town together and ended up in a bar where they were playing songs by the great band Oasis. The song was 'Don't look back in anger' both me the Fireman, and the two Police Officers loved this tune at the time and having done and completed the Hadrian's Hike that day we were in fine spirits and we had had a few drinks between us. The song came on, and we felt in fine voice and sang along at the top of our voices like a bunch of teenagers.

"So Sally can't wait, I'm sure it's too late as we were walking on by. Her soul slides away, but don't look back in anger, I heard her say......!" WHAT A NIGHT OUT WE HAD! Thanks for that Oasis. It just goes to show that Policemen really are human beings when they are not on duty!

It was after I had arranged and done a number of these events that two of the girls who worked at our Brigade Control told me that they would like to come on a walk with us. I had no problems about this at all. The events were open to anyone who expressed a desire to take part. So, we went off to do the Malhamdale Meander in Yorkshire, and Joe and Jan came with us. The Meander is a 26 mile route which included some stiff climbing up the hills and was a tough event. Unfortunately Joe had to pull out before the end of the walk, but Jan made the distance. I was impressed with Jan's fitness and we soon became friends and later a 'couple'.

It was about this time in my life that I brought a new car, well not new as in just off the production line, but new to me. It was a Citroen 2cv. The 2cv was a nice little car which had a white body, black roof and green wheel arches. I had always liked 2cv's and saw it advertised in a local paper. The seller wanted £900 for the vehicle which I thought was a bit too much, but when I viewed the car I fell in love with it immediately! The mileage was quite low and it was in reasonable condition. So, I paid the man for the little car and drove it home.

My new little car outside the house

To this day, I still have that car, but it has been somewhat revamped, but more about that later.

It was in the summer of 1994 that my girl friend Jan and I expressed a desire to walk a long distance trail and decided that we would walk the trail of the North Downs Way. Having done a bit of walking between us we thought that we would be capable of taking it on.

The trail runs along the ridge of the northern chalk hills in the south of England. Now, I know that that sounds like a bit of a contradiction, but there is a lot of chalk countryside in that part of England and there is also a trail called The South Downs Way on the coast of southern England.

Jan and I had never taken on a long trail before, so we worked out what distances we would walk each day. We knew that we were capable of walking twenty five or twenty six miles in a day as we had done this on plenty of occasions.

The North Downs Way is a footpath that runs from Farnham in Surry to the Kent coast at Dover over. Why do I always say Dover over? It's a bit of a hang up from my Fire Service days in Kent. Because for some reason, regarding radio procedure, we always used to say it for a bit of a joke on the radio. When speaking to our Control at Maidstone on the radio we would say, " Hello Control this is 802 at Dover over." Or something like, "This is 802 mobile and available in Dover over." The silly things you do when in the Fire Service sometimes.

Anyway, Jan and I had decided that we would walk from Farnham to Dover (over). What we did not think about was that although we had walked many challenge walks of about twenty five or twenty six miles, to do it in consecutive days would push you to the limit. But Jan and I had a plan that we would work to and stuck to it like shit to a blanket!

We made the necessary arrangements for our travelling and started the trail, carrying our packs. The first section of the trail we walked twenty five miles from Farnham to Westhumble. We arrived absolutely shattered! We had something to eat and then got our heads down in the pre-arranged accommodation. Then we set off the next day to try and stick to our plan.

Here is Jan at the North Downs Way sign.

We set off in bright and clear sunshine and not feeling too bad. After our first hard day. We were going to do eighteen miles today, not too bad we hoped. But it turned out to be tougher than we had imagined and suffered a little. We found our accommodation at Oxted for the night and collapsed into bed like a falling drunkard!

The next day we had planned was to be from Oxted to Cuxton, a day of twenty nine miles! Jan and I were already feeling pretty exhausted by now and starting to realise that we might have bitten off more than we could chew! I was getting a touch of shin splints. We made it to Cuxton and at least no blisters so far!

Here is me taking a rest and cooling my feet off.

When we managed to get ourselves out of our beds we got our kit together and knew that we had another day ahead of us of twenty five miles to Charing.

Could we keep it up? HOLY SHIT BATMAN!

Jan and I tried to get an early start that day so that we could have plenty of rests along the route, which we did. We rested on a regular basis and eventually made it to Charing. It was not that either of us had blisters that was making it a hard trail. Just that we were trying to walk too many miles in one day after another and another. Not having walked a long trail before, I think that we were a little nieve about the effort that it would take to walk a long distance trail.

The next day we were going for the finishing line Dover (over). Twenty nine miles that day. We set out early, to allow plenty of time for resting along the way.

Here is one of the marker stones used on the North Downs Way

God alone knows how we finally made it, but at the time of writing this, I have to say that I did shed a few tears, because we suffered on that trail, but we made it to the end and I learnt a valuable lesson from that experience on the North Downs Way. Don't bite off more than you can chew if you want to walk a long distance trail. Keep it at a reasonable distance each day and enjoy the walk. Not try to prove that you are a superman, or superwoman in Jan's case! We had finally made to Dover over, and now it really was OVER! HOORAY!

It was at about this time that I decided that I would do away with my solid fuel central heating system and go for an alternative. The solid fuel boiler in my cellar was a 'pain in the backside' because with solid fuel you have to go down there once a day and pulling on the lever 'riddle' out the ash and then using the hopper fill the boiler up with fresh fuel. Not only was it a pain but also very messy and made a mess in my cellar.

Obviously gas was out of the question as there was no gas out there at Petham Stone Street. So the only option was oil. There was just one problem that had to be overcome. How was I going to get the oil tank I needed into my back garden? If I could achieve this getting the oil in the tank would be no problem because the delivery man could park his lorry out the front run the supply pipe down the ally between number one and two Chequers Cottages, because legally I had a right of access and then up my garden and into the tank at the end of my garden. However, getting the oil tank itself down the ally was out of the question because the ally was too narrow to facilitate this. Hmmmm.

I had a think about this and came up with an idea that broke the mould a little. It was a little bit off the wall, and out of the thinking box! Between my back garden and the car park of the Chequers Inn was my neighbour Chris's garden. So short of taking the two fences down there was no way of getting the tank in that way, or was there? Being in the Fire Service and working at Canterbury I had some connections in the right places. I knew that a Turntable Ladder could also double up from being used as a method of rescue to be used as a crane. Well one of the 'specials' at Canterbury Fire Station was a Turntable Ladder. How convenient!

When I was on duty I had a chat with my colleagues and put my idea to them. We all got on very well on that large watch and they seemed pretty enthusiastic to give it a go. I had a chat to the now new owners of the Chequers Inn, John and Maureen. With whom I got on well as they owned the house just across from me and a little bit further up Stone Street. I put my idea to them and asked for their permission to do what I had in mind. They thought that it was a blinding idea and would be good fun! As long as it was done before opening hours which it would have to be, because the car park would have to be empty.

So I contacted some people who were selling central heating oil tanks and brought the one that I wanted which they delivered to the car park of the Chequers Inn. Then next time that our Watch was on duty we came over to Petham in the pump 802 and the Turntable Ladder. We then craned the tank over the two fences and into my back garden and lowered it into position. JOB DONE!

Just for the record, this was of course a training exercise for the duty crew at using a Turntable Ladder as a crane and of no personal benefit to me.

Craning in the oil tank.

The next mission that I had to achieve was to put an oil fired boiler in the house somewhere? Hmmm well I had thought about this before buying the tank and had decided that the best place for it to go would be in the fireplace of the dining room. There was just one drawback. The fireplace in the dining room was not large enough to take the boiler that I wanted. There would have to be some structural reconfiguration here.

I started bashing out the fireplace in the dining room between my house and number two. To take the fireplace back to the original nine inch pillars that supported the chimney. There was just one drawback with my plan here. I actually made a hole in the back of the fire place that allowed us who lived at Chequers Cottages to see through from one property to the one next door! Richard and his wife Jane next door at numbers one and two were not impressed! I told them not to worry, and that I would make good the damage, which I did.

Then I had to find a way of supplying the fuel from the tank to the boiler. This involved digging a big trench in the lawn and laying a plastic coated copper pipe from the tank at the end of the garden to the boiler, now in place in the old fireplace. Once all this was done and the trench was filled in, everything was connected up and I was ready for the big FIRE UP!

I had my first delivery of oil from a local company and setting all the controls of the Honeywell system, I started the boiler up. The system worked, I was now an oil fired centrally heated house. No more ANTHRACITE YIPPEEE!

CHAPTER TWELVE

THE PENNINE WAY (1996)

Everywhere is within walking distance if you have the time!

It was at the beginning of 1996 that I decided that I would like to walk the Pennine Way. The Pennine Way is a continuous route of 256 miles of open countryside that runs up the backbone of England. The Way has become a victim of its own success over the years as much erosion has occurred due to the number of people walking sections of the Pennine Way. Many people use a part of the Pennine Way to form a circular walk in some of the more picturesque parts. But to walk the Pennine Way in one continuous attempt is not something that should be taken on by the faint hearted! At the time that I walked it there were many improvements being carried out by the laying of flagstones along the more eroded sections.

The flagstones come from all the large disused mills that were torn down. They were transported to the place where they would be laid by a helicopter and then a team of volunteers would take the time and effort to lay the flagstones to form the path. The whole project was a huge and time consuming effort which was being worked upon at the time that we took the Way on.

Some have complained about the laying of the flagstones to create and artificial surface, however no one would ever enjoy wading through water logged peat so the improvements that have been done have a good side of the argument. I will leave it up to you to make your mind up about this when you walk the Pennine Way.

THE ORIGINS OF THE PENNINE WAY

The Pennine Way was the first national trail in Britain, officially opened on 24th April 1965, (Blimey I would only have been three years old!) at a gathering of over 2000 walkers at Malham Moor in the Yorkshire Dales. The project to open the route gained Ministerial approval in 1951 but it took a further 14 years for local authorities to open up the 70 miles of new paths required to complete the continuous route.

The idea for the Way was the brainchild of a rambler and journalist Tom Stephenson and an article appeared in the Daily Herald written by Tom in 1935. Tom had been so impressed by similar trails in the United States he had the vision to apply the concept of a wilderness path to the English Pennines. The country was ready, and the suggestion was carried forward on the same heady wind of change that had demanded access to the hills and the establishment of the National Parks. Most of the research required to find the route for the way was carried out by the Rambler's Association and the Youth Hostels Association. In 1949 the Act was carried through Parliament.

I got hold of a video that was based on the route, which showed all the scenery along the route taken from a helicopter. Jan, who as I said earlier worked at out Brigade Control, was living with me at this time and she said that she wanted to walk the Pennine Way with me. So, arrangements were made. We booked our annual leave to allow us plenty of time to complete the route, and for travelling at either end. I had a copy of the Pennine Way Companion written by Wainwright and just before we started the walk I obtained two more books about the route to provide maps of the route we would take. These were written by Tony Hopkins and produced by Aurum Press Ltd in association with the Countryside Commission and the Ordnance Survey. One book was Pennine Way South. Edale to Bowes. And the other was Pennine Way North. Bowes to Kirk Yetholm. Using these two books when on the Way removed the need of having to carry reams and reams of Ordnance Survey maps the size of a bed sheet that would blow all over the place in the high spots of the route.

I was intending to keep a diary of our journey so I brought a small hard back book that I would write the diary in each evening about things that we had encountered along the route. While we were researching the books to plan our route and the places that we would stop each evening I wrote this in the front of the log book allocating a page to each stopping place and writing the distance we would walk, the type of accommodation we would have, a contact telephone number (if applicable.) and the grid reference.

The equipment that we would carry on the walk required a large back pack as we were intending to camp a lot of the nights that we would be on the Way interspersed with the occasional bed and breakfast to give us an opportunity to have a good meal in a pub and get a hot shower or bath and also to clean up our kit and to dry it out if necessary. As it happened I did possess two rucksacks, both of them were the old style framed rucksack and both of them were yellow. As the route of the Way goes up the back bone of England some of the areas are very remote and there is no hotel or bed and breakfast accommodation. So, the walker must deviate from the way to get a roof over his or her head if he or she is not carrying a tent and sleeping bag. It was for this reason that Jan and I had decided that we would camp along the way when necessary.

Walking the Pennine Way in its entirety is not something that should be taken on without due consideration. The Pennines can be a dangerous place and the weather can be unpredictable. I would certainly suggest that if a person is considering attempting to walk the Way they should make sure that they are physically capable by doing plenty of training walks. Ensure that their map reading and navigational skills are up to scratch, and that they are capable of using a compass and can take a magnetic bearing and a grid bearing when required.

This is where being an ex-infantry man became useful as I had been trained in navigation way back in my army training year in 78/79. Again there was one of our little army sayings that we used to remind us about grid and magnetic bearings. "Grid to mag add, mag to grid get rid." What this means is that if you are converting from grid bearing off the map, to magnetic bearing on the ground, you add the variation. If you are converting from a magnetic bearing on the ground, to a grid bearing on the map, you get rid of the variation. 'Grid to mag add, mag to grid get rid.' As clear as the mud on the Pennine Way right?

Ensure that you have the correct equipment in the form of a good pair of boots that have been worn in, but not worn out. A couple of pairs of socks without lumpy seams. A first aid kit is best if it is one that you have put together yourself so that you know what is in it and should contain such things as a strip of breathable plaster and a pair of scissors, midge repellent, Vaseline to sooth chapped skin, some sterilization tablets for running stream water if you have no method of boiling it. Etc. With regard to clothing two pairs of trousers that can be converted to shorts is a good idea and also some underclothing that will wick sweat away from the body to help you stay warm and dry. Obviously a good waterproof jacket that is breathable is a must.

Jan and I had done a lot of day challenge walks and also the North Downs Way previously and had nearly all of the kit that we would require. We did shop around and replace some of the more worn out items that we considered needed replacing. We also brought a reasonably good tent that would provide us with our accommodation on the nights we weren't at a B and B.

We paid heed to the hard lesson we learnt when walking the North Downs Way about the distances you walk each day when on a long trail. So we planned to walk on average about fifteen miles a day. Obviously this is somewhat predicted by the terrain and seventeen miles was the longest planned day and eleven miles the shortest. Once we were all packed up we were ready for the off!

We were starting the route on Monday the 13th of May (Lucky or unlucky thirteen hmm) and had to travel up on the train the day before carrying all our kit that we were taking with us. After making all the necessary train changes eventually we arrived at Edale. Once there at Edale we stayed at the Cotefield Camping Barn. Monday morning dawned with sunshine streaming into the Camping Barn, and Jan and I packed all out kit into our large (yellow) rucksacks and with some excitement and I must say, apprehension, made our way to the official start of the Pennine Way.

The first few steps of the Pennine Way are reckoned to be from outside of the Old Nags Head at Edale.

The start of the Pennine Way

Most people who take on the challenge of the Pennine Way in its entirety give up during the first few days if they are going to give up at all. The Dark Peak of Derbyshire can be a lovely place to be in early summer sunshine, but a leaden day of mist, rain and cloying peat can test any walkers resolve. I have written in this book about the Pennine Way in a format that is a section of my diary for each day, followed by a paragraph or two of comments or explanations of things that are mentioned in the diary.

Diary. Day One. Edale to Crowden 16 miles.
Excellent weather today. Hurrah! We woke up to bright sunshine streaming into the bunk barn. A good night's sleep was had in the Bunk Barn after a night in the Old Nags Head where we had a good feed and water. The packs were heavy and stops frequent when we were climbing up 'Jacob's Ladder'. Great views while walking along from Edale Rocks to Kinder Downfall. We stopped for a brew at Kinder Downfall and Jan bathed her feet in the stream. We met a guy called 'Vic' from Derbyshire who was including the Way as part of his route while walking the length of Britain in one continuous effort, from Lands End to John 'O' Groats! (Must be Mad!)

The ascent to Bleaklow Head was quite tough with huge peat groughs blocking the way.

The campsite is quite nice, hot water showers (Hooray!) No Pubs (Boo) The dreaded 'Black Hill' tomorrow!! We saw the Legendary Derbish's Cave today, no sign of the Whirling Derbish himself though.

Don't ask me what the legendary Whirling Derbish is, because I have no idea! I can only guess that he must be some sort of monster that lived near the Way in Derbyshire? The second section of the Way we planned to walk on day two was from Crowden to Standedge where the Way reaches the northern edge of the Peak National Park including a long ascent over Laddow Rocks to Black Hill. This section includes the famous Woodhead railway tunnel about Woodhead Reservoir and was built between 1838 and 1845. Twenty eight people were killed in a cholera outbreak during construction of the second tunnel and most of these people were buried in the little church of St James.

Diary. Day two. Crowden to Standedge. 11.5 miles.
The weather was very hot today which made it a long 12 miles. Jan's legs got burnt due to her very short shorts! The dreaded climb up to Black Hill was not as tough as expected as the route has been improved a lot by the laying of the flagstones to combat the erosion. In fact it was quite pleasant laying in the

grass at the top of Black Hill. Crowden Great Brook looked good from the top of Laddow Rocks. We saw a lot of grouse today. The climb up Blakley Clough was longer and tougher than expected and Jan had an energy crisis half way up. Ha ha. The campsite at Glebe Farm was nowhere near as nice as Crowden. It will be a long day tomorrow if the hot weather persists. Now that we are in Yorkshire I suppose we will never see the Whirling Derbish! If of course he exists, or he ever did! Ummm call me Mr Sceptical, I'm not sure that the Whirling Derbish ever existed. I think he was just invented by the locals to pull in tourists!

Our third day was to be a fifteen miler from Standedge to Hebden Bridge this section of the Way sticks to the high moors and grit stone edges. The reference points being the arterial roads to be crossed and the high level reservoirs of Green Withen's, Blackstone edge, White Holme and Warland.

Diary. Day three. Standedge to Hebden Bridge. 15 miles.
The weather was not so good today. Very windy and overcast, but still no rain as yet. We had a good meal last night at Glebe Farm and were provided with a packed lunch for today. They sent home some gear that we had packed and decided that we had packed too much and wanted to lighten the load a little. The day went fast today. Done the fifteen miles from eight a.m. to three p.m. We had to keep going and stepped it out because it was cold in the wind. The highlight of the day was Stoodley Pike. As I said we stepped it out today and to do it in that time shows that we must be getting fitter. No real problems so far and I'm feeling good and Jan seems fine. B and B tonight at the Woodman Inn. It's a bit of a dump (shame) but a bar downstairs (Hooray!) All the kit is washed and dried, which is nice.

Day four is to be another fifteen miler from Hebden Bridge to Cowling and after miles on the rooftop of England we would now find ourselves down in the boiler-room, crossing a ribbon of road, rail, canal, river and industrial terraces.

Diary. Day four. Hebden Bridge to Cowling. 15 miles.
The weather today was clear and sunny at first anyway. After a large cooked breakfast we donned the shorts and set out. It was a very stiff climb out and up onto the moor. By the time we were up the leggings and fleecy were back on! We stopped at High Gate and signed The Pennine Way visitor's book. We had lunch at 'Withens' the ruins reputed to be Emily Bronte's Wuthering Heights.

The 'Withens'

We also passed Ponden Hall. Quite a few climbs today, short and steep, but a tiring fifteen miles. We have the campsite to ourselves at Cowling. A fellow walker called Steve overtook us today only to be beaten in at the end of the day by 'the yellow rucksacks' which is how refers to us when he could see us in the distance ahead of him.

At this stage we varied from the guide to even out the distances that we would walk each day. The guide had advised to stop at Ponden, which would have made yesterday a short day, but we had pressed on to Cowling. Now we were going to do a long day of 17 miles to Malham. When we had stopped at 'Withens', as I had mentioned in my diary, according to local knowledge this was reputed to be the place that was where that Heathcliff and Cathy fell in love and if you have ever read the story of Wuthering Heights you will know this. If you are reading this book and enjoying it, then I would recommend that you read Wuthering Heights at some stage. I don't know if that any of it is true, and whether if 'Withens' ruins high on the moor really is the place, but if you are a person of romantic tendency, then it is worth a visit. I, being a man of romantic tendency would like to think that it really was the place. It was high on the moor in a bleak and barren place of the Pennines, and to live there back then would have been something extraordinary.

127

Diary. Day five. Cowling to Malham. 17 miles.
The weather was changeable all day and it was waterproof on, waterproof off, on, off, on, off. There was lots of climbing in the first half of the day with great views of Pen-y-Ghent in the distance and we will cross it on Sunday. We stopped at Thornton-in-Craven, but no café here to get some grub. We asked a chap if there was somewhere we could get a cuppa and the man in the post office with no stock in his shop made us one. Ha Ha. I wrote a message to Steve who was now behind us on a rock. (I hope he sees it, will we ever know?) Passing the Leeds and Liverpool canal we saw all the nice long boats. We went to a Café we saw advertised and it was closed on Fridays! (Grrrrrr). However the lady who runs it made us a cuppa and a sandwich anyway (Hooray). Last night at the end of day four we went to a pub called the Black Bull and met a nice bloke called Dave who had walked the Way previously. He must have thought that we were kindred spirits because he kept buying me beer all evening! We swapped addresses and I promised I would send him a postcard at some stage later on the Way.

When we planned our walk of The Pennine Way I planned in two rest days. These would be the two days that we would do no walking. However, after our first rest day at Malham we changed our plans and cancelled the second rest day. We found that now we were getting so fit that we just wanted to press on and couldn't be bothered sitting around resting for another day.

Diary. Day six. Rest day. Miles 0.
Rest day today. We got up late and went into the village for a look around. We found a great shop called the Cove Centre, but managed to get out only £100.00 lighter having brought a new pack each, some small bits and pieces. Also a new stuff sack for my sleeping bag. This afternoon we went and sat by the river about a mile from Malham to wait for Steve and Marion to catch us up. (the yellow rucksacks) Steve came through about four O'clock. Marion had got on the bus at Gargrave. (Blisters 'again'!) A bloke called Derrick we met earlier on the trail came bimbling along just as I was thinking how he was doing. He is going slow, but still going. I hope he makes it, he is a nice bloke. Now back at the tent and new rucksacks packed and ready for the morning. (no more yellow rucksacks!) Looking forward to Pen-y-Ghent tomorrow. Steve didn't see the message I wrote on the rock. Shame.

The reason we changed from the yellow rucksacks is that they were old fashioned framed rucksacks which are somewhat out of date at the time of doing the Way, so we opted for some more modern non-framed rucksacks to see if it would make the going any easier. If you are going to stop for a day at any stage on the Way Malham is a good place to do so. Where it used to be a place of mills and mines it now caters for tourists. The two major attractions being the nearby Malham cove and Malham tarn. The Pennine Way includes both of these tourist attractions.

Diary. Day seven. Malham to Horton in Ribblesdale. 14 miles.
We had a rough night in the tent, very wet and windy. Woke to high wind, mist and rain. Had a close look at Malham cove. The climb over Fountain Fell was shrouded in mist, so no views there. Weather cleared on the approach to Pen-y-Ghent. We climbed the steep face of Pen-y-Ghent in a howling gale! It was quite tricky. Took a small diversion off the Way to have a look at Hull Pot, very impressive! Still raining at present. Spilt curry all over myself and the tent at dinner time, (bummer!) Hope the weather improves tomorrow.

The climb up and over Pen-y-Ghent that day was great. Hard work in that howling gale, but very exhilarating! The good part about that day on the Way was that the weather had cleared when we had gone up and over the mountain, so that had provided us with and opportunity to take some great shots. Our new tent took a right bashing in the gale that night

Day eight is to be another day when we varied from the recommended stopping place in the guide at Hawes. We pushed on through the village of Hawes for about another two and a half miles to the village of Hardraw. This would make the day a sixteen miler. The reason for this was that the guide makes day nine a 19 miler so, by going on for another two and a half miles on day eight we would chop this distance off day nine.

Diary. Day eight. Horton-in-Ribblesdale to Hardraw. 16 miles.
8.41 a.m. Woke this morning to absolute downpour. Been raining all night. Waiting to see if it will ease off for 9.00. We considered a bus or taxi to Hardraw, but couldn't bring ourselves to do it and walked anyway.

It's always too soon to quit. (Norman Vincent Peale.)

I rang the Green Dragon and changed our booking from camping to B and B expecting to be soaked by the time we arrived! Togged up in all the waterproofs and set off. By the time we had walked the five or six miles to Ling Gill Bridge the sun was out and the waterproofs off! (yippee) The traverse across Cam Fell was great and the also Dodd's Fell excellent with great views all around. Having started late we expected to finish late, but we made good time and stopped in Hawes village to shop and have tea. I forgot to say we saw a great cave in full flood which was unexpected. The Green Dragon is nice, got all the gungy gear washed and a good bed. Hardraw Force waterfall was fantastic after all that rain last night.

Hardraw Force

As I said in the diary, we did consider a bus or taxi to Hardraw, but what is the point in that! You will have walked about two hundred and forty miles and then still at the end of it not be able to say that you had walked the Pennine Way. If you really want to be able to say "I have walked the Pennine Way." You need to have really done that from end to end. 256 miles!

The centre piece of Hardraw is the waterfall of Hardraw Force which the beck tumbles down a wall of yoredale rock which is just upstream from where we stayed at the Green Dragon. The vertical drop is over 98 feet and can be accessed by a private foot path from the Pub. The waterfall is reputed to be the place that was used for the time that Robin Hood Prince of Thieves took a bath in the film starring Kevin Costner. I don't know if this is true or not, but it certainly looks like it could be.

Diary. Day nine. Hardraw to Tan Hill. 15 miles.
Left the Green Dragon after a good breakfast and a fire drill (burnt toast ha ha!) It took us two hours to climb up Great Shunner Fell. Excellent views but very windy as usual! The bimble down to Thwaite was tricky as the track was very rough. Had a cup of tea and a scone in the café in Thwaite and chatted to a bloke from Liverpool who was also walking the Way. (another kindred spirit) It was a steep climb out of Thwaite into Swaledale. Great traverse to Keld looking across to the Coast to Coast path on the other side of the dale. Sun now out and shorts on and legs out too. Got to Keld and the sun is now in again (bummer). Boggy route through to Tan Hill. We met Ron and Pauline about half a mile from Tan Hill Inn walking towards us. They brought us some Dinner in the Inn. Tan Hill Inn is great, real flag stone floor and oak beams. The highest Inn in Great Britain at 1724 feet!

I wasn't to know it at the time, but the Coast to Coast route was one of the paths that I would walk later in life with my mate Lloydie from the army I mentioned earlier in Chapter five, but more on that later. Ron and Pauline are Jan's parents and we arranged to meet them at Tan Hill Inn because it was the nearest spot to the centre of the total trail that was convenient. The dinner they brought us in Tan Hill Inn was great. Yorkshire puddings the size of a dinner plate, filled with plenty of nice succulent sliced roast beef and thick gravy, then topped off with chunky chips, delicious! That's the sort of dinner a Pennine Way walker wants in the evening. We did not have a good night sleep though at Tan Hill Inn because the camp site was just a bit of rough ground at the back of the pub and the ground was rock hard! So hard that some of the tent pegs bent when I had to hammer them into the ground with a rock! We called the geezer from Liverpool 'Scouse' and bumped into him again later.

Diary. Day ten. Tan Hill to Blackton Reservoir. 11 miles.
The most miserable day so far. Woke this morning to cold wind and drizzle. Jan's heel blister quite bad again (Due to wet boots!). Nearly froze to death packing up the camping gear. The drizzle quickly turned to hard driving rain. Boots soaked again (Bummer!). We considered making for Bowes to get a B and B to hole up, but in the end pushed on the Blackton Reservoir as planned. The only good thing about the day is that we are still on schedule! On arrival at the Hostel it was full for the night. So its another night in the wet tent. We need some supplies when we get to Middleton tomorrow.

There is not much that I can say about that day at the time of writing this book. I think by reading the diary I wrote at the time you can tell what sort of mood we were in by the end of day ten. Pretty much down in the dumps!

Diary. Day eleven. Blackton Reservoir to Cronkley Scar. 14 miles.
We woke up to beautiful sunshine (thank god!). Got our packs packed up with all the gear dried out from the Youth Hostel drying room. Met up with the bloke called Scouse (don't know his real name) after half a mile. He had spent the night sleeping in a sheep pen after a wet day poor bugger! He was on the Way and heading for Middleton for a launderette to wash and dry all his gear. Crossed from Lunedale into Teesdale and stopped at Middleton for an early lunch and get supplies. The weather is now cloudy but dry. Set off up Teesdale along the river where we saw and photographed Wynch Bridge, Low Force and High Force, all excellent. Upper Teesdale is lovely and we stopped for the night and wild camped at the base of Cronkley Scar. The scenery is great here, now raining though. Looking forward to Cauldron Snout and High Cup tomorrow and Dufton for a B and B (Hooray). We have had no shower for 3 nights. Passed halfway on the trail today. Perhaps we will make it?

Poor 'Scouse' had to sleep all of the Pennine Way wild camping, because he had no money to be able to sleep in a B and B even if the situation required it. He was unemployed and obviously pretty hard up. However I admire him for his tenacity. Just because in those times he couldn't get a job in the area where he lived, he didn't just sit on his backside and moan about things, he still got off his butt and got on with it. Good on him. I don't know if he made it to the end or not, but I would gamble on the fact that he did in the end. If I had taken a contact number and address from him, he could have had a copy of this book free of charge!

Teesdale is great place to go if you like dramatic scenery. Wynch Bridge is a little suspension bridge which was built in 1830. The original bridge that was there and used by the local miners collapsed in 1820 killing one man. As I mentioned in the diary there are several waterfalls that you see as you follow the Way up Teesdale. The first you come across is Low Force which is pretty, but the most impressive is High Force further up the dale.

High Force.

Diary. Day twelve. Cronkley Scar to Dufton. 13 miles.
Another great day today. One for the memory album. Woke up to light rain showers which fizzled out and had a good breakfast at the local farm at Widdy Bank for £2.50 each. Very reasonable! We set out along the upper Tees section with great scenery all the way. The waterfall of Cauldron Snout lived up to its name as it was most impressive.

Cauldron Snout.

I have to say that the walk up through Teesdale in my opinion is one of the best sections of the whole Pennine Way. At this point we crossed into County Durham and picked up Maize beck which we forded by removing our boots and gaiters to pick up the better path on the other side (Brrrr, water was freezing!). After a few more miles reached High Cup. Fantastic! The drop down to Dufton was fast and easy. I forgot to put earlier that when we forded Maize beck we stopped for a brew in the sunshine. By the time the kettle had boiled we had had a hailstorm and the sun was out again! Changeable weather in this part of the country! Also saw the fish (trout I presume?) feeding in the pools of the small mountain stream. What a great day! Cross Fell tomorrow.

When you reach High Cup Gill you find yourself at a pivotal point of the landscape. The whole world suddenly opens out beneath you with whinstone cliffs sweeping left and right with cascades of scree falling away on both sides and Ravens and Peregrines soaring above the cliffs. It is a fantastic site and well worthy of the effort required to go there to see it. I have to say that at the time of writing this section of the book I dug out all the photographs of the time on the Pennine Way and was looking at the photographs of our progress up Teesdale. Thinking back to the times we were there in 1996 I had a bit of an emotional outburst and shed some tears.

Diary. Day Thirteen. Dufton to Garrigill. 15.5 miles Had a good breakfast at Dufton Hall Farm and a very nice B and B for only £16.00. Climbed all morning to Cross Fell via Green Fell, Great Dunn Fell and Little Dun Fell, very tough mornings walk. We met our old mate Derrick at the top who we had not seen since day six at Malham! He is still going, good on him. There was extreme wind and very cold too much to linger up there for long. It was a long descent on a rough track down to Garrigill. It was hard on the feet and legs. We have decided to change our plans regarding taking a rest day at Garrigill as the is no proper campsite with any facilities. So we will push on tomorrow to Lamley Common or somewhere around there. We could possibly be in Kirk Yetholm and the end of the Way a day earlier than anticipated.

The small village of Garrigill is derived from Gerard's Gill. Gill being an old Norse word for a narrow valley. It is a nice enough little village and worthy of a look, but it is not the place that we wanted to linger for a day due to the lack of a campsite.

Diary. Day Fourteen. Garrigill to Greenhead. 20 miles.
We changed our original plans of having a rest day today and went all the way to Greenhead (possible mistake!) Twenty miles today. Raining all day and not a particularly nice walk. The last section across Hartleyburn Common and Blenkinsopp Common was wet and boggy. Jan suffered with tiredness and bad towards the end. Decided to find a B and B for the night but they were all full. We went to the Youth Hostel but that was full also. So we have ended up at a campsite outside of the village. Raining all night and most of the gear is soaked. I strained my back climbing out of the tent. Nothing serious though. It must have been an accumulation of the long wet day.

We over did it that day on day Fourteen and paid for our mistake. That is one problem you have to face when walking The Pennine Way. The amount of hiking that you do each day is dictated somewhat by the availability of accommodation and campsites. Unless of course you are lucky enough to have a full time back up crew who will come and pick you up at certain pre-planned meeting points along the route. But that would not be the same achievement of doing it on your own would it? Cheating, some might say.

Diary. Day Fifteen. Greenhead to Steel Rigg. 7 miles.
A short easy day today. Only seven miles. (We need it!) It was still raining when we woke and packed up our kit, but it soon cleared to a broken cloud and sunny day. Boots and socks drying out at last (Yippee). Hadrian's wall was excellent. Jan took some of the weight from me to help ease my back strain which worked.

We are staying at the Twice Brewed Inn Tonight. Mainly for my back, as sleeping on the ground will not be good for it. Should be o.k. for tomorrow. Over the 200 miles mark now and only four days to go! Saw our mate Derrick on the road again and he is still bimbling along. Good on him.

The walk along the crest of Whin Sill following the route of Hadrian's Wall is an interesting part of the of the Way with all the good conversation points that the Wall provides.

Diary. Day Sixteen. Steel Rig to Bellingham. 14.5 miles.
We had a good nights rest and a good breakfast at the Twice Brewed Inn. On the road at 09.15 a.m. This is the best preserved section of the Hadrian's Wall and Jan and I stopped for a couple of photographs. Derrick caught us up when we stopped for a breather. I found an amulet on the path that someone persons unknown had dropped. (Now around my neck). We finally left the Wall at Rapishaw gap. After a while we went into Wark Forest which we will pass through a number of times on the Way. Saw a deer, but not close enough to get a picky. No real Highlights now until the Cheviots. We did pass through Horneystead (funny name) and had tea which was served in the hay shed surrounded by dogs, horses and chickens! While we were sitting on straw bales. We also passed through Shitlington Hall (Unfortunate name!). Stayed at the campsite.

Horneystead dates back to 1873 and lies adjacent to the ruin of a fortified bastlehouse built about 1600. These bastlehouses where built as a result of the troubles between the Crowns which came to an end in 1660. Despite this, new farmhouses where still built solid and square which reflected the lack of trust in human nature and the local weather. Shitlington Hall with it's unfortunate name can be misleading it sounds like you would expect to find a grand Hall with sweeping lawns and well clipped hedges. It is in fact only a farmhouse!

If any walker would like to know a bit more about the Wall they can take a diversion where the route of the Way leaves the Wall at Rapishaw Gap and carry on along the Wall to the fine excavated fort of Housteads.

Diary. Day Seventeen. Bellingham to Byrness. 15 miles.
I didn't have very great expectations for today. I thought it would be a 'fill in' before the Cheviots, but it was very enjoyable which is good. Weather was fine and dry. The first half of the day involved the climb up and out of Bellingham. (Got away late as we had to wait for the bank to open). The crossing of the open moor land across Whitley Pike and Padon Hill was very wet underfoot so we

had to do some bog trotting. Great views of the Cheviots in the distance. In the afternoon we entered the forest again, but it wasn't boring as expected with views out to the climb up out of Byrness. Now in B and B in the one horse town of Byrness and the Cheviots looming above us. Only two days to go!

The town of Bellingham is pronounced Bellinjum and is a grey little town of only a thousand or so people. There are shops and pubs there and also a 13th century Church of St Cuthbert which has an unusual stone-slabbed roof which was constructed centuries ago to replace the previous ones burned down in Scottish raids as mentioned previously about the building of the Bastlehouses. As said in the log we stayed at a Bed and Breakfast place that was run by an old lady. I think she regarded us with some scepticism, but she was nice enough.

Diary. Day Eighteen. Byrness to Clennell Street. 14 miles.
We woke up to rain and mist. The mountains enshrouded at the tree line. The climb up and out of Byrness was steep and taxing making us sweat under our waterproofs! The day involved a gradual climb up over several peaks, toward the 'Cheviot' itself (promising great views). All we could see was about 100 yards, then just white with the rain and mist lashing us all the way. It was really boggy underfoot and our boots soon became soaked. Too wet and cold to stop we pushed on to the Bothey (Mountain shelter hut) at eight miles and had a brew and eats in relative comfort all the time our clothes steaming! Met Derrick and another chap at the Bothey. At Windy Gyle it lived up to its name and we got blown away as we made for the summit! The weather improved a bit in the afternoon and we managed to dry out a little. Now lying in our tent looking up at the Cheviot with the top still enshrouded in mist. Wind gusting strongly. I hope the tent can last one more night of this! 12 miles to go to the end tomorrow.

The village of Byrness that we left that morning was a specially created village for workers to build a the Catcleugh Reservoir and then to plant the Border Forest. As the trees grew the village melted into the darkening forest. This made the number of foresters decrease and several of the houses either fell vacant or were sold. Along that section of the Way from Byrness to Clennell Street we passed and ancient maize of earthwork which the Romans built to create a marching camp. My god, the Romans were pretty amazing way back then I think. How did they get this far north in Britain?

Diary. Day Nineteen. Clennell Street to Kirk Yetholm. 12 miles.
What a day! We had to move the tent at nine O'clock last night due to the rising wind. We dropped down into the woods which seemed o.k. Got to bed after being nearly run down by a low flying aircraft! We got about three hours kip last night as

the wind was blowing like crazy and threatening to flatten the tent. We got up at 6 a.m. made a brew and pushed on. Gale force winds and gusting hampering our progress through the boggy terrain. Made the turn at Cairn Hill and headed for the rescue hut for breakfast. The wind was now of Phenomenal proportions and it was impossible to walk in a straight line and very exhausting. Made it to the rescue hut for soup and sarnies (sandwiches) The climb up the Schil extremely windy and tough, but once over all down hill to Kirk Yetholm. Now safe and sound in the B and B. Wind still blowing. We made it!! Here at last, home tomorrow.

At the time of writing this book I do not remember the decent into Kirk Yetholm being windy? I remember it as a bright sunny day, how odd, selective memory I suppose, but I have to go by the diary that I wrote at the time when things where fresh in my mind. I do remember that as we approached Kirk Yetholm and it became apparent that we had actually made it along The Pennine Way, Jan burst into tears, and I really feel for her, bless her. Which is not surprising, as to walk the Pennine Way in one continuous effort is an amazing feat of endurance for any person to achieve.

The strange thing is that at the end of the Pennine Way I did not cry at that time. However, at the time of writing this, reading through my journal that I wrote at the time and thinking back to May 1996 when we walked the Pennine Way, I cried on several occasions and I don't mind admitting it! Not because they are tears of sadness, but just a tears of emotion at what we had achieved back then, and the highs and lows that we experienced along the Way.

As I said at the end of day eight you cannot say that you have walked the Pennine Way if you have taken a day out somewhere along the line. So I was, and still am extremely pleased that we 'bit the bullet' at that time, and carried on regardless. Jan and I can put our hands on our hearts, look someone in the eye and say "I have walked The Pennine Way." There are not a lot of people around that can say that!

It is strange how people who have walked the Way form this type of 'bond' between them. It is almost like an unofficial club that you join when you have walked The Pennine Way in its entirety. But I like it because Jan and I certainly deserve to be members of The Pennine Way Club!

At the time of writing this book, I am a considering going out there and walking The Pennine Way again. I don't know why that is, but that is what I am thinking about. How strange is that?

CHAPTER THIRTEEN

THE MID-NINETIES

It was in the mid-nineties that I got another dog for company for Lucy dog. I had been In the Chequers Inn for a pint and got chatting to a fella who told me of some Labradors that were going free. I said "Going free! Surely no one gives Labradors away." Anyway he told me that they were at a farm that he knew down in the valley. I wrote the address down and then looked them up on the Ordnance Survey Map.

Jan and I went down there and found the farm concerned. I made some enquiries to the Farmers Wife and asked if there were any black Labradors going as this is what the chap at the pub had told me. She said "Well they are not black and we only know for sure that the mother is a Labrador, father unknown!" I said "Oh o.k. well can I have a look at them anyway?" She took us to the barn and we went in. Lying on the floor was the Golden Labrador mother of the litter and all the pubs were milling about trying to find a feed.

They looked like normal Labradors to me so I thought well it don't matter that they are not black. So I said to the lady "How much do you want for them?" She said "Just pick one and you can have it." So I looked them over and said "What about that one." Pointing my finger at it. She said "That one is spoken for." So, pointing again I said "What about that one over there?" That one was spoken for also. "O.K. which ones are not spoken for?" Pointing into the corner of the barn she said "That one is still free." There, in the corner of the barn looking forlorn and lonely was a big fat puppy with its belly protruding. She looked like a Buddha. Hmmm I went over and picked her up and she promptly peed

139

on me. Love at first sight! I said I would have her and Jan drove us back to my house. I climbed out of the car and handed the puppy to Jan and the Puppy was promptly car sick on her.

When inside of the house I had to come up with a name for my new pet. What was I going to call her? I had a good think and tried to come up with a good name but the only thing that seemed to produce a response what-so-ever was Puppy. Well, I thought I can't call her Puppy all her life! She will soon grow into a dog. I know I will call her Poppy like the flower as that is like puppy and she responded to it quite well. I introduced Poppy to my old Lucy dog and they did not seem particularly keen on each other but they got on alright in the end. At the time of writing this book, Poppy is still going in 2010, but the poor old girl is getting on now and I don't think she will be around much longer, so keep your fingers crossed!

SPORTING EVENTS

It was about this time that I met a Fireman who had just joined White Watch at Canterbury. His name was Jim and Jim was a good sailor. He lived on the Isle of Sheppey and had been sailing at the sailing club there for years. Long before I had learned to sail, he really knew what he was doing. Unlike me who used to spend a lot of time in the 'drink'. I liked Jim as he was a nice and funny bloke and we decided between us that we would enter the Fire Service National Sailing Competition. The competition would be held up in London on a lake that was up in that part of the country. Now, I was used to offshore sailing and so was Jim, but this would be inshore sailing. We decided that we would go for it anyway.

To Quote Princess Diana; "Only do what your heart tells you." So that is what we did. We went for it.

I had done sailing in the past, so I knew the fundamentals, but Jim was sailing all the time at the club on the Isle of Sheppey so he knew his onions. (For those who don't know who are reading this, knowing your onions means really understanding something.) So, therefore even though in the working Fire Service environment I was the boss, it was decided between us that in the yacht he would be the boss. He would helm and I would be the crew. A wise decision I think! We placed our entry for the competition and it was accepted. Prior to the event itself I made some inquiries to the London Fire Service about them providing some accommodation for us. And as Firemen the world over are all like brothers in arms they said that they would put us up at the Fire Station no problems.

The Bosun yachts we would be sailing would be provided by the club concerned and Jim and I carrying our buoyancy aids and sleeping bags, travelled up to London from Kent and found the Fire Station that would put us up for a couple of nights. We got to the Station quite late at night and I remember that it was dark at the time and the night Watch was on duty.

On arrival I was somewhat 'gob smacked' to see that in the Appliance Bays where the Fire Appliances are normally kept was a London Fireman underneath his car working on the engine. Something that would never be allowed down in the Kent Fire Brigade! My initial reaction was that things are certainly more relaxed than they are in Kent. Anyway Jim and I introduced ourselves and were given a cuppa by the duty crew and then shown where we could lay our sleeping bags and get our heads down.

The next morning on the day of the race Jim and I got our sailing gear together and drove to the inland water where the race would take place. We were given a Bosun yacht in which we would sail and had some practice time to get used to the thing. Then the sailing race itself started and off we went.

It was a windy day that day and Jim as the helmsman timed it well and we crossed the line just as the starting gun went off. A good start was had. We knew the course and that we had to complete three laps. Jim at the helm and me providing the crewing. We sailed the course and although I was very fit at the time, toward the end, having to be hiked out for so long my stomach muscles were getting really tired. Jim was the captain and when I was leaning in because my stomach muscles were killing me he REALLY SHOUTED at me! "YOU BLOODY WELL HIKE OUT THERE IF YOU WANT TO WIN THIS RACE!!" A Fireman does not shout at his superior! (I don't bloody care Jim and I were very good mates.) I did the best I could but my abdominal muscles were killing me! I hiked out with my guts burning like THEY WERE ON FIRE! AAAAAAAH!

We did alright, we got second place in the race and I am very proud of it, but would to have loved to have won! Jim did not hold any grievance against me because being an experienced sailor he knew how hard it was to hike out like that for so long. It was a combination of excellent helmsman ship, crew fitness, and team work that got our sailing yacht across the line in second place. We had had a wonderful time and were really glad that we went. After the race we sorted out the Bosun yacht and stowed the sails. Then there was a presentation ceremony where First, Second and Third award shields were issued. Jim and I were presented with our shield with a shake of the hand. On the shield there was a picture of a yacht and underneath it said 'Shield for F.S.S.A.A. Sailing Section National Dinghy Championship. 2nd-1996. (F.S.S.A.A. Fire Service Sports and Athletics Association.)

As they say in my part of the world, "If ya can't cut the mustard, get on ya bike, and sling ya hook!"

Clutching our awards, we returned to the London Fire Station where them London boys were putting us up, we had a good shower and then some other funny things happened there in that London Fire Station. We said to the duty crew that we wanted to go out for the evening. They looked at us sideways and a bit sceptically and one of them said, "Well, if I were you guys, I wouldn't go out in the pubs and clubs around here! You being southern softies, you are certain to get beaten up, mugged or worse!" Then they said, "Look just jump on the fire pump and we will run you up the road to a safe bus stop and you can get a ride to the posh part of the city where you can have a night out and enjoy yourselves."

Now, to take a person not in uniform on a fire pump would be something that we would not dream of doing in Kent! Anyway Jim and I got our 'glad rags' on and the coloured gentlemen, of the London Fire Watch, all jumped on the pump with us with their fire kit on and we set off.

When we exited the Fire Station, they had automatic doors, and as we were leaving the doors started coming down and they caught on the roof mounted ladders and causing some damage to the doors the driver nearly tore the doors off! The guys on the pump said, "Oh shit! But sod it, we will worry about that when we get back." They were a rough tough bunch those London boys! And I really mean, really rough tough London Firemen! Not like us guys. But what can you say about men like that! I have nothing but admiration for them. They took us about a mile up the road and dropped us off at the bus stop and told us which bus to take.

We caught the bus and went to the 'posh' part of town and the ladies must have thought that we were a right bunch of commoners because they didn't want to talk to Firemen and Sailors like Jim and me. So Jim and I just had a few beers and listened to the music and talked about our sailing that day. Then later we called a taxi and he took us back to the Fire Station.

The night crew let us in and Jim and I decided that it was time to 'hit the hay.' Finding our sleeping bags we went to bed. Climbing into my sleeping bag I found all these strange objects that I didn't know were in there? In our absence the London Fire boys had filled our sleeping bags with loads of aluminium plate warmers from the kitchen! We had the same thing in Canterbury, aluminium disks that are used to keep your dinner warm in the hot plate if you had got called out to a 'Shout'. Those London Firemen! The bastards! Ha ha ha. God bless 'em! Jim and I had some laughs with those London Firemen. It just goes to show that Firemen are the same the world over. Thanks boys if you ever get to read this. I really appreciate what you did for Jim and me at that time.

It was about this time that my mate Nick, (The Copper and ex-army mate) had asked me if I would like to have a kitten because he and Heidi's two cats were constantly having litters! I told him on the telephone when he called me, no, I did not want a cat. He was rather persistent and in the end I relented and said "O.k. I'll have one of your bloody kittens, but only on ONE condition, it has to be a ginger tom." I had said that because I was fairly confident that he would be unable to meet my requirements. After a while, Nick turned up at my house carrying a box. I opened it up and there he was the new addition to the household a ginger kitten. He was strikingly vivid in colour. He was so ginger that he almost glowed! So a name for him came straight to mind. I will call him Scorcher because he was like a fire, scorching.

As mentioned previously I had been involved in doing a lot of challenge walks. I decided that it was about time that Kent Fire Brigade organized a Challenge Walk of their own. I spoke to Jan about this and she thought it would be a good thing. We contacted a few of our buddies that had done some challenge walking to see if they wanted to get involved, most of them that I had contacted wanted to be involved in the event in someway or another.

We then formed our own little committee to do all the organizational side of the project. At that stage we had no idea about the amount of work that it took to put together a National Challenge Walk. Believe me it was a lot more work than I had suspected it would be!

The first committee meeting was held and we had a little chat. The first thing we had to come up with is a name for the event. All challenge walk events have a name such as: The Wirecock Challenge, Hadrian's Hike, Malhamdale Meander, and The Dales Traverse. The list goes on. I suggested that we call it 'The Kent Hop Challenge.' Which the rest of the committee thought was a good idea. Why The Kent Hop Challenge? Well in Kent they grow a lot of hops, not so much these days as they used to but there are still a lot of Oast Houses that contained the hop drying kiln to dry out the hops ready for packing. So that was the name that was given to our event. It did not mean that those taking part in the event would have to hop all the way around the route as they would never make it!

The next thing that we had to do was to decide on which weekend of the year we would host the event. Now, the trouble was I thought that it would be unwise the have it on the same day of one of the other existing events as that would put us in competition with other Brigades for entrants into the event. We looked into it and through the summer months there was an event on somewhere in the country on every single weekend! So we opted for the 26th of October. The reason for this is that the countryside in Kent can look lovely at this time of year with all the leaves turning red and gold and on a sunny day it looks great.

Now we have to form a route. This was a very time consuming task, as we were not just going to get a map and work out a route, we were going to actually walk the route section to prove that the final route we would be creating could in reality actually be walked and the walkers were not going to be walking around our route and come across a stile that had disappeared and was now a barbed wire fence! In my experience this can happen at times, when the stile has collapsed with rot and the farmer wanted to keep his stock in the field.

Following much walking of the route we finally decided what it would be. There needed to be check points along the route which would be manned by volunteers to check the walkers through. We strategically placed the check points in places that would ensure that no walker would take a short cut. Not of course that I think that any entrant would want to try that, but just in case. The final route we had come up with was twenty six miles long.

Obviously we wanted as many entrants into the event as possible, and the committee decided that to do this it might be a good idea to come up with a shorter half distance route which we did. The two routes would be a circular ones starting and finishing in the same place and this would be at the Kent Fire Brigade Fire Station at the little village of Wye.

Another issue that we had to face was the problem of communication between the base at the Fire Station and the check point operators out on the ground. This was achieved by using radios. We contacted a local Radio enthusiast group called RAYNET and asked them for their help with the communications which they were more than happy to do.

Now we had to organize some advertising to attract as many entrants as possible. The Brigade produced and information Bulletin on a regular basis and any sporting events could be advertised in there so we on the 'Committee' of The Kent Hop, designed an advert for the event and informed whoever did it to put in the Bulletin. Also I put an advert in the national walking association magazine. We were all set for the off.

The day of the event dawned clear and bright with a good weather forecast for that time of year. There were plenty of volunteers to help with the running of the event and come the day we all went the Wye Fire Station and set up the control point. The Fire Engine was pulled out of the bays to make room for setting up of all the collapsible tables that we had brought with us. We set these up in the bays and put all our paper work for the registration of the entrants onto the tables. From somewhere, I am not sure where, we had got a board which had a load of tallies on for the walkers to be allocated one each. We had probably borrowed it from someone who was in the service that held some similar sort of event. The Raynet guy set up all his communication equipment on a small table and put up a board with the information on.

The Raynet man.

All the walkers that had entered the event turned up in good time to register and be allocated their tally. When all the necessary paper work had been done and everything was prepared The Chief Fire Officer of Kent Fire Brigade stood up in front of all the walkers and made a nice speech, for which we were very grateful. To have our Chief Fire Officer turn up to open the event was somewhat of a surprise! He must have been impressed as to the amount of work that we had put in. Then with some pomp and circumstance the walkers were off!

As I said there were some check points along the route that we had arranged and we had a checkpoint operator at each one. They checked the tallies as each walker came through. There was a large group of retained Firemen from our station at the village of Aylesham that had entered the event and on seeing these guys I was somewhat baffled at why they were all carrying such big packs for only a single day out, but this would become apparent at a later stage.

Janice and I had the job of staying at the Fire Station all day and monitoring the progress of the walkers and how the event was going via the Raynet chap. Not the most exciting role in the world but someone had to do it.

Jan and I at the control desk having our lunch.

When we had been organizing the event we had arranged for a Brigade mini-bus to be available. This was done for emergency purposes, so that should one of the walkers twist and ankle, get bad blisters of even something worst and had to drop out of the event we had the ability to go and pick them up. After all you don't really want to be calling 999 for an ambulance for someone who has got bad blisters!

In general the event went extremely well, and I don't remember anyone having to pull out at any stage. However, there where some very weary looking walkers that rolled in at the end. The weather was very kind and it was a beautiful sunny day all day. One thing that did strike me as odd was that the group of retained firemen from Aylsham, on arrival back at the start point all seemed somewhat tipsy. That was why they had the big packs for the day. The large packs had been full of beer!

The Kent Hop was a great event and I felt proud that we had arranged for it to happen. And that our Chief Fire Officer had deemed it worthy of his attention to come and set The Kent Hop off. So there.

It was in 1997 on the 4th of April, that I was given the best birthday present that I have ever had, and it was somewhat of a surprise! As you know Jan and I and Simon and Alison where doing a lot of days out walking in the countryside and we had arranged to go for a walk on my birthday. I was getting to that stage in life where I didn't make a big deal out of a birthday anymore, just treat it like an ordinary day. So, off we set with our picnic and other bits and pieces. Well as it happened I had not arranged the route that day which is unusual as it was normally me that did the route planning. The route that we walked just happened to pass a small airfield at where there happened to be a red Tiger Moth G-ASKP. For those who are unaware a Tiger Moth is an old bi-plane like they used way back in the early days of aviation. Jan said to me "Take your pack off, you are going up for a flight!" I said "You got to be kidding?" However she was not kidding and the pilot gave me a leather helmet and a pair of goggles and I climbed in.

Me in the cockpit of the Tiger Moth.

The pilot took off and we were away, soaring in the sky in a bi-plane, something that I had wanted to fly in all my life! Since I was a young boy I had been building model bi-planes from balsa wood and then crashing them! During the flight the pilot said, "Do you want to loop the loop?" I was not sure about this, would I be able to hold onto my lunch? Of course I agreed and we looped the loop twice, and he even let me take the joy stick and fly the Tiger just to try and keep her steady and in a straight line. What a gift! That was the best gift that anyone has ever brought me. And probably the best one anyone ever will. Thank you Jan.

It was about this time that my dog Lucy had to be put down. She had become so blind in her old age that I thought it was cruel to keep her going any longer. I took her to the vet and he agreed that I was making the right decision. So it was done. I phoned Ma who was now living in Wales and told her the bad news. At that time she was being visited by my sister Sarah and she told me later when I was writing the book, that they had both cried when they heard what I had had to do, and I cried when I was writing this, I was typing away with the tears running down my face remembering Lucy dog.

On a brighter note one of the things that I did at this time was my first ever open water Triathlon. For those who are unaware a Triathlon is a sporting race that involves three disciplines. A swim, a bike ride and lastly a run. There are two types of Triathlon an Iron Man Triathlon which is a phenomenal event that finishes with running a full marathon. Or an Olympic standard Triathlon that is not such a long event and finishes with running 10 kilometres. I did several Triathlons, but only of the Olympic standard, never an Iron Man. You must be completely bonkers to do an Iron Man!

To take part in a Tri you need to do a fair amount of training and get yourself good and fit. I did some training in the local public swimming pool, lots of cycling and plenty of runs. After doing a few Triathlons where the swim is in a pool, I entered the Dover (over) Triathlon in which the swim is in Dover Harbour.

Before the event I brought a wet suit and thought it would be good to go down to Dover Harbour and do some practice swims. I went down there one day and feeling brave and rather silly at the same time, wearing my wet suit I went into the water. I have to say that swimming in a wet suit was not the easiest thing to do. The neoprene of the suit affected your buoyancy in the water and made swimming awkward. That day the water was extremely choppy and I was really struggling to make any progress! After nearly drowning I gave up. All I could do was hope that on the day of the event the water in the harbour would be somewhat more settled and that I would be able to swim the course.

The day of the event dawned and I loaded my bike and wet suit and other bits and pieces into the car and drove down to Dover (over). After registering for the event and being allocated my competitors number and putting my bike in the rack, I put on my wet suit and I was ready for the off.

Now, of the three disciplines involved in a Triathlon, swimming was my weakest point, and running my strongest. All the competitors gathered on the beach most of them wearing wet suits but some of the braver ones were not. I was somewhat concerned as to how far out the red marker buoy appeared to be, it seemed to me to be a long way out there! However I was pleased that on the day of the event the water in the harbour was a lot calmer than on the day of my last training swim.

The starter gun went off and all us brave, or was it mad, competitors ran down the beach and plunged into the water. I swam out to the buoy plodding away with my slow, laborious swimming style. I eventually rounded the buoy and swimming back to the beach I realized that I was probably near to, if not the last in the field of competitors. When I exited the water and started to strip off my wet suit as I ran up the beach a girl shouted out "GO ON MATE, YOU ARE DOING REALLY WELL!" I was somewhat touched by her enthusiasm, as I knew I could well be the last in the field to finish the swim.

Exiting Dover harbour

I then found my bike in the rack, stripped off the wet suit and donning my vest and trainers (tied up with elastic laces.) as fast as possible, I jumped on the bike and started to pedal (I CAN RIDE MY BIKE! As in chapter one, but I had improved somewhat since then.). I soon started to take over some of the other competitors as I had done quite a bit of training on the bike. The course that we would have to ride was well marked on the public roads and navigation was not a problem. Having completed the ride in a reasonable time, I got back to the dismount area and ran pushing the bike to the rack. I dumped the bike in the rack and going through the strange sensation of changing from cycling to running began the 10 kilometre run.

I felt that I was doing alright now, well at least I hadn't drowned in the harbour! Or I hadn't caved in the front wheel of my bike! I had caught up quite a number of the other competitors on the bike section, and was now warming into the run. When I got going with the run section I was flying! Passing lots of the men that had exited the harbour long before I had and I felt like I had wings on my heels like the Greek God Hermes! I knew that the running section would be my strongest point.

If you look at this picture that is Dover Castle in the background.

115 on the run.

I completed the course and obviously I was not the winner. To be the winner of an open water Triathlon you need to be the best in all three disciplines. Well if not the best in all three, then at least the best all rounder. However I did finish in a respectable place in the middle of the field of competitors and I was happy with that. It was a good day out and I was just really pleased that they did not have to fish me out of Dover Harbour, and that my bike was still intact!

After this things carried on as normal being a serving Leading Fireman getting 'Shouts' to this that and the other sorts of incidents that were attended as usual, and I was really enjoying my work in those years. I know some people think that it is strange that a Fireman would enjoy his work, but that is not so alien to me, and I am sure not to other Firemen. We joined the Fire Service to achieve certain missions and to do that provides a certain amount of satisfaction.

In the summer of 1997 we all went up to the top of the university hill and took a picture of the Watch with the Cathedral in the distance.

That's me second on the left, next to Austin on my left who gets a mention later and my sailing buddy Jim is kneeling down on the right. Fire Service life was good back in those days.

CHAPTER FOURTEEN

More walking!

It was in 1998 that I was to walk two trails in one year. In the spring I was to walk part of a trail called The Ridgeway and then later on Coast to Coast but more about the Coast to Coast later. Firstly about The Ridgeway.

I walked The Ridgeway with my two friends Simon and Alison, just the three of us. Originally when we first planned the trip my then girlfriend Jan was going to come with us, but times change and due to our change of personal circumstances Jan did not come with us.

Unfortunately I did not keep a diary of our walk, which is a shame because they have been very useful in jogging my memory while I was writing this book. So therefore I will have to write this section of the book about our trip working from the memory banks of Simon, Alison and I.

The Whole Ridgeway runs from Overton Hill near Avebury to Ivinghoe Beacon. Or it can be walked the other way starting at Ivinghoe Beacon and finishing at Overton Hill. We did not have the time available to walk the whole of the Route, so we had decided we would walk the first half of the route in reverse. Starting at Goring and finishing at Avebury. I don't know why but that is how it felt the natural way to do the path, strange but true!

There is a lot of ancient history along this path more that three other paths put together, or so they say anyway. The Ridgeway is an ancient track so old that no one can even put a date on it! All that can be said is that it was almost certainly a trading route in the New Stone Age. That began about 6000 years ago. Blimey!

There is certainly a lot to see in the way of ancient monuments along the Ridgeway and Simon, Alison and I looked at all of the ones that we passed.

The three of us made our way to the start of our planned section of the Ridgeway at Goring. We managed to achieve this by doing some juggling around with two vehicles to ensure that when we had reached the other end of the linear walk we would have transport to take us back to the beginning to pick up the other car.

We drove the two cars Alison's Laguna and my little 2cv to the finish of the walk at Avebury. Then I drove Alison and Simon to the start of our walk in my 2cv, a ride that I am sure they enjoyed immensely! When at the start of our trip we left the 2cv there and would come and collect it when we had finished. So we were all set for the off!

Here I am at the sign of the Ridgeway.

Well we set off and had to complete the first section of our walk to the B4001 which is about three miles before reaching Uffington White Horse Hill. As I did not keep a diary I cannot accurately say about the mileages that we walked each day. Having walked a number of trails in the past and learnt my lesson when doing my first long distance trail with Jan on the North Downs Way about trying to complete twenty five miles each day I suspect that we were aiming to do about fifteen miles each day.

The reason we aimed for the B4001 was that it was about two miles out of the village of Childrey where my sister Sarah and her family lived and they would be giving us a bed for the night. John as mentioned earlier in the book, who was my sister's husband, came and picked us up and took us down into Childrey. To stay at their much improved house.

The next day the weather was fine for that time of year and again John ran us up in the car to the point that he had picked us up and we continued on along the Ridgeway. I took some more pictures and here is one of Alison walking along the Ridgeway.

Of course for me having lived in Childrey when I was at primary school this was familiar territory to me. I had been up on the Ridgeway many times when I was a boy and new the area like the back of my hand. Anyway navigation on the Ridgeway was not a problem because it was so obvious which way you had to go you could only get lost if you tried to. You can see by the picture of Alison that the Ridgeway is as clear as day.

We had a good look around when we walked along the top of White Horse Hill at the ancient white horse that had been carved out of the ground in the distant past. This is still a place worthy of a visit because the monument is maintained still to this day. Also there is a strange mound of grass covered chalk at the foot of White Horse Hill which is reputed to be the place where Saint George killed the Dragon!

Simon, Alison and I carried along the Ridgeway to continue our walk and had a look at Wayland's Smithy. Wayland's Smithy is one of the most impressive and atmospheric Neolithic burial chambers in Britain. Somehow this ancient

155

grave became associated with Wayland, the Saxon god of metalworking, from whom it takes its name.

I think it was at this stage that Simon got in touch with his ancestors, because he suddenly became a tree hugger to get in touch with all the things that had gone before! Perhaps the long gone god Wayland had sent a message to him from the great beyond!

Having finished getting in touch with our ancestors we carried along on the Ridgeway. Passing under the M4 motorway we reached out destination for that day, at a nice cottage at Ogbourne St George. We stayed in the bed and breakfast and had a good night's kip.

The third and final day of our walk along the Ridgeway was good, no rain and no bad weather. I do seem to remember that it was fairly windy that day, but who cares! To do a long walk in April in England and not get a good soaking is a blessing from the Gods. Perhaps Wayland was on our side after all.

On arrival at the end of the Ridgeway I had a bit of an emotional burst and shed some tears, as I usually do about completing long trails. I wish that I had had more time on my hands at that time and had been able to walk the Ridgeway in its entirety. We had a good look around the stone circle at Avebury. A meal in the local pub and crashed out in our pre-arranged accommodation, and then the next day went off in Alison's Laguna to pick up my 2cv from Goring.

If someone is big into walking and also likes a bit of ancient history thrown in for an interest factor, I would recommend the Ridgeway. It is a great walk and you don't need to be a superman or superwoman to do it because there is lots of accommodation available along the trail so you don't need to carry a tent and a lot of other gear. You don't even need to be that good at navigation as it is fairly apparent all along the way where you need to be going.

Having done our walk of half of the Ridgeway, we returned to work and got on with carrying out our Fire Service duties. I don't remember much of anything worthy of writing about being in the Service between walking the Ridgeway and doing my next long distance path that was surprisingly to happen later that year. I am sure that when on duty I was sent out on the pump to attend all the usual incidents that I attended such as grass fires, chimney fires, cat up a tree! Etc etc.

The strange thing that did happen later in that year was that my ex-army friend Lloydie, and now Metropolitan Police Force Officer who was a friend, as I mentioned earlier in the book, turned up at my house and explained to me that he was actually suspended from duty due to something that had gone on, and he now had some time to kill.

I have to say here that Lloydie was later exonerated from any blame that he may have been suspected of, and he was returned to duty. Completely, and absolutely exonerated! Lloydie was a good cop and had received many mentions in dispatches during his time in the Force. We had been in South Armagh together in the Army, and seen some shit there. He had been in some riots in The Big Smoke where the rioters where charging his diminished group again and again, and again, and again, and again as if it was never going to end. Lloydie held his shield and also his nerve and they held on. He was a good Police Officer and I would not want anyone in anyway who is reading this to doubt it. He is the sort of man you would want as a blood brother. Certainly if you were in trouble of any sort! You knew that you could call Lloydie and he would come and sort it out for you. I was always extremely proud to have him as my best mate and I would fight anyone who thinks otherwise. SO THERE!

So Lloydie and I decided that we would take on the Coast to Coast. Which I think was a good idea.

COAST TO COAST (1998)

No man goes further than he who knows not where he is going (Oliver Cromwell)

Having completed the North Downs Way, The Pennine Way and the Ridgeway previously, I really had the bug about walking long distance trails anyway and had heard about Wainwright's Coast to Coast route. This is a route that goes from one side of England to the other and incorporates the Lake District National Park, Yorkshire Dales National Park and the North York Moors National Park. Officially the route runs from West to East as the order of the parks indicates. However my mate Lloydie and I decided that we would walk it in reverse order than what Wainwright's guide is written.

He was now at a bit of a low ebb in his life and I felt sure that a good long hike along the Coast to Coast would give him a pick me up. Lloydie had never done a long distance trail before but he was an incredibly fit guy as he used to keep himself in good condition to be able to carry out his police duties.

He told me about some times that he was on duty in London and on a number of occasions had come across a crime in progress, and had shouted at the culprit "Stop what you are doing, you are under arrest." And the culprit had took off at the run to avoid being arrested and Lloydie just used to chase the man down, keep running and running and running, until eventually the person ran out of steam and Lloydie 'nicked' the guy! So, knowing that, we were fairly confident that he was more than fit enough to be able to complete the trail as long as there were no unforeseen disasters. For some reason, Lloydie had said that he would not have a shave all the way along the trail until we got to the end. Why? I don't know why, but that is what he said and that is what he did!

We got all our kit packed up and sleeping bags and the tent and caught the train up to Robin Hoods Bay on Sunday 28th of June and stayed at Hook's House Farm and camped for the astronomical fee of £2.50 each.

While writing about the journey across England on the Coast to Coast I have used a format similar to that when writing about the Pennine Way with a section from the diary that I wrote on the way followed by a paragraph or two of comments and explanations of things that may need some clarification.

Robin Hood's Bay is known locally as Bay Town or just the Bay. The Bay is a picturesque little town with its red roofed buildings perched one above the other and the town is a labyrinth of small passageways and steps. The Bay started off as an obscure fishing village and had a reputation of being a haunt for smugglers.

In more modern times it started to earn a secondary livelihood from visitors and attracts a lot of tourists. We had a look around the town in the evening and then went to a Pub for a good feed and a few beers and then the next morning we were ready for the off! I was to use a guide written by Alfred Wainwright in which at the end he wrote:

"I finished the Pennine Way with relief, the Coast to Coast Walk with regret. That's the difference." God bless Alfred Wainwright, a wonderful man. I wonder if I shall feel the same about both the trails? I think not, because I did not finish the Pennine Way with relief, I finished the Pennine Way with regret, and Jan finished it with a few emotional tears. And all these years later I also finished it with some emotional tears.

Diary. Day One. Robin Hood's Bay to Grosmont. 16 miles.
Lloydie and I felt that we should get out feet wet first before we set off on the Coast to Coast, so this morning we went down to the sea front in the Bay and stood in the North Sea. We had asked a chap to take a picture of us standing in the sea with our packs on. It was not too bad going at first but then as we climbed up onto the North York Moors National Park we were enshrouded in mist which soon became rain. Then mist and rain all day. On arrival at Grosmont we found Fairhead Farm and put up the tent for a charge of £1.50 each. Grosmont, not bad, nice pub which only had one lager and one

bitter! People 'brash' but friendly though. No showers at the farm. (bummer)
However the working steam railway was quite impressive.

Not the best picture I know, but the person that took it was no professional
photographer, but it does give you an idea of what it was like.

The working steam railway at Grosmont is part of The North York Moors
Railway Society and the railway runs from Whitby to Pickering. The line
threads a tortuous course through beautiful scenery and would look lovely
on a sunny day. Another thing that I feel I should mention here is that
Lloydie and I were using a different tent from the one that Jan and I had
used on the Pennine Way because that last night on the Pennine Way was
so windy that the tent that we had tried to sleep in had been so flattened
by the gale that it had to be thrown away!

Before we had decided that we would walk the Coast to Coast, I had been
out and brought a new tent. O.K. it was not cheap, but it was made by the
company The North Face. It was of such good design and quality, that on
many of the occasions that I have used that tent I have never even had to
put the guy lines out and still possess that tent today. It is light, weather
proof and incredibly strong. It was a bit snug for two chaps sleeping in it,
but we coped!

I remember at some time on the Coast to Coast there were a couple of girls
camped in a tent near to ours, I think they were Dutch. I asked them for
something, I can't remember what. But they did say to me at that time.
"Are you both going to sleep in that little tent?" Lloydie and I did not mind

things being a little cosy. After all, it is only to keep the rain off your head while you get your head down for the night and have a good kip! Once you are asleep who cares? The most important thing that I had learnt on The Pennine Way, with Jan, is that your tent must be able to take anything that the weather can throw at it! And that little tent could take anything that the weather could throw. I think you could have been at Everest base camp and still been alright!

Diary. Day two. Grosmont to Blakey 13 miles
Rain and mist on the tops again today. I hope this weather improves in the near future. We crossed over Beggars Bridge which is a cute little early 17th century bridge which the river usk flows under. We arrived in good time at the Lion Inn after a good 'bash' across the hills. Camped by the pub and watched England get tragically beat by the Argies in the world cup football. Again no shower! That's 3 nights in a row now.

The Lion Inn is the most obvious halting place on this section of the route. However if you have not booked and are camping you don't get a shower as we found out. Dating back to 1553 the Inn is a located in a bleak and isolated spot on the open moor it is an obvious port of call for motorists and walkers alike. If I remember correctly that might have been the 'hand of God goal' but if I am wrong don't worry about it, as I am not really a football fan. The world cup is good though.

Diary. Day three. Blakey to Ingleby Cross 21 Miles
Another day on the tops. Rain, mist and wind all the way. Got tragically lost after about ten miles in the mist and went miles out of our way. Lost the path completely and had it not been for the geezer (Geezer, is southern English slang for man.) we met, we would have carried on in the wrong direction for miles! Cut down off the hills and done a large loop with no map! B and B at Broughton coz pissed off and wet and tired. Ended up behind Schedule by about 8 miles (sad) but great B and B (good!). Cutting across country tomorrow to pick up the C to C tomorrow at Ingleby Cross.

As you can see day three was not my best feat of navigational skill. It is not often that I get lost when out in the hills, but it happens to everyone at some stage. The lucky side of the thing is that the day we had planned for day four was only a short day of ten miles so adding on eight more would make it an eighteen miler, not the end of the earth! Good job that day four was not planned as a twenty miler.

Diary. Day four. Broughton to Danby Wiske. 17 miles.

After a long hard 'bash' along roads we got to Ingleby Cross by midday (back on route). No rain so far today (Yippee!). We are now back on the Coast to Coast and made the nine miles to Danby Wiske by four p.m. We had planned to camp at the White Swan and although the pub its self was actually shut the landlord was good enough to give us a pint anyway! Ha-ha. Signed the Coast to Coast visitor's book. The sun is shining and back on schedule!

There is not much that I can say about that day, just that we did cross over Cold Moor and Cringle Moor where you see The Wainstones which are rock pillars which rise up out of the moor in a pillar like structure which is quite interesting and worth a photograph. Particularly if it's not raining!

Diary. Day five. Danby Wiske to Richmond. 11 miles.

Set out early at eightish probably due to the fact that the pub was shut so we got an early (and sober!) night. Walked the low lands across some lovely rural scenery. Saw some trout in the river. Got lost (again!) just before Richmond and had a good argument with Lloydie about it! (hot sweaty and tired!) Weather is much better now and improving. Richmond town and castle brilliant. Took plenty of piccies. Going up Swaledale tomorrow, should be good, but twenty one miles! Didn't see Dr Death all day.

Do not go where the path may lead, go instead where there is no path and leave a trail. How true, and Lloydie and I left quite a few trails on the Coast to Coast!

Lloydie and I had had a BLOODY GOOD ROW THAT DAY! I suppose because I had got us lost again. Walking a trail with Lloydie was the first time that I had done a long trail with another man, and I suppose with chaps tempers can fly a little bit more easily than between a man and a woman, I don't know! Lloydie was my best mate at the time and I know him very well. I know that he can be a bit of a firery character at times. But we did have a good laugh about it later and no hard feelings.

Robert Louis Stevenson said, and I quote; "We are all travellers in the wilderness of this world, and the best we can find in our travels is an honest friend." How true.

That's what it's all about walking a long trail. Post Script to this, IT WAS ME THAT HAD TO DO ALL THE NAVIGATION! At least he didn't completely loose his temper and THUMP me! I am glad to say! Ha ha ha. We camped at a farm again the night we were at Richmond and had a good night out in the town. Plenty of drinking going on in the pubs and there was a big fight in a pub, the name of which escapes me. It must have been a couple of rival gangs or something because it was like a brawl in a western saloon! Lloydie likes a good fight and dived in, which was funny to watch. I think in retrospect that he had dived in and thumped someone else instead of me! I think that my mate just needed to blow off a bit of steam! I just stood back and watched them at it ha ha. With regard to my reference to Dr Death in the diary, I have no idea what I was referring to there. Perhaps it was some chap that we had met on the Coast to Coast and named him Dr Death.

Diary. Day six. Richmond to Keld. 21 miles
A long day today 21 miles. 10 miles in the morning with a stop at Reeth to take on supplies for the nights camp at Keld. First ten miles were great, up Swaledale from Richmond. The afternoon was good for the first five miles and then Lloydie started suffering on the unexpected climbs and descents. Stopped at sheep pen for a rest and Lloydie said, and I quote; "Here lies the man that is well out of his league!" Ha ha. Pressed on to Keld and got in about 7.30 p.m. Lloydie suffering. Camp site absolutely crawling with midges. (Nightmare!). Drank neat Vodka and reminisced about things. Lloydie soon recovered. Half way now and only six days to go!

That is true, he really said that. "Here lies the man that is well out of his league." Lloydie did have a sense of humour. I remember that the official campsite was little more than a spot by the river and the midges were swarming there. Lloydie and I thought 'sod this' and picked up the tent and moved up the hill away from the river and the midges. There were another couple who were walking the Coast to Coast and they stayed by the river and as you will see, this is mentioned in my diary of the next day. I know that is not the best photograph in the world, but it had to be taken propped on the back pack with the camera timer, as there was no one else around to do it! Perhaps if Lloydie had not dived into the brawl the night before he might have had a bit more energy the next day!

Diary. Day seven. Keld to Kirby Stephen. 12 miles.
Broke camp after battling the midges all night. Talked to the couple who had stayed by the river all night, they were midge bitten to hell! Long haul across boggy moor land all the way to Nine Standards Rigg where we stopped for lunch. Saw our midge bitten friends with their 'mascots'. Weather was misty and windy on the tops. Dropped down into Kirkby Stephen by 2 p.m. Great campsite! Hot showers, cut grass etc. (Yippee!) We saw an Australian couple on the hill and the woman's pack made us laugh. Monty Python and the Holy Grail style! Coconuts and all!

The young couple that stayed by the river really were bitten to hell by the midges. They had red lumps all over their faces and regarding their mascots, they had little teddy bears propped on top of their packs. 'How cute'. If you have ever seen the film Monty Python and the Holy Grail then you will know what I am talking about regarding the Australian couple. They were carrying just about everything but the kitchen sink in those massive back packs. My philosophy when back packing on a trail is 'travel as light as possible, with just the minimum equipment that makes sure you are safe and you can cope with all situations.'

Diary. Day eight. Kirby Stephen to Shap. 19 miles.
A good day today, weather was fine and good views all around. No real good laughs though. Didn't see many people but did meet some nice Dutch people who were camping at The Bulls Head as we are. We can see the Lakeland Mountains in the distance and will be there tomorrow, for a tough 18 miles. Lloydie threw away his meatball dinner! Disgusting ha-ha.

On the route that day we passed a place which is known as Robin Hoods Grave. Which is mentioned in the guide but it also says that this is in fact not the grave of Robin Hood. (How do they know that? Have they dug it up?) Why it is called Robin Hoods Grave is a bit of a mystery. At Shap there was a place worth a look, Shap Abbey. Built in the 12th and 13th centuries, the tower has fine proportions although little remains above the first floor height.

Picture of me taken at the time.

Why I was wearing that bandana and those sunglasses and had the goatee beard at the time on the trail is now a mystery to me at the time of writing this. I think that I look a bit like Dennis Hopper who was in the war film Apocalypse Now as the crazy reporter! Perhaps in my own way, I was blowing off steam as Lloydie had done earlier, who knows. I blow my steam off in a slightly less aggressive way than my mate! However, it doesn't matter really. What really matters is that overall I had a great time walking the Coast to Coast with Lloydie, and he didn't thump me once. NOT ONCE! I think that it was because we thought ourselves as blood brothers and at one time in the distant past when we were both drunk. We had cut our hands open with a knife and then swapped blood like the Indians did in the western films that we saw when we were boys.

Diary. Day nine. Shap to Patterdale. 16 miles.
Excellent days walking today. The best so far, good old Lakeland! Weather this morning looked grim, but soon brightened. Crossed to Haweswater and followed the bank to the head. Didn't see our Dutch friends though. The climb up to Kidsty Pike was not as tough as expected and outstanding views from the summit. Weather now bright sunshine and little wind. Great traverse across before dropping down to Patterdale. Going to do the Helvellyn alternative if the weather holds. Lloydie having trouble with his Knees and is wearing knee supports.

We camped that night at home Farm at Patterdale. They only charged us £2.50. Very reasonable! Lloydie had been struggling with his Knees at this stage and had to wear knee supports on both knees. It was not that he was an unfit man. It was just the weight of the pack and when you are descending carrying a heavy pack the strain is all on your knees.

Diary. Day Ten. Patterdale to Rosthwaite. 18 miles.
A nightmare day today! Started well enough with the climb up to Striding Edge with the Dutch couple called Daniela and Luke that we met on the trail. Then we met Dave at the hole in the wall. Lloydie did not take on the alternative route up Helvellyn due to his knees. Mist and wind drove us off the ridge and so we had to haul up again to the summit of Helvellyn. I left the others to drop down to meet Lloydie, but took the wrong path and after emerging from the mist had to double back about a mile and a half to the summit again! (bummer). I ran down the mountain to catch up time. The remainder of the route was tougher than expected and we got in about 6 p.m. totally knackered!

Striding Edge is a route up the mountain of Helvellyn and as the name suggests it is a knife edge of rock. Not hard to navigate in clear weather but can be deceptive in the mist and rain. If you ever walk the Coast to Coast and consider the alternative route up Helvellyn don't bother if the summit is enshrouded in mist. Stay low down in the valley. If it is a good clear day then I would recommend that you do it. Helvellyn is wonderful on a nice day and well worthy of the effort required to get up there.

Diary. Day Eleven. Rosthwaite to Ennerdale Bridge. 14 miles.
Rain last night. Got soaked walking back to the tent from the pub after watching France get through to the world cup final. Not much dry gear left! We got a good early start and made the crossing over the pass to Ennerdale in mist and rain. (Again!). Got a lick on through the forest section to Ennerdale water where the weather brightened. Nice walk along the lake shore. (No sign of Dutchie!) Weather now bright and breezy. Good for drying out all the gear. Spirits high. Last day tomorrow.

When I wrote my diary on the trails I of course knew exactly what I was referring to. However, reading my trail diaries now, many years later, I wish I had put in a bit more detail, because reading them now, sometimes I am not sure about who or what I was referring too. Like for instance, who the hell is Dutchie? I can only think that it must have been Luke the Dutch guy that I met on the trail.

Diary. Day twelve. Ennerdale Bridge to St Bees Head. 14 miles.
Great last day in which we passed some interesting places and saw some fantastic scenery due to the bright and clear weather. Lloydie's knees held out to the end and when we reached St Bees Head we walked into the Irish sea. Someone took a photograph of us standing in the sea. We looked like a couple of tramps, me with my bandana and sunglasses and Lloydie with his beard.

It had been a great trail and despite falling out that one day when we got lost, overall we had had a great time. Long distance trails are like that. It is not all Sunshine and Sangria all the way, but it is worth it for the sense of achievement one gets when finally reaching the finishing post! I am glad that we did the walk in reverse order to what Wainwright had written it as I think that is the best way to walk it. The only draw back is that you are walking into the weather coming at you most of the time. However, you keep the best to the last.

It is good to have an end to journey toward, but it is the journey that matters, in the end.

When people meet other people who are attempting to walk a long distance trail, strangely enough they immediately seem to find some sort of bond between them. I can understand this feeling as I have experienced it on many occasions. I have walked the North Downs Way, the Pennine Way and The Ridgeway and obviously the Coast to Coast. Even later still I walked the West Highland Way and The Cumbria Way with Tracy. Which is in this book later, it is strange, but you feel like you are soul mates because you are all trying to achieve the same mission. Just to beat the weather, the countryside, and even the mountains just to make it to the end of the path.

I have to say that I am a fairly emotional geezer and I cannot read a lot of the things that I have written in this book without tears. They are not tears of sadness. I find it hard to explain, it is just tears of pure emotion!

CHAPTER FIFTEEN

BACK ON WATCH

Now I was back to work and on Green Watch. It was about this time that I attended an incident that warrants a mention. The main road that runs through Kent from London to Dover (over) is the M2 A2 and near to this is a small airfield at a place called Dunkirk. Not the infamous Dunkirk near Calais, France, another Dunkirk, Kent, England.

The bells went down and we were tipped out to a 'Shout' which was in some woodland on the opposite side of the A2 from the airfield. Apparently a small aircraft had crashed into the woodland when it was taking off. We zoomed up the A2 to the woods where we thought the crash had happened. On approaching the incident we could see a spiral of smoke rising up into the summer sky. We assumed the crashed aircraft had caught fire.

It was as sure as day is light and night is dark.

How right we were! When we had taken the Fire Appliances as near as we could get, we had no option but to go through the woods on foot. Grabbing some fire extinguishers and a first aid kit from the lockers we set off running as fast as we could go through the woods and up the hill toward the smoke. There was a very strange and sickly smell that reminded me of roast pork that pervaded the whole area. On arrival at the crash site it became apparent that we were obviously too late.

The small aircraft was well alight and almost burnt to a shell. One guy was lying nearby in the woods with a few minor injuries and a broken ankle and the other guy, the pilot of the aircraft, was still sitting in the pilot's seat. Due to the severity of the blaze the poor man was completely burnt away. It must have been the aviation fuel that had caused the severity of the fire. He was the cause of the smell of the roast pork that had spread through the woods for a radius of about half a mile!

There was little that we could do at the incident other than give the guy that had manage to crawl clear of the aircraft some first aid. The poor man must have been absolutely traumatised by having to witness his friend die in the fire. Once the fire was out and the fuselage of the plane had cooled sufficiently for our chaps to get the body out, two of the guys had the grisly job of getting the cremated body out of the aircraft and into a body bag. This was then carried through the woods to where it could be put into an ambulance for transportation to the morgue. Not a job that I envy them of having the task to do, and I am sure that they remember that incident as vividly as I do.

It was the smell that sticks in my mind more than any visual image of the occasion and since that day I have never managed to bring myself to eat roast pork again.

Another thing I remember about the same time that I was moved from Green Watch, to White Watch as a Leading Fireman, and something that happened when was when I was on duty, was the day my crew of the day and I call 'The day the county burned!' We had had a long hot and very dry summer that year in Kent. I went on duty as normal at 09.00 for a day shift. When going on duty we would always do a parade to be allocated who would be riding on which Fire Appliance. The Sub Officer would ride in charge of the Water Tender Ladder and the Leading Fireman in charge of the Water Tender. The remaining Firemen would be allocated to be either one of the drivers, the Breathing Apparatus Crews or to ride one of the specials. That day as I was the Leading Fireman on duty I would ride in charge of the Water Tender.

The normal routine on a Fire Station is to do the Taking Over Routines after the parade. On the Taking Over Routines, or T.O.R.'s as we called them, the crew would check over the Fire Appliance they are to ride, checking all the equipment and a Breathing Apparatus set. Filling in the B.A. entry tally with their name, making sure the cylinder is charged to the correct pressure and write on the entry control tally the correct cylinder pressure. Also, that the pump is as it should be and the water tank is full. So that should we get tipped out to a 'Shout', we would be prepared. Well, 'the day the county burned' we didn't even get time to do the

T.O.R.'s before the 'bells went down' and myself and the Water Tender crew were tipped out.

Where exactly we went on that first 'Shout' escapes my memory, it may have been to a fire, or it may have been on a standby at another station. What I do remember about that day is that as the crew of the Water Tender 802 we were out all day going from one fire to another and then on to another and another and so on, and so on! If a Fire Engine has attended an incident the crew must make sure that they find a nearby hydrant and ensure that the water tank is full by connecting to the nearest hydrant and charging the tank. They will be able to tell that the tank is full in two ways. One by the overflow valve will operate and surplus water will spill all over the road and two, by the site tube which is located on the rear of the pump.

The Officer in Charge will not book 'mobile and available' on the radio until the water tank is full. That day, as soon as we had attended one incident and sent a 'stop message', and then sent a 'mobile and available' message to Control, we would be mobilized to the next job. So it would go like this. "Hello Control 802 now mobile and available 802 over." "Roger 802 informative message over." "Go ahead Control 802 over." "802 you are mobilized to a fire at ....blah de blah de blah!" Was it ever going to end?

All the fires that day were either grass land alight, crops alight or woodland alight. Not one of the 'Shouts' were to a building fire. The County of Kent was absolutely tinder box dry! We worked so hard my crew and I, that we had to drink water from the Fire Engine pump outlet valves, because we were getting dehydrated from all the sweat that we were loosing!

I remember clearly that as we drove past Leeds Castle near Maidstone the hill nearby was ablaze with all the trees burning like HELL ITSELF! There were about fifteen pumps already in attendance so we weren't sent to that one. Fortunately! I sort of looked the other way and pretended that I had not seen what was happening, and hoped that control weren't going to mobilize us to the job. The crew and I were absolutely shattered! We finally got back to Canterbury at about 8 o'clock in the evening to hand over to the night watch that had come on duty at six o'clock. What a day! That was 'The day the County burned!' Jesus, we earned our money that day! I have to say that I know that it was such a day that it sticks in my memory even now at the time of writing this, but secretly, Shusssssh. We all absolutely loved it! That's what we joined the Fire Service for, to put out as many fires as we possibly could.

Another incident that in a strange way was to change my life for ever was when in the spring of 1997 a shop selling telephones was gutted by a savage blaze. I attended the incident as crew commander of the Water Tender 802. The shop was just at the bottom of Dover Street where I used to rent out that dump of a house years back before I brought my house at Petham. The gutted shop was located just across the road from the pub called 'The Flying Horse' but we used to refer to it as 'The Flying Divorce.'

Once I knew that the fire was out I thought I would see if I could 'scrounge' a cup of tea for the crew. It was about ten in the morning and I went to The Flying Divorce and peered through the window where I could see someone cleaning the carpet with the vacuum cleaner. 'Ah the cleaner' I thought. I tapped on the window and a very attractive cleaner came to the door and unlocked it.

She must have thought I looked a right sight because at the time I had a large scab down the centre of my nose due to an injury received at a previous incident. The cleaner opened the door and in a very curt and impatient voice said "YES, WHAT CAN I DO FOR YOU!" In my best possible 'posh' English accent, I said "Well, I was wondering if I could impose on you for a cup of tea for me and my fire crew. If that's not to much trouble of course?" She looked me up and down and then curtly said "Come back in five minutes." And then slammed the door.

On my return I went in and there were five cups of tea on the bar. I quite fancied the cleaner and I said "Thanks, I'll take three cups out for the crew and drink mine in here with you if you don't mind." She looked at me a bit odd and said "Do what you want!" On my return for the mug of tea I got chatting to her and said "So, how long have you been the cleaner here then?" She nearly exploded! "THE BLOODY CLEANER! YOU CHEEKY MONKEY I AM THE LANDLADY OF THE PUB!" I could not be more apologetic. After much vocal boot licking I got her to calm down.

Her name was Tracy. She was very attractive and I was very interested in her situation. She was not a married woman, but did have a male friend, but nothing serious she told me. After that day my mate Lloydie and I started to go to 'The Flying Divorce' somewhat more frequently. It was at times like this that having the presence of my intimidating policeman friend who had walked Coast to Coast with me was useful. He did not actually have to hit anyone, he was just a man that emanated a sense of power and strength that no one wanted to challenge, and he was my best mate, so eventually Tracy and I started dating each other.

It was about this time that I made some major changes to 3 Chequers Cottages. I was getting a bit cheesed off with having to keep painting the wooden boards which made up the part of the weather resisting structure of the house. I would spend about 4 days each summer redecorating it by going up the ladder with a paint brush and a pot of paint. Then by the end of winter it had all started to peel off again! Grrrrr. So using the internet I did a bit of research to look for an alternative cladding for the house and discovered just what I was looking for.

There was a product out there that could replace the wooden boards, but it had the effect of looking just like Shiplap boarding. It was synthetic and completely rot proof unlike the original wooden boarding. I contacted the company concerned and asked them to come over and quote me a price. They did just that and quoted me a price that I was happy with so they got the job. They soon started work and the first thing that they had to do was to erect some scaffolding and rip off all the old weather boarding. As you can imagine I was somewhat taken aback by the drastic action that was required, but it had to be done. Once they had all the original boards off, they then started to replace these with the synthetic boards.

The men doing the work also had to do the back top half of the house over the kitchen and bathroom extension. They had to do some crafty scaffold building to achieve this. When the house had been completely done it looked great. No more painting for me. (Yippee!)

After a while Tracy came over to Petham to visit me and to see where I lived. Tracy had a dog that used to live with her at the 'The Flying Divorce' and his name was Tom. Tracy brought Tom with her over to Chequers cottages and to ease the meeting between Tom and my dog Poppy I thought it would be a good idea to introduce the two dogs on neutral ground as Poppy could be a bit aggressive with other dogs when she first meets them. I think this was due to the fact that she was a bit possessive about her territory! So, to ease the meeting on the arrival of Tracy and Tom I suggested that we all go out for a nice walk where the dogs could meet. Tracy agreed.

However I made a bit of an error that day in the fact that Poppy had a favourite toy that she used to like to take out on a walk, which was a red rubber hoop. We had the two dogs on the lead and walked down the lane to the field. No problems so far. When we got to the open field I threw the rubber hoop for Poppy to go and fetch. This went alright for a short while, but then on one occasion Tom beat her to the hoop and picked it up. Poppy went absolutely BALLISTIC! and attacked poor Tom and took a large chunk out of his backside! Yelping Tom ran away so fast that he crashed into the field fence and lay there whining with blood running out of the wound he had received. Poppy just picked up the red rubber hoop and carried on as normal.

That was the Status Quo established as far as Poppy was concerned, she was in charge right? Wrong Poppy! After a couple more meetings where they regarded each other with some suspicion, Tom decided that he had had enough of being the underdog and let loose at Poppy and with teeth and spit flying they had a real good set too. Tom came out on top and the Status Quo had been re-organized and Tom was now the top dog in their relationship and strangely enough things were fine and they got on very well just like their mistress and master Tracy and me!

It was about this time that Tracy moved in to live with me at Chequers Cottages and our relationship moved on to a more permanent basis. The number of occupants at 3 Chequers Cottages had swollen from three to five. There was now myself, Tracy, the dogs Poppy and Tom and also Scorcher the cat.

Unfortunately in November of this year the cat Scorcher had a bad accident. Across the road from Chequers Cottages was an open piece of ground that the owners would let go fallow. Scorcher used to like to go over the road to hunt there. He would often bring home mice and birds he had caught and dump them half eaten on the patio. Which I had the unpleasant task of clearing up.

To get there to his hunting ground, Scorcher would have to go out of the cat flap in the back door, across the patio, squeeze under or jump over, the gate that was between my rear garden and the rear garden of numbers one and two which had been converted into a single dwelling. Pass the rear of their kitchen and up the ally.

Then he would cross the road to the fallow ground where he would hunt. I knew he used to go over there at night because there were times when in the dark I could see his eyes glowing. I knew that it was dangerous for him to cross the road, because Stone Street is a long and very straight road made originally by the Romans. But short of keeping him locked in the house there was little that I could do to stop it.

In my cottage there was no upstairs bathroom or loo, and if you wanted to go to the loo in the night you would have to come down and use the loo in the bathroom in the extension.

Originally when the cottages had been built, there had been a small brick building to the rear of the cottages that had been the two loos which served all four cottages! Things had been improved somewhat since those days and now the small brick building served as a shed for number three and I would keep my push bike and garden tools in there.

One night in November of 1999 I needed to go down to the loo for a pee, it was in the small hours at about four or five in the morning. Previous to that I had made a big bed for both the dogs to sleep in which was under a table in the kitchen. When I reached the kitchen I new something bad had happened. There was Scorcher lying on the floor near to the dogs and I immediately knew that he had been run over as I could actually see the tire marks across his little body.

Scorcher was in a bad way I could see that he was in a lot of pain and one of his legs was laying at a funny angle. I examined him as best I could without causing him more pain and I established that his leg was broken. His femur was snapped clean in two. How he had managed to crawl back off the road, down the alley, under the gate, across the patio and through the cat flap with that injury amazed me! Obviously the boy had a real fighting spirit for life and I was 'DETERMINED' to save him.

The poor lad was suffering and I had to get him to a veterinary surgeon fast! I went and woke Tracy up and told her what had happened. We both got dressed and picking up Scorcher as carefully as I could we transported him to the vet that I had all the animals registered with. This was about four miles away in a small village called Bridge. The vet took a look at Scorcher and he said "It's entirely up to you to do what you want. I can put him down now and save any further suffering, or I can keep him here at the animal hospital and do an operation on the leg to try and save it."

There was no doubt in my mind what to do, I loved my little ginger Scorcher and there was no way that I wanted him put down. I told the vet to operate on the leg and try to save it. He said it could be quite expensive. I was on tender hooks and I flew off the handle and shouted "HANG THE BLOODY EXPENSE SAVE MY BLOODY CATS LEG!"

After a while, I think it was about two weeks the vet rang me and told me to come over and collect Scorcher. It was with some apprehension that I drove over in my little 2cv to collect Scorch. On arrival at the vets I went in and he informed me that Scorcher was on the mend and then he showed me the x-rays that had been taken of Scorcher and they clearly showed the snapped femur and also that he had suffered some damage to the hips. Then the vet showed me another two x-rays which had been taken after the operation.

He had made a surgical steel plate with finger like extensions that he had used to bond the femur together and I was very impressed at his veterinary skills. He had obviously had to open up the leg somewhat to get the plate in, but the repair job had worked! (Hooray!) He told me to keep the cat in for a while to keep him immobile to allow the leg to heal completely. So I invested in a tray and litter from the pet shop on the way home. Before leaving the vet I had to settle the bill to the tune of six hundred pounds! Where I got the money from I don't know.

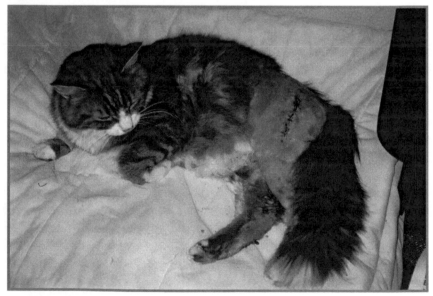

Scorcher with his injury.

Things went well for a while for little Scorcher, and he seemed to get better. However things took a turn for the worse and it was a couple of weeks later, exactly a month from the accident and on Christmas Eve, that Scorchers leg swelled up like a balloon, it had obviously gone septic! We telephoned the vet but he was closed for the holiday period. Phoning all around the area to find a vet that was open on Christmas Eve, we eventually found one on the London Road out of Canterbury. We rushed poor Scorcher over there and took him in.

The vet was of Indian origin and had a very strong Indian accent. Not that I hold that against him of course! I explained the history of the Scorchers problem and he looked him over. On seeing the infected wound and seeing how much it had swollen, he kept sucking in air though his teeth, while prodding the wound. Then he said "It doesn't luk gud, it doesn't luk gud!" At this stage I flew off the handle again with a vet, grasping him by the front of his shirt and shouting I said "I KNOW IT BLOODY WELL DOESN'T LOOK GOOD! IM NOT BLOODY STUPID! BUT WHAT THE BLOODY HELL ARE YOU BLOODY WELL GOING TO DO ABOUT IT!!!!!! I think he was somewhat surprised at my emotional outburst. He picked up a syringe and fixing a needle to it he pierced the infected area and drew out a syringe full of yellow puss. This generated another bout of teeth sucking! I think that the poor vet was thinking that after my emotional outburst, that if Scorcher died, I would come back there and kill him as well!

He told us to leave the cat with him and he would do what he could. So, it was Christmas with no Scorcher. Not the best Christmas that I have ever had. I called the vet a few days later and he said that he had operated on him, cleaned and flushed the wound, and that Scorcher was still alive and he would call us in a few days. A few days later he called us and told us to come and collect Scorch. We picked up Scorcher and brought him home.

The poor cat had obviously been mentally affected by his ordeal, because when I let him out of the box all he would do was go round and round and round, in tight circles. Tracy and I decided that we would give him a little bit of time to see if he got any better, before making a decision.

The upshot of it was that it would be a long, long road of recovery for poor Scorcher and his 'bionic' steel leg. Gradually over a period of months he very slowly got better and better. I think the trauma had affected his vision somehow and he couldn't see any more than a few feet in front of him, but gradually and gradually he got better. He never left the property again after that. Simply because he couldn't see well enough to be able to jump up on anything. However, I think he was happy enough in himself and always had a healthy appetite.

It is incredible to know, but at the time of starting to write this book it was only about three months ago that he finally died, probably from old age. That was ten years ago that all that happened so he had lived for another ten years since his accident! I found him dead on the living room floor when I came down in the morning one day. That happened shortly after I had had to leave the Fire Service. Shedding a few tears, I dug a hole and buried him in the garden. I then planted a few foxgloves on top of the grave which should flower next summer. I have always been fond of foxgloves.

CHAPTER SIXTEEN

2000

Today is your day, your mountain is waiting, so get on your way. (Dr Seuss.)

Another long distance trail that I walked was the West Highland Way which Tracy and I did in June 2000. The West Highland Way is as its name suggests in the West Highlands of Scotland and runs from the outskirts of Glasgow to Fort William. The W.H.W. at 78 miles is not a long trail, nowhere near as long as the massive Pennine Way, but as it was to be Tracy's first trail I thought that it would be a good one for her to take on.

The route starts off quietly from the edge of Glasgow and builds to a crescendo by arrival at the foot of Britain's highest mountain, Ben Nevis. Another advantage of the way for Tracy's benefit is that there is a pack carrying service called Travelite, which will carry your heavy kit for you and drop it off at a prearranged destination. This means that you can still camp along a lot of the Way, but not have to carry all the gear every step of the way. Obviously you will need to take a day sack with you for your water bottle, lunch, waterproofs, insect repellent for the midges, a wallet and a few other things.

We had decided to do the walk in the first part of June as this will provide some relief from the midges. As it was Tracy's first long trail I made sure that we did some training and we went out walking on plenty of occasions to build her up. After lots of training walks she could cope quite well with a fifteen miler which was the distance that we were aiming roughly at on each day of the

W.H.W. Some days would be longer and some shorter. Obviously this would be depending on the terrain.

We were going to go up on the train to Glasgow and would be taking the overnight sleeper. With spirits high we set off from Canterbury on the 17.26 to London and arrived at 18.47 where we got to Euston on the underground and departing at 23.21 arrived in the morning at Glasgow Central at 06.59. On arrival we had to get to Milngavie (pronounced Mull guy) to the start of the W.H.W.

As you will now know, I had kept diary about Jan's and my time on the Pennine Way and Lloydie's and my time on the Coast to Coast. So I kept a diary on the West Highland Way again. Here in the book I have used the same format as with the Pennine Way Trip and the Coast to Coast writing a paragraph from the diary followed by a back up paragraph or two, to explain things.

Diary. Day one. Milngavie to Drymen. 12 miles.
The overnight 'Sleeper' was a bit of an exaggeration! We managed to get a couple of hour's kip. Finally arrived at 'Mull guy' after a bit of trouble with the time tables. Started the walk in the rain which eased off after a while. Pretty uneventful day as a 'warm up' Found the campsite a bit rough but adequate. We went into Drymen in the evening for beer and food. Talked to a local chap who confirmed our beliefs that the walk gets harder as it goes on. Rain forecast for tomorrow. (Bummer).

Travelling to Scotland from London on a train called the overnight sleeper is not the best way to travel. Sleeping sitting up in a train seat can be a bit of a challenge! With regard to the pronunciation of Milngavie as Mull-guy, this is mentioned in the guide, but it does say that no one seems to be able to come up with a rational explanation why this is so! We made our way that morning to the start of the West Highland Way where we took some pictures. Then having dropped our large sacks of at the pre-arranged Travelite drop and pick up point we set off.

Diary. Day two. Drymen to Rowardennan. 13 miles.

Forecast was correct! Rained nearly all day, but fortunately stopped over Conic hill, but fairly midgy through the woods beforehand and head nets came in handy, or heady as it were. Stopped at Balmaha and had the worst burger and chips in the world! Yuck. The National Trust campsite was by the river and under the trees. Ideal Midge country and we were swarmed! Sat in the tent and drank cider for me and girlie pops for Tracy fortunately carried by Travelite.

Through the section at Balmaha there are now two alternative routes, though walkers may not be given the choice. During the lambing season, the more attractive route over Conic Hill that we took is closed for about a month between mid-April and mid-May. The alternative follows the more obvious track from White's Plantation and eventually becomes a surfaced road at Milton of Buchanan and then you have to hump along the road to the large car park at Balmhaha where the two routes join. So my advice would be to anyone thinking of walking the Way, wait until after mid-May and then go to avoid the alternative route and avoid the midges!

Diary. Day three. Rowardennan to Inveranan. 13 miles.

Fine weather for most of the day. The 'high' route along Loch Lomond turned out to be boring. Stopped at Inversnaid for a cheese and onion sarnie and a pint. On the last six miles Tracy had a sense of humour failure and told me to "Stop walking like trying to catch last orders!" ha ha. I took the piss and then she was fine! The remaining walk up the Loch was quite tough but enjoyable. Nice campsite and hot showers, clean undies since Sunday. Great! Went to the Drovers Inn for supper which has not changed since the 1700's!

The guide says that the final section of Loch Lomond has a somewhat fearsome reputation for being rough and difficult, but walkers will find that the obstacles have been somewhat exaggerated. It is not easy walking, but then there is no really tough part that has not been improved by providing wooden steps in the really awkward places. And to anyone who reads this book that is not familiar with some southern English colloquial terms. 'Taking the piss' means making fun of someone.

Diary. Day Four. Inveranan to Bridge of Orchy 18.5 miles.
Rained all night again! Woke up to a soaked tent again! Packed up and set off. Tracy had a knee problem and had to pull out at Crianlarich. She took the bus in the rain to The Bridge of Orchy. I took the road to catch up some time and re-joined the Way just outside Tyndrum. Rain still coming and feet soaked and very wet all round. Had a low outside Tyndrum. Got a knee support at Tyndrum and met the biggest MIDGE in the world. (Scottish man). After Tyndrum I got going again and had an easy six miles to the bridge. The wet weather finally broke about four miles out from the Bridge and all my gear dried out in the breeze. Arrived to find that that Tracy had been pestered by the Big midge. Met some nice people in the evening and the Big midge reappeared. I told him in polite terms to "go away." We are staying the night in the bunk house at the bridge of Orchy.

The man we referred to as the 'Big midge' was a Scottish guy that seemed to have made it his mission in life to pester people who were walking the West Highland Way. He would just go from stopping point to stopping point blathering on about the Way because he was the world's authority on it. Self appointed of course. I think that he never actually walked any of the way himself. Fat Bastard! He just liked to take the bus from one place to another. He was a big man and like the other midges, pestered you who were walking the West Highland Way to a point of distraction. So we called him the big midge. So eventually I had to shout at him and told him quite bluntly to "GO AWAY!" I think he got the message because he didn't pester us after that.

Here is Tracy at the Bridge of Orchy.

Diary. Day Five. Bridge of Orchy to Kingshouse. 12.5 miles.

The Bunk house at the bridge was o.k. but got woke up in the middle of the night by the slamming of the doors! Some silly cow had left the window open and infested her room with midges! (not a camper obviously!) The trail started o.k. with Tracy with her bad knee getting up the hill o.k. Great views and weather fine. Steady uphill to Rannoch Moor and more good views of the mountains. Took our time to walk the day and Tracy done well with the 'trusty staff' that I cut from some mountain ash. Took loads of piccies of snow topped mountains. Not seen Mr BIG PACK yet. Dunked our feet in an ice cold stream. I had a laugh with Tracy with me playing at being the Beast of Rannoch Moor. Got to Kingshouse in plenty of time. Tent dry. Mats dry. We had a bit of a scary moment when we recovered out packs as there was one of the sleeping bags missing! Fortunately we found it as it was where the packs had been delivered by Travelite, but had become detached from the pack, but was in fact still there. (phew!) Met these two fellas in the hikers bar who had just come back from a wild couple of weeks canoeing in north isle of Scotland. Good conversation and loads of laughs. Went to the 'posh' hotel (no dogs, no boots, no laughing and definitely no enjoying yourself!) Tracy had a doggy bag Chicken in her coat pocket. A good day and the devils staircase tomorrow!

That is the day that sticks in my mind most about the West Highland Way. We had great weather that day and to cross Rannoch Moor in good weather is a treat. There have been times when people have got lost, sunk and died in the bogs of Rannoch Moor never to be seen again! I think that is why the myth of the Beast of Rannoch Moor was invented. To stop or discourage people from going onto the bleak and barren moor in the first place. So we were very fortunate that day. When we stopped to cool our feet in the stream and I played the Beast of the moor it still makes me chuckle to this day. That's the tops, you can't have a better day on a long trail than that!

The Beast of Rannoch Moor.

I remember it as vividly as if it were yesterday. We had gone to the 'posh' hotel to get a meal that evening, but being outdoors types we would have rather had stayed in the hiker's bar if there was food available, but unfortunately not. We slept that night at the grounds of the Kingshouse Hotel where there was permissive camping but no facilities for a shower for us smelly back packing types!

Diary. Day Six. Kingshouse to Kinlochleven. 9 miles.
Met the two canoeing fella's again later in the evening last night after some grub at the hotel and enjoyed a whisky. Saw them again in the morning and their mate they were waiting for still hadn't shown up. Rain first thing, but soon cleared to leave a nice day. Glencoe was superb and the 'Devil's Staircase'

was not as bad as feared. Great views over to Ben Nevis. Long decent down
into Kinlochleven. Tracy got down in a combination of me helping her with
an arm support, and the 'trusty staff' and a Fireman's lift on the really steep
parts! I literally had to give her a Fireman's lift and carry her down the steep
parts on my shoulders! Got in about four p.m. and got a result with cash back
at the Co-op. Nice campsite, got the tent up and stowed and then the heavens
opened and rain, rain, rain. Hope to get some dinner sometime tonight! The
picture of us on the route up Glencoe was taken with a timer on the camera
with the camera resting on a rock. That is why it's not quite lined up straight,
but that doesn't matter does it?

That is the truth what I wrote in the diary. I really did at times have to put
Tracy on my shoulders with a Fireman's lift and carry her down the mountain
on the steep parts. Not that I was bothered of course, I just wanted her to
make it to the end of the trail! I wonder what she would think about that if
she were to read this book so many years on. I am just glad that she is quite a
small woman and I was able to do it. Had she been a fifteen stone man I think
that would have been the end of it!

Diary. Day Seven. Kinlochleven to Fort William. 14 miles.
Last leg today, raining hard (bummer). Got a good early start on the climb out
of Kinlochleven, got near the top and realized that I had no wallet! (Shit!). Ran
back down the mountain and found it rolled up in the wet tent we had left for

Travelite to take. (Phew). Climbed back up the hill to find Tracy and carried on. Long Traverse up the Glen to the forest. Awful weather, rain and wind. Took the 'alternative route' to Fort William and got a bit worried we were going the wrong way then suddenly we were there! Took a B and B and had a good night at McTavishes Kitchens. Great trip! Met Julian and Kirsty in the Grog and Gruel on Monday afternoon while waiting for the train. We shared a few stories about the walk and had a good laugh.

That was the end of the West Highland Way. Another long trail to add to the memory. The reason we went to McTavishes Kitchens is because it is almost obligatory that if anyone visits Fort William they must go and have a night out at the Kitchens. It is a place where they provide a traditional Scottish Dinner and have real Scottish entertainment with singing and dancing. A great night out and I would recommend it to anyone.

Can you see the 'trusty staff' leaning against the wall?

In McTavishes Kitchens with the trusty staff leaning against the wall

You can see by the picture that Tracy and I both look pretty weather beaten at the end of the West Highland Way! But it was a great trip and I have written some more about it.

A funny thing that occurred when we were walking the West Highland Way was that when we got toward the end of each day and Tracy was starting to get tired, I would sing a song at a good marching tempo to help lift her spirits and carry her along the Way. The song was by the Proclaimers, which was appropriate as we were in Scotland as they are a Scottish band. I mentioned the Proclaimers earlier in the book in chapter seven. I would sing the lyrics from the song 'I'm gonna be (500 miles)'. The thing about the Proclaimers is that they sing their songs with a Scottish accent. So, I would have to change my slightly Cockney accent to a Scottish accent for the song. What a laugh we had.

It was a great song and Tracy would join in and sing with me while trailing along behind. (Bless her little cottons.) It lifted our spirits and helped us along to the end of the day. So, if the Proclaimers ever read this book I have to say thank you for your brilliant songs that have provided so much happiness and help over the years. I love your music and listen to it regularly.

On our return home to Chequers Cottages we decided that we would have a barbecue, as a way of celebrating our completion of the Way, as the weather down in Kent was somewhat more reliable than on the West Highland Way! So that's what we did and Tracy wore the shortest shorts in the world! After walking the West Highland Way and doing the previous training she was now tuned and fit and looked really good!

You may ask yourself when reading this 'I wonder if the author laughed much when he was writing this book?' Well I will tell you this. Laugh? I laughed so much at times I nearly laughed my head off!

But I would walk five hundred miles, and I would walk five hundred more. Just to be that man who walked a thousand miles and fell down at your dooooooorr.

It was about this time on our return from The West Highland Way that Tracy and I started to get into dancing classes. We felt that we would like to dance to classical music and as you can imagine, having heard my mother play on the piano when I was young, I loved classical music. We found out that there was a couple who did classical dancing classes in Canterbury and we joined up.

Those who dance are considered insane by those who cannot hear the music!

They taught us how to do the Foxtrot, Waltz, Merengie and many others. Now, the Merengie was a bit of an oddball because this was a Latin American style of dance, but we loved it and after we had learned it we entered a competition held locally to see if we were any good. Tracy and I gave it our best shot. As it happened we won the competition! When we were presented with our award by one of the judges, leaning over and whispering in my ear, she said "I just loved your tight butt doing the Merengie!" Well anyone who had walked The West Highland Way would have a tight butt! I think that I might have touched a nerve there! Ha Ha.

Back at work it was about now that someone suggested that we take a picture of White Watch. So we backed the Water Tender pump out of the bays and after clambering over it we took a picture. That's me, on the roof trying to look cool with the sunglasses on.

It was about this time in the year 2000 that I had an unexpected visitor to Chequers Cottage. Tracy's Parents were visiting us and it was the first time that they had come over to Chequers Cottage to see us. We were sitting in the living room having a cup of tea and someone knocked on the door. I thought to myself, 'I wonder who that could be?' as I was not expecting any other visitors. I opened the front door and an old man wearing little round spectacles was stood there.

The man looked a bit like a mad professor as his hair was long and sticking out in all directions! I was thinking who is this mad geezer? He said "Mr Haines?" and I replied "Yes, I am Mr Haines, and who might you be Sir?" He said "Mr Haines". I thought this guy really is a mad professor. So I said, "No Sir, I'm Mr Haines, what is your name?" And again he said "Mr Haines". It was then that I twigged it. My God it is my Father! You could have knocked me down with a feather. I had not seen my Father for about twenty seven or twenty eight years, way back when he had left the family in 1972 or 1973. How the hell he had found me God knows.

I thought that I had best invite him in but I took him to the dining room, because I didn't want Tracy's Mother and Father meeting my mad professor of a Father. I sat him down at the table and made him a cup of tea. I think it was about now that Tracy's Mother and Father beat a hasty retreat and headed off home. My Father Alan was now living in the North of Kent in Rochester. He was still going fishing on the canal at Rochester on occasions. He even asked me how my head wound following the falling rock was.

After that day I kept in touch with my Father and went to Rochester to visit him at the flat on a number of occasions. Alan was O.K. for a few years after that, then suddenly he became very ill and died in December of 2004. He left his only son all of his fishing gear that he had. I suppose he hoped that I would go fishing and use it one day. Who knows, perhaps after writing this book, maybe one day in the summer I will.

CHAPTER SEVENTEEN

MEMORABLE INCIDENTS

When a man is serving at a busy Fire Station he will attend many incidents over the time of his career, but there will always be some in particular that will stick out in the Fireman's memory. Here are a couple that even though it is many years back I remember as if they occurred yesterday.

One was to a house fire in a small housing estate on the outskirts of the city called Sturry Road estate. It was late in the evening when we were on night duty and about 11 p.m. the bells went down. 801 (Water tender ladder) and 802 (Water tender) where tipped out to a domestic dwelling fire on the estate. I was riding as Officer in Charge of 802. The call had been received by our Control at Maidstone as 'Person's reported'. A 'Persons reported' call means that whoever put the 999 call in to the Fire Service had said that the building was on fire and it was known that there was someone still in the building or that someone was missing.

We made best speed through the city with my old mate Keith with his undress cap on, to cover his unarranged walnut whip, driving like a thing possessed. On arrival at the address given we could see that the house was well alight. There was a woman hanging out of the first floor window shouting "HELP! HELP!" In auto-pilot we slipped and pitched a ladder to the window and colleague of mine called Austin scaled the ladder, while I footed the ladder on the ground. With exemplary skill Austin got the woman onto his shoulder with a Fireman's lift, then carrying the woman down, he descended the ladder to the ground. The woman's face was a black as your hat and she was obviously in a state of some distress. She must have been suffering from being mentally unstrung, because as soon as he put her down she started swinging punches at us and we had to restrain her until the ambulance crew could calm her down and get her in the ambulance. That was the one and only time in my career that I witnessed a live carry down at an incident. Something that fortunately is incredibly rare in the Fire Service these days.

After the rescue, the Breathing Apparatus crew were then committed to the building and went in and put the fire out. It was then that it became apparent that it was arson. There were two seats of fire, one at the bottom of the stairs on the ground floor and one at the top of the stairs on the first floor. You don't get two fires break out in a domestic dwelling at the same time! F.I.R.T. (Fire Investigation and Research Team) were called in.

Once we got back to station after the incident we discussed what had happened and talked about the bonkers woman and her black face, but we knew that she would be alright and we all had a good laugh about it.

That may seem like a callous thing to do, to laugh at someone else's dilemma, but being a Fireman can be a very stressful occupation and the times that they experienced danger the stress can be diffused by turning a job into a laugh over a cup of tea in many circumstances.

Another incident that I particularly remember was another night time 'Shout' when we got tipped out when 'the bells went down' to The Borough, in Canterbury on the 23rd September 2000. It was late at night, possible even in the early hours of the morning, I don't remember exactly, but I do remember attending the incident as if it was last night. The bells went down and we were called to a domestic dwelling above a shop in The Borough.

At that time we were a bit short on manning and only riding four on 801 and four on 802, whereas normally we would ride a minimum of five on 801. This meant that the Sub Officer would be the Officer in Charge of the incident, his driver would operate the pump and do the radio messages and his two Breathing Apparatus crew would be the Emergency Crew. The Emergency Crew were the Firemen that stood by wearing Breathing Apparatus ready to come in and save the other B.A. crew if required. My crew would be the driver operating the pump and doing the entry control board for the B. A. and my B. A. crew would go in, taking a hose reel, and fight the fire and do any searching necessary. I would do what ever I could!

During this time we had to avoid what can happen at an incident that can cause the compartment involved in fire to 'Flashover'. This is the most dangerous time for a Fireman to face during an incident. In America they call this phenomenon 'Backdraught', and I am sure that some of the readers will have seen the film, but in the U.K. we call it 'Flashover' which I think is a more accurate way of describing the Phenomenon. The American Firemen call it 'Backdraught' because that is describing the rush of oxygen from the atmosphere that can rush into a room or compartment large or small when a door is opened that will change the atmosphere that a fire is occurring.

The way this happens is that radiated heat from the fire is absorbed into the actual structure of the room and contents. So the walls, ceiling, floor and contents of the room are heated to a point where they actually start to emit flammable and unburned gasses. When it reaches a certain temperature point, the compartment of the building will 'Flashover' and within an instant the whole compartment and all the contents are ablaze. When 'Flashover' occurs it can be a strong enough blast to blow the windows out, and certainly kill or maim anyone who is in that compartment at that time. At a previous time, I had lost some colleagues due to this happening. One died, and the other two got burnt so bad that they could not stay in the Service. It is a very sad time for a Fireman to lose one of his mates due to this. Burns are just about as debilitating as any injury a man can receive.

Obviously a Fireman wants to avoid being in a compartment when a 'Flashover' happens. So to do this the fire should be attacked from the doorway. If possible of course, as sometimes this is not so. One member of the B.A. team will crouch down to one side and grasp the door handle. The other Fireman will also crouch down and holding the branch will point it to go through the gap in the door, then after hand signals of one, two, three, Fireman one will crack open the door and Fireman two will open the branch and put a jet or spray of water into the compartment that is on fire. After another count of three, he will close the branch and the other Fireman will slam the door shut.

The idea of fighting the fire like this is to minimise the chance of the perfect triangle of fire forming in the room (Heat, fuel and oxygen.) and 'Flashover' occurring by using two methods of extinguishing the fire here. One, you are cooling the fire, and two, you are smothering the fire, by keeping the available oxygen in the compartment of the building to a minimum.

This process would be repeated a number of times until the Firemen involved, using their skill, experience and judgement, would feel that the risk of a Flashover had been reduced or hopefully eliminated by reducing the temperature and available oxygen in the compartment, and that it was now safe, or as safe as it can be, to go in and extinguish the fire.

An important thing to do when attending a fire such as this is to do a good reconnaissance of the area to see if there is anybody hanging out of a window somewhere. As I was the only one available while the B. A. crew where in the building fighting the fire. I made my way to the rear of the building. There was no sigh of any activity there, so I went back to the front of the building and tried to keep contact with the B.A. crew of my pump 802 who had gone through the front door and up the stairs to the seat of the fire.

Fortunately for us that night there was no chance of a 'Flashover' occurring, not with the fire venting like that through the broken window so I knew that the B.A. crew could go in and make any necessary rescues with the confidence that the fire was not going to BLOODY WELL 'Flashover'. Excuse my French! I have to say that we were frightened. There is no way that we can say that we were not! We all knew that it was a dangerous job, and we just got on with it and achieved the mission that we had been tipped out to.

After some time, the B. A. crew from my pump came down the stairs carrying a casualty. Jesus, it was hell that night.

It was a bloody grim night that night and it was raining hard. They laid the naked man on the pavement in front of the building and went back in to attempt to put out the fire. I was the only one available to administer first aid to the man. The poor guy was in a bad way.

The B.A. crew had found him unconscious laying hanging out of the bed with his feet in the fire. His feet were virtually burnt away, it was just the bare bone from his shins down that was left. I assumed that he was dead but somehow I went into auto pilot and checked for his vital signs. No carotid artery pulse in the neck that I could feel. Well I must go through the motions anyway. I ran to the Fire Engine and got the oxygen resuscitation equipment.

I put the mask on the man, opened the oxygen valve, and started to do compressions to the heart. WHERE THE HELL IS THAT AMBULANCE! To my amazement after about five minutes his eyes opened, HE WAS ALIVE! WHERE THE HELL IS THAT BLOODY AMBULANCE? The man started mumbling incoherently about things that I could not understand. After a while my B.A. crew, having extinguished the fire exited the building and stripped off their B.A. sets and started to administer first aid to what was left of the man's feet by wrapping them in bandages. WHERE THE BLOODY HELL IS THAT BLOODY AMBULANCE?????

In all my career in the Fire Service I have never know it to take twenty minutes for an ambulance to arrive, but it did that night. My B. A. crew where exemplary Firemen on that grim and dark night. I can only have the greatest admiration for Austin and Steve. At the time of writing this I still cannot think of that incident at the Borough without a tear coming to my eyes even though that was nearly ten years ago.

Austin, Steve and I were to receive a commendation from the Chief Fire Officer later in July of the next year.

CHIEF FIRE OFFICER'S CONGRATULATIONS

3819 Leading Fireman Haines

You are formally congratulated for your actions at the incident at The Borough, Canterbury on 23 September 2000.

A male adult was rescued from the fire by the breathing apparatus crew and was unconscious when brought to safety. Your actions as a first aider were in the highest traditions of the service when assisting with the resuscitation of the casualty prior to the arrival of the Ambulance Service.

You demonstrated considerable initiative and determination in performing your duties.

Chief Fire Officer

1. 07. 01

Date

Making Kent Safer

So, there you go. And my crew at the time Austin and Steve got a similar award. The three of us had to go to our Fire Service Headquarters to receive it from the Chief Fire Officer. I must say that I am extremely proud of it. The four things that I have in my life that I am most proud about at the time of writing this are my three medals from the Queen of England, and my Certificate of Congratulations from my Chief Fire Officer.

That is Austin on my right and Steve on my left.

What Firemen they were that night.

CHAPTER EIGHTEEN

GETTING MARRIED?

It was about the time of the incident at the Borough that I was having serious considerations about my relationship with Tracy. Did I want to marry the girl?

I had to find a way to get my head straight about things. I was in a bit of emotional turmoil at that time. So I booked some leave from the Fire Service and packed up my back pack and headed off to Wales to walk the Pembrokeshire Coast Path. I drove up to south Wales from Kent in my little 2cv and went to the Fire Station at Haverfordwest and parked up.

I spoke to the Officer in Charge and explained that I was a Fireman from Kent and asked if I could park my little car there for a while, because I wanted to walk the Pembrokeshire Coast Path. Now, Firemen the world over are kindred spirits. Just like my old London colleagues from my sailing times, and he said of course I could leave my car there for as long as I wanted. However, he did warn me that I should be very careful when walking the Path as the coast of Pembrokeshire can be a hazardous place, and to treat it with the respect that it deserved. I would imagine that there had been a number of occasions that they had been called out to the cliffs to do rescues there. I thanked him for his advice and he even ran me down to the bus station in his staff car. After taking the bus to the start of the walk I set out on my way.

Why did I do this, well there is a song by the great Johnney Cash that I know, perhaps this could help explain how I felt at the time. Here is an excerpt from the song 'The Wanderer'.

I went out walking with a bible and a gun

The word of God lay heavy on my heart

I was sure, I was the one

Now Jesus, don't you wait up, Jesus I will be home soon

Yeah, I went out for the papers

Told her I'd be back by noon

Yeah, I left with nothing

But the thought you'd be there too

Looking for you

Yeah, I left with nothing

Nothing but the thought of you

I went wandering

My diary of the Pembrokeshire Coast Path reads as follows.

Diary. Day one. St Dogmaels to Newport. 15 miles.
The Fire station at Haverfordwest kindly agreed to let me leave my car there and the Station Officer even ran me down into town to the bus station. I took a bus to Cardigan and then another to St Dogmaels. Finally got walking at 11.50 a.m. Hard going up and down, up and down! I had forgotten how much a 36 lb pack weighs! Highlight of the day was seeing the seals swimming in the Witches Cauldron. Mummy, Daddy, and Baby seal! I was not lonely there as there was plenty of company of the insect variety. Moths and Butterflies were nice, but not the billions of big black hairy arsed flies that plagued me! I was just about chin strapped when I rolled into Newport. Nice little campsite with hot showers.

The guide to the Pembrokeshire Coast Path does say that this section of the way is tough. You would think that a man of my experience in trail walking would be able to handle it fairly well. Well that's what I had thought at the time of taking the path on. Obviously I had got somewhat out of condition and it was hard. The trail involves no mountains, but it does go up and down the cliffs a lot which are steep and demanding. If you are wondering about the expression

'Chin Strapped'. It's and infantry expression for completely worn out. Which is if the chin strap of your infantry helmet or I suppose even your fire helmet, hits the ground, you are worn out!

Diary. Day two. Newport to Goodwick. 13 miles.
Rain during the night and mist and rain in the morning. Kicked away at about 9.00 expecting an easier day (not so!) Dinas Head which is a national park of Dinas island was shrouded in mist and so I considered missing it out, but by the time I got there it had cleared so done it anyway. And put a couple of extra miles on the day. More ups and downs. Gave the campsite a miss as it is 2 miles out of town and tonight I am staying at Steve's backpacker's hostel. He is a fellow 2cv owner! Great night out in Fishguard (Abergwaun in Welsh) with a live Caylee group in the red lion.

It is strange how us 2cv owners stick together! It's a bit like I mentioned earlier in the book about how Firemen across the world stick together, so do people who own a 2cv feel some form of unity. That is the way things are and they will never change. Own a 2cv and you are my friend for life.

Diary. Day Three. Goodwick to Trefin. 17 miles.
The forecast was wind and rain, and got the wind but no rain I'm glad to say. An excellent days walking. Blue sky, blue sea, high wind and high waves. Great! The best day so far for the scenery. I coped with the back pack much better today, so it seems that after three days I have become accustomed to it again. Still struggling with 'being alone' factor though. It's much nicer when you are on a long trail to have someone to chat too about the things that you see and experience. Saw some more seals today. I am going to make it the last day tomorrow and travel home to Kent on Friday.

Why did I feel like that on that day? I think that by that stage I had decided that I was going to propose to Tracy, and ask her if she would be my wife. It is strange how these things come to you. Perhaps the walk along the way had cleared my mind and I then knew what it was all about.

Princess Diana once said; "Only do what your heart tells you."

Diary. Day Four. Trefin to Whitesands Bay. 11 miles.
Packed the tent away wet in the rain. I was going to head for St Davids to find a site for tonight and cut the day down to about 10 miles due to the weather. Not many people out today! Got an early start at eight, and was in St David's by 12.30. Caught the bus to Haverfordwest to find the 2cv at

the Fire Station and had half a mind to drive some of the way back before finding a camp site, but being a lover of the brilliant Gilbert and Sullivan, as they say "Faint heart never won fair lady." I ended up coming all the way home to Kent. Six and a half hours! The little 2cv went like a bomb. Sixty miles an hour all the way!

Never underestimate the power of passion. (Eve Sawyer.)

Well, what can I say about that day. I think that I had made my mind up about what I really wanted to happen. The very next day I went to a jeweller in Canterbury and brought an engagement ring. Following a telephone call to her, Tracy came to my house and I knelt down and proposed to her! I wanted to marry the girl. She was somewhat gob smacked, but she said YES!

Tracy and I decided that we would like to get married abroad as we had both been married previously and did not fancy the rigmarole of a Church wedding in the United Kingdom. After some discussion we decided on St Lucia in the Windward Islands of the Caribbean. We made all the necessary arrangements and had arranged to be married on the forth day of the trip.

On the first couple of days of the trip Tracy and I met a couple called Keith and Karen. They were a lovely couple and we asked them if they would help us on the wedding day by Keith being my best man and Karen being a bridesmaid for Tracy. They were over the moon and more than happy to oblige and said that they felt honoured to be asked to do so. How nice.

On the day Karen videoed the wedding ceremony while Keith signed the register and then they swapped and Karen signed the register. Once all the signings were completed the steel band played 'Feeling Hot! Hot! Hot!' which was appropriate for the occasion and Tracy and I danced in front of the band clutching glasses of champagne. Then the guy in charge of the steel band said "We want you to play with us" so we went round the other side and started to play. Keith shouted "GO ON MICK SHOW EM!" Which I did and its all on the video! After all I am completely bonkers. Tracy looked stunning in her wedding dress and I looked cool in my shorts. After the ceremony we went down to the beach with the photographer and he took some snaps of us under the palm tree.

All of the others who where getting married at the resort were wearing the full English wedding suit and dresses and the poor guys were sweating away like a freshly run race horse in the hot Caribbean sun. So, I think my option to go for a cool shirt and shorts was a good idea!

Later that week we all went on a sailing trip on a massive catamaran to the twin peaks at the end of the island and had a barbecue on the beach. Then after we had returned to the resort in the evening when the sun had gone down there was a massive beach party and I had a go at the limbo competition with all the other guys which was great fun! Then we danced the night away and Tracy looked gorgeous and I just looked like a Muppet, but that doesn't matter as we had a great time. If you read this Keith and Karen, thanks for the video it's great. Also thanks for the letter that came with the video that was very thoughtful of you.

It was at this time that I was considering putting in for a transfer. Why was I thinking like this? I shall explain. My previous neighbour and friend Chris, whose garden I had had to crane the oil tank over, had recently moved up to Shropshire. He had done this because he had recently married a lady whose name was also Chris. Christine and Christopher, Chris and Chris. They had wanted to go somewhere nice and rural because Kent was starting to become somewhat over crowded. They had been able to do this because Chris made furniture to order in his workshop and Christine worked as a charity aid worker all over the world so she had to go away from home a lot. Therefore they could live anywhere in the country and it made no difference.

After Chris and Chris had moved up to Shropshire where they had brought an old stone barn that they were going to convert to a house, I went to Shropshire and paid them a visit. I liked the area. So I was starting to think, Hmmm It would be nice to live on the border of Wales somewhere.

I put this to my new wife with some trepidation, expecting her to say 'Not on your Nelly my son!' (That's Kentish speak for 'no way.') The reason I thought I would get this reaction is because all of her family lived in Kent and she would not want to be parted from them. However, to my surprise she thought it was a good idea. So, I looked into it in a bit more depth.

I wrote a letter to the two Fire Brigades that I was interested in possibly getting a transfer to. The Hereford and Worcester Fire Brigade, and the Shropshire Fire Brigade. I received a letter from both Brigades, Shropshire declined my offer, but Hereford and Worcester offered me an interview.

CHAPTER NINETEEN

Change in life.

Strangely enough I do remember the day that I went for my interview for a job in Hereford and Worcester Fire Service. I think that most people who read this book will remember that day. It was September the eleventh of the year 2001. The day that the attack on the World Trade Centre happened.

I had driven up from Kent to Droitwich for my interview at the training centre. Not being overly familiar with the area I was not exactly sure where the training centre was, so I called into a taxi office on the outskirts of the town to ask for some directions. When I went into the office the guys there were glued to a television. I said "What's going on guys?" They were not really sure at that time, but they did know there was a big fire happening in the World Trade Centre. I looked at the screen of the T.V. that they were watching and said "Wow! That is one hell of a fire!" I asked them for directions to the Fire Service Training Centre which they gave me and I left the building.

At that time I had no idea that the fire and the following collapse of the World Trade Centre was a terrorist attack. I just thought that is was a fire in a large building, and fires do happen in buildings! But I was in a hurry and had to get to the Fire Service Training Centre for my interview!

I arrived at the Training Centre on time and following a successful interview, I was offered a job as a Fireman serving at Hereford Fire Station. That meant I would have to take a drop in rank from Leading Fireman, but I was willing to do that as I was sure that after some time I would be able to regain my rank.

Arrangements were made and I found a place for me and my new wife Tracy to live. I made several trips up to Herefordshire over the next couple of weeks to seek out a house for us. Eventually we found the house that we wanted and it was called 'Rosehill' which was just over the border into Wales and was on the outskirts of a small town called Knighton. The house was in a lovely location and faced up the River Teme valley into Mid Wales.

The house was of late Victorian construction and had three bedrooms, an upstairs bathroom, a living room, dining room, utility room with a downstairs loo, which is always handy! The house also had a large cellar which was not damp and never flooded. The kitchen of the house was large and had been added to the side of the property at a later stage, but fortunately had been constructed in keeping with the original house and did not look at all out of place.

Regarding the exterior of the property, the house was approach by way of a long drive which was accessed from the road by way of a large gate. As you came up the drive initially there was a double garage, then the gate, an open area then a large twenty seven foot workshop which had electrical power, and plenty of power points, then on the left a set of steps which allowed you to go down and access the road by foot. After this further up the driveway it opened up into a large turning area in front of the house.

To the rear of the property was a large long garden which you accessed by a small gate to the side of the house, or the back door. The garden gradually rose uphill towards the town and at the top of the garden there was a gate that you could use to walk to town. So, effectively there were four ways that you could leave the property. The bottom of the drive, the gate to the side, the garden gate at the top, or there was a door out of the cellar that opened onto the pavement at the side. It was rather like a split level property, but just what we were looking for and also it had stunning views from the front window out up onto the hills and Offa's Dyke Path.

The whole property itself was rather run down and the gardens needing some serious work, but the house was sound which is what was important, and the state of the property was reflected in the asking price. We new immediately that it was the property that was the one we wanted. So we approached the agent to discuss things. We said that it was too much for us, but the agent said not to worry too much about the asking price as the house had been on the market some time and that the owners would be open to offers. Tracy and I put in an offer on the property which was accepted and we were over the moon!

There was one hiccup though, when the marketing agent Mr Parry had put a sold sign attached to the for sale sign, suddenly there was another offer put in at ten thousand pounds more than our original offer. Obviously someone else had been eyeing up Rosehill and seeing the sold sign had panicked and put in the inflated offer. By now we were back in Kent and when called by Mr Parry and told that the offer had been accepted, we knew that we had been Gazumped! We were FURIOUS! We called the vendor and they were very apologetic. After some discussion they said that they felt bad about the situation and that if we were to match the offer of the second buyer they would honour the original agreement and sell to us. Tracy and I did some 'very fast' mathematics and decided that we could raise the money and upon informing the agent we had the house. Phew!

Tracy and I did a bit of juggling around at that time because we still needed a buyer for Chequers cottage. Obviously I had to work my notice in the Kent Fire Service before moving jobs to Hereford and Worcester Fire Service. Somehow we managed to wrangle it and when we had a buyer for Chequers Cottage we were able to move.

Then came the time that I had to break the news to all my work mates at the Fire Station at Canterbury. I had up until then been keeping my cards very close to my chest about the transfer. So it was only a week before I was to go that I told all the guys on the watch. We did our normal parade in the morning and I stood out the front with them lined up and read out the runners and riders for the day. The before I fell them out to do the Taking Over Routines I made the announcement. I said "Well men, I am afraid I have some sad news to tell you. After this tour of duty I will be leaving the Watch and going to pastures new up in Herefordshire". You could have knocked them down with a feather!

Without telling me what they were doing the men had a whip round amongst themselves and then one of them went to our Brigade shop at Headquarters and brought me a parting gift. On the morning of my departure after my last nights duty with my colleagues on White Watch, they all gathered together in the dining room and called me up from the office.

One of the guys had a little speech prepared. Then they presented me with a foot tall figurine of a smoky old Fireman clutching a baby rescued from the fire. There was a brass plaque on the side on which was written. Good Luck from White Watch E80 Canterbury. I too had a little speech prepared in my head, which I delivered not without a tear in the corner of my eye and my voice quavering a little. "Thanks for that men, it is not without some regret that I leave you all at E80. It has been a pleasure and an honour to serve with you. Thank you all for this gift I shall always treasure it." And I do treasure it to this day the gift from my old colleagues from Canterbury. We saw a lot of shit together, and dealt with it together over the years.

So that was it! I had left all my old colleagues at E80 and I don't mind admitting that at the time of writing this it brought it all back in a wave of emotion and I burst into tears and had a bloody good cry! Over the years me and the boys had seen a lot of shit together and been through some hard times and some good ones, and it was very, very sad to leave all my old buddies.

At the time of my transfer to my new Brigade circumstances dictated that my new wife and I would have to be parted for a while, during the times that I was on duty for the four day period. Fortunately this was not for long as things went smoothly with my sale of the old house and the purchase of the new one. Being new to Hereford and Worcester Fire and Rescue Service even though I was an old hand I was treated well by my new colleagues and even offered a temporary bed during my transitional period by one of the guys on the watch called Richie. That is the thing about Firemen. They are all in the same hazardous occupation and in times of trouble they will help their comrades if they can, no matter what part of the country or even the world they come from. A Fireman is a Fireman and that's that.

When all the property issues had been resolved and we were ready to move I had a word with an old mate of mine who used to live just around the corner from us at Chequers Cottages, at a small row of houses called Chequers Orchard. Ian, who had helped me with the boiler, worked as a motor engineer in his own business fixing and spraying people's cars. Ian and I had become mates over the years that I had lived at Chequers Cottages. He had after all helped me get the old anthracite boiler into the cellar. Ian had a son called David who lived with him. I said that as we lived in a small cottage we did not feel that the amount of stuff we had, warranted a professional moving service and that with their help, we could all move Tracy and I between us to our new location.

Ian was a good sort and he agreed to help us. We hired a Luton van for all the heavier furniture and boxes and come the day before the big move we loaded all the things up. The only thing that I regret about that move at the time of writing this, is that Ian and I did not stay in contact later in life, but that's men for you.

The plan was as follows. Ian would drive the van. David would drive their car with the loaded trailer of Ian's attached. Tracy would drive our Berlingo loaded to the gunnels, and I would drive my 2cv with the animals in the family, Poppy and Tom on the back seat, and the amazingly alive cat Scorcher in a box on the front seat. Tom used to love to go in the car, but Poor Poppy hated it and quivered all the way.

On the 15th of December 2001 we set off as planned in convoy. Me in the 2cv in front, followed by the van and then the car and trailer driven by David, and finally with Tracy in the Berlingo bringing up the rear. What a sight of rag tags we must have looked!

I would like to say that the trip up to Wales went without event, but this was not the case! We stopped at a motorway café for some grub about lunch time and then the police pulled David and the trailer over because they thought that it was an unsafe load! But after some negotiation with the Police Officers, they allowed us to continue on our way.

We finally arrived at Rosehill in the pitch dark and Ian tried to reverse the van up the quite steep drive. The van had also been loaded to the 'gunnels' and with the drive being of gravel the van just wheel span and the drive was barely wide enough to get the van past the workshop. After much cussing and cursing, much more wheel spinning and 'HEATED' conversation between Ian and I, the van clutch finally burnt out and nearly caught fire! Oooops.

At that stage it was obvious that the van would be going no nearer the house. Consequently the entire van load which contained some heavy objects had to be carried by hand up the rest of the drive to the house in the dark. My old neighbour and mate Chris from Chequers Cottages, was waiting for us to help unload all the gear, as his new home of the stone barn was only about fifteen miles away over the border.

When we finally got all the things into the house we went into Knighton town to get some dinner as there was no way of making a meal in the house the power was all off and the house had no gas supply and we had no gas cooker anyway!

The next day Ian managed to get the drive unblocked by rolling the van down the drive and across the road into a convenient lay-by at the other side of the road. It was there that the van was abandoned and Ian and David set off back to Kent in the car towing the now road-safe unloaded trailer. I can only thank Ian and David for their efforts during that move from one side of the country to the other. There were some disasters along the way, but we made it in the end.

CHAPTER TWENTY

SERVING AT HEREFORD

So now Tracy and I were in our new home and I have to say freezing to death! There was no central heating at Rosehill and it was ten days before Christmas. Although the house had no central heating, it did have two open fires, one in the living room and one in the dining room. We used to heat the house by buying logs from the town and lighting the fires, but in my opinion not really adequate for the large Victorian detached house.

The house would need central heating installed and I was the man to do it. After all, I had installed the central heating at Chequers Cottages and I did know what I was doing. Right? Apart from the squirting leaking joints! Rosehill house, being in a quite remote location had no gas supply available, so I knew that it would have to be an oil fired system, as was the case at Chequers Cottage. Before I could do that I needed to get myself entrenched with my new Watch at Hereford.

I must admit, that things in the Fire Station at Hereford were not the same as that I had been used to down in the Fire Station at Canterbury, as they were somewhat different from what I had experienced with the Kent Firemen and the London Firemen. When you are a Fireman in the service you get used to certain routines and methods of working. My god! They don't even have cheese rolls here at elevenses! They have toast at the eleven o'clock cup of tea. I was under the impression that all Firemen across the country had a cheese roll at eleven O'clock with their cup of tea. I really missed my elevenses cheese roll and had to adapt to toast instead. (Bummer!) Also a thing that I really missed about being in the Service was that volleyball had been banned due to all the injuries caused.

However, even though I was the stranger on the Watch, they treated me well. Jango was the old Fireman and me and Jango got on well, He had an attitude that I liked and although things were much more relaxed at Hereford than they were at Canterbury, the job got done when it needed to be. I think that my new mates at Hereford thought of me as a bit of an oddball due to my southern accent 'twang' from Kent, which was very much different from their country accent at Hereford. But this did not matter at all! We were all Firemen and that is what mattered. The fact of the matter is, when the bells went down, we all knew what we had to do and when we had to do it. I hope that Jango reads this book and remembers me, like I remember old Jango. What a bloody good Fireman he was.

Fire 'Shouts' were much less frequent at Hereford Fire Station than they were at Canterbury. Which is good isn't it? No Fireman wants to have to go out on a 'Shout'. It's not that we are lazy, but we don't want to have to go into a burning building to save someone unless it's necessary. God knows, I have the scars and memories to prove it!

At the time that Tracy and I had moved up to Rosehill in Knighton I did a bit of research and found that not far from our house was an area of allotments owned by the local council. For the benefit of anyone reading this book that may not be familiar with the way things work in the United Kingdom, an allotment is an area of ground that you rent off the local council and can use to grow vegetables. I put in for one of the allotments and was given one.

The allotment had been left unattended for some time by the look of it and needed some work. It was quite a large allotment and to try to dig it all over by hand tools would have been a back breaking experience. So, I though what I need here is a rotavator. I scanned the local press and found one advertised by a chap in Hereford. I went for a look at the thing and he showed me that it was in good working order. "How much do you want for it?" I said. "Forty Quid" he replied. For those who are unaware, a quid is slang for one pound sterling. I thought that it was a good buy and brought the machine from the man. It was the best forty quid that I have ever spent! I loaded the rotavator into the back of our Berlingo and took it back to Knighton. Soon I was up on the allotment and rotavating away. I soon had all the earth turned over and ready for planting.

I met a man called Neil who lived in a house that backed onto the allotment. He had an old shed that he wanted to sell and my shed on the allotment was in a rather dilapidated state. Neil said "Just give me a tenner and you can have it" I thought that was a very reasonable price for the shed and gave Neil his tenner (ten pounds). Then I destroyed the old shed and Tracy and I started to erect that shed we had brought off of Neil.

As things progressed it became apparent that there was a problem. The so called shed that Neil had sold us was not in fact one shed, but in fact a combination of parts of two different sheds! I had to do some reconfiguration of the shed components to get the thing to go together, but the end result was that we had a weatherproof shed that was far better than the old shed that leaked like a sieve.

I spent a lot of time up on the allotment in the summer months. It was a nice place to be, with views out over the mountains and Offa's Dyke Path. I made friends with a man who had the allotment next to mine. His name was John, Big John. Big John was what Tracy and I called him, because he was a big man. He was about six foot six tall and half as wide. Big John worked on his allotment nearly as often as I did and we talked about things regularly. He was seventy years old, but fit as a fiddle and as strong as an ox. Big John must have thought it was a bit strange having me next to him on the allotments because of my strong southern England drawl, but regardless to that he saw that I was working the ground and reducing all the weeds and probably thought that it was a good thing.

Big John had a standpipe outside his shed and he kindly gave me permission to run a hose pipe from it to enable me to water my allotment in the hot dry periods. I must say that I loved my time up on the allotment. I would take some sandwiches, flask of coffee and a bottle of water and go up there for the day. It was wonderful to be out in the good clean air and have views out over the mountains. There can be no better place to have an allotment.

With much use of the rotavator and much hard work I soon began to produce lots of vegetables from the allotment which Tracy and I benefited from. There is nothing better that a diet of good veg that you have grown yourself and know what has gone into it.

Meanwhile, I had to find how to heat our house Rosehill for my wife to make it warm and comfortable for her. As I mentioned earlier I had decided that I would install a central heating system in the house, fuelled by oil. I did some research about installing a system and having done some work before at Chequers Cottages, I felt that I was more than capable. I designed the system myself and did some drawings of how the system would be laid out. At this stage I contacted a local plumber who was called Roger. I asked him to come and visit the house. Which at an agreed date and time he did.

On meeting with Roger I liked him immediately and showed him my drawings about the plan for the central heating system and he seemed impressed. He said "Not bad for a guy who has only done part of a college course on plumbing." I said "YES, BUT WILL IT WORK!" He replied "Yes of course it will work, what do you want me to do?" I explained that my plan was that I would install the system on my days off from the Fire Service, doing all the radiators and the pipe runs and then he would come and install the boiler and fire up the system. He was more than happy with this arrangement, and so the work started.

There was a lot of upheaval at Rosehill while the heating system was installed. With floorboards up here, there and everywhere. Eventually the system was installed and Roger came to the house with the Honeywell boiler and fitted it in the downstairs loo. He fired up the boiler and with anticipation and crossed fingers I awaited the results. Slowly and gradually the radiators got warm and then hot. IT WORKS! My central heating design was a success. I can't say how pleased I was that I had designed and installed a working central heating system. Tracy and I were made up! (Being from Kent we have certain colloquial expressions that we use, and 'made up' is an expression we use meaning being extremely pleased) I paid Roger his very reasonable fee for his help and he went on his way.

It was on 13th November 2002 that the Fire Service went on strike for the first time in twenty five years. The strike started at six p.m. when the day shift went off duty. The then deputy prime minister, John Prescott, branded the strike as "unnecessary and unreasonable and that it put lives at risk!" Well did Mr Prescott think that the Firemen where stupid and did not realise that this would be putting lives at risk?

Up to 50,000 Firemen where then on strike for 48 hours and with the emergency cover no longer in place the vintage green goddess tenders where brought back into service by the army. I think that Mr Prescott thought that the Firemen would not ever actually go on strike, because he said, and I quote. "There is a very real remedy in your own hands, don't put people's lives at risk. Be reasonable, not unreasonable, suspend the strike. Don't walk, talk!"

But the Firemen had had enough by then of all the 'bullshit' that they were being fed by the government. They did not see why the Government wanted to make them work longer hours for crap wages in sometimes extremely hazardous conditions, and extend their retirement age! So they walked.

That was the one and only time that I was ever on strike in my life and something that does not happen much in the modern working climate these days. Not like back in the 1970's when work forces were striking on an almost regular basis! I have to admit, and I am saying this off the record, I did actually not understand the politics that much about it all, because I was not that interested. All I knew about was being a Fireman, but if my colleagues were going 'out the doors' then I would go with them.

Following some negotiation with the union officials and the Government eventually it was decided that Firemen that had been working in the service for a certain number of years would fall into group one, and Firemen (and by then also female Fire-Fighters) would fall into group two. Those in group one would stick to the original pension scheme and go when they had done thirty years or reached fifty five years old, and those in group two would have to work until they were sixty and also be put on a different pension scheme.

Fortunately for me I was in the group one and they would honour all the large chunk of my wages that I had been paying over the years and give me my pension. SO THEY BLOODY WELL SHOULD IN MY OPINION! It's no good entering a burning building and complaining to the owners that the building is on fire! Or moving the goalposts after the football has been struck. If you want to change the pension scheme you should have thought about that earlier and then applied it to the new members that were coming into the Fire Service and not try and back date it.

It was about this time that I was to receive my second medal from the Queen that I could pin to my undress uniform. It was 2002 and the time of our Queen's Golden Jubilee. The Queen was giving all the Firemen who had served more than five years service at the time of the Golden Jubilee a Jubilee Medal. It is a lovely looking medal, Gold in colour with a red, white and blue ribbon. (The colours of the Union Jack.) The medal came internally set in a little white box with a card that read as follows. 'This certificate guarantees that this medal has been hand crafted in the British Royal Mint to the highest standards of quality and excellence.' I was extremely pleased and honoured that the Queen of England had thought that her Firemen where worthy of a medal on her Golden Jubilee and I wear it with much pride.

So, that was that sorted out and I was most happy to get back on Watch and do my job as a Fireman. Shortly after the strike, things were to change for me in the Fire Service. Sniff, Sniff, "Do I smell promotion in the wind?"

After about two and a half years on Green Watch at Hereford the opportunity for promotion arose. The organization was starting up a new initiative called Community Fire Safety. The idea of the project was to educate the general public in the prevention of fires in the home and a post was created to achieve this. The post would require a Sub Officer and that was the rank on offer and a rank I wanted, after all I did have the (hard earned) qualification. Anyone who applied for the post would have to attend an interview hosted by a panel and put forward their ideas and initiatives to educate the public. I put in for an interview and was given one.

I had a good think about things before attending the interview and came up with a few ideas. So, on the date and time allocated and putting on my best undress uniform. (and medal ribbons.) I attended the interview at the Brigade Training Centre at Droitwich.

After the formal introductions to the officers on the interview panel I went into my pitch for the job. I explained to them the ideas that I had about Community Fire Safety. Using the white board and pens provided by the interview panel, I drew some diagrams explaining that with my methods and ideas of education of the public, how we could balance out the need for more Fire Appliances and therefore provide a reduction in the financial burden to the organization. This would in due course provide more finance available for Community Fire Safety, which would save the lives of the public and also put less Firemen at risk, and so on and so on.

There was only two ways that my interview could go. Either down like a lead balloon, or up like a sky rocket. They would swallow it like a cup of cold sick, or drink it down like a nice pint of beer. I could tell by the look on the faces of the interview panel that I had made quite an impression on them, but good or bad I couldn't tell! When I had finished my 'spiel' I thanked them for their time and left the interview room with my bum cheeks clenched tight, so I didn't shit myself as I was 'Sooo' nervous.

Fortunately for me it was option two that the board of officers went for. They thought that I had some great ideas for Community Fire Safety and I had a nice letter a few days later offering me the post of Sub Officer Community Fire Safety West District. (West District being the whole of Herefordshire) This of course I accepted and turned up for duty in my new post on the 1st April 2003 as instructed. Were they serious or were they playing a very elaborate April Fools Day joke on me? Fortunately for me it was not an April Fools joke and I got stuck in at my new post.

So once again I had to leave my colleagues on the Watch to move on. It was not the end of the earth though, as the District Headquarters was only on the third floor of the Fire Station at Hereford and that was where I would be based. So, occasionally I would see my old mates when they were on duty in the day time. The biggest change in my life regarding my promotion was that I would no longer be doing shift pattern work. I would be working nine to five, Monday to Friday.

I enjoyed my time as Community Fire Safety Officer in West District as the job involved a lot of travelling around the county and meeting different people from all walks of life and promoting Fire Safety to all parts of the community.

CHAPTER TWENTY ONE

TIMES OF CHANGE.

It was at this time of my second promotion in the service that I had to make some changes in my life. I was no longer working the four on four off shift pattern and this meant that I had less time available for other activities and after some consideration I had to let the allotment go. It was a shame because I loved the time in the summer in Wales that I used to spend up on the allotment working the earth and producing all our vegetables.

When we had brought the house the garden at the rear of the house was like a jungle because the poor old lady that owned it previously had been unable to look after the garden as it should have been. So what would happen now was that I would get this garden sorted out at weekends when I was off work.

Halfway up the garden was a large shed or small barn almost that was in very dilapidated state. In fact it was almost falling down. So, I attacked the shed and tore it down. Keeping all the timber that was re-useable I built a much smaller shed at the top of the garden by the rear gate. I then burnt all the rest of the large shed that was unusable for recycling. Being a Fireman by trade, there is nothing like a bloody good bonfire to make a Fireman happy!

I cleared the garden of all the things that I thought would have to go, and had lots of bonfires to burn all the timber, branches and twigs that I had cut down. Keith who worked at the garage at the top rear end of the garden came over and leaning over the wall said to me, "You just bloody love it don't you, you just can't stop burning stuff!" He had hit the nail on the head. How right was he!

217

When I had cleared the garden of all the things that I thought should go. I then got in a small mini-digger and started to landscape the garden. Not being an expert mini-digger driver, I did experience some problems with the landscaping of the garden. All I seemed to be doing was pushing the soil from one place to another and back again! At one point I nearly managed to tip over the mini-digger with me in it! I had to tie the mini-digger to a tree with a length of line to get myself and the mini-digger out of the shit. I don't know how, but somehow I managed it.

When we lived at Rosehill Tracy and I used to take the dogs for a walk down to the river on a regular basis. From the bottom of our drive you could cross the road to a stile and walk across the field and you would then be on the Offa's Dyke Path, which ran along the side of the river Teme. This was a good place to take the dogs as it provided an opportunity to give the dogs a wash in the river.

Poppy loved jumping in the river to get wet, but Tom was not so keen. Poppy had an amazing talent that I could never quite grasp. I would select a stone from the bank at the side of the river and show it to her and rub my hands all over it to get my scent onto the stone. Then I would throw it into the water. She would jump in and swim out to the point where the stone had gone in and when she was about in the right spot she would dive under the surface and swim underwater and find the stone, then swim back to the bank, bring it back to me and drop it. It was uncanny. It would be the exact same stone, not one of the thousands of other stones that formed the river bed. No, it would be that one particular stone. How the hell she did it is beyond me!

Like I said, Tom was not so sure about going in the water. When Poppy was fishing out my stone, Tom would stand on the bank, Barking. Woof, woof, woof. What I used to do is just pick him up and throw him into the water. He would go in with a big splash and surface and start swimming around chasing Poppy when she was stone fishing. Once in he was in he was fine and loved it. We had some great times with the two dogs fishing for stones, and it was good exercise for us.

After we had been living in the property of Rosehill for about two years that in 2003 Tracy and I decided that we would like to go and walk another long trail. I did a bit of research into the various long trails that were available in the U.K. and was looking for one that I had not already walked. We looked at all the options and opted for The Cumbria Way. The Cumbria Way was a trail of seventy two miles, most of which would be within the boundaries of the Lake District National Park, a beautiful part of the country. The reason it is somewhat different from the Cumbria part of the Coast to Coast route that I had walked years earlier, is in that the section of the Coast to Coast in Lakeland goes from East to West. Whereas The Cumbria Way goes the other way across Lakeland and is walked from South to North.

The Cumbria Way runs from Morecambe Bay in the south to Carlisle in the north and the trail as I said is a total of seventy two miles. For any one of a reasonable standard of fitness it can be walked in five days. The trail starts off fairly easily and then reaches a crescendo at the middle of the trail and then slowly tails off towards the end. There is a good guide to the route which I would advise anyone who is taking on the way to purchase and take with them. Produced by Aurum Press, with Anthony Burton the author as in the guide of the West Highland Way. In the guide there are some excellent photographs taken by Rob Scott that if you buy the guide, and you look at the pictures, you will be getting your boots out and preparing to take on the way as soon as you can. You will be getting itchy feet in the winter waiting for the better weather to arrive!

Once we were ready for the off, and had packed all our gear we drove up the M6 to where we had arranged to leave the car. Looking at the diary that I wrote back then about the journey I am not clear in my memory as to what went on that day but it reads as follows.

THE JOURNEY TO CUMBRIA.

M6 busy until we reached Cumbria, then a nice drive and lifted the foot to see the scenery. We had a bit of a fright at the railway station when I asked for a ticket to Ulverston. The man misheard me with my strong southern drawl, and thought that I said Alston! He said "No trains there today or ever." We cleared that up and got two tickets to Ulverston. Where we met Donna who was very helpful. Train to Lancaster was a nightmare as the air conditioning was broke and everyone was moaning. Met a nice chap at Lancaster rail station, who decided to tell us all about the passengers. We think that he was pissed because all he said was that the passengers were rich, educated, fit and unfit! Don't really know what he was on about. Finally got to Ulverston and met up with Billy who gave us a key and left us to get on with it. Good pub across the road called 'The Laurel' named after Stan Laurel who was born in Ulverston. (Claim to fame.) Walk begins tomorrow, weather fine at present.

I know that that probably does not make a lot of sense to anyone reading this book. Because to be honest it now does not make a lot of sense to me, and I wrote it! Like I said earlier, I wish that when I was walking the long trails on which I had written the diary that I had kept them in a little better English Language, so that reading them later in life it would be clearer as to what it was that I was blathering on about. But it will get written in my book exactly as I read it from the diary.

Diary. Day one. Ulverston to Coniston. Fourteen miles.
Had trouble finding the start of the Way at Ulverston. Are we going to make it to the end? A really long fourteen miles, probably the longest ever! Met the four fellas on the Way who steamed ahead of us, but the fat one of the four suffered for it at the end. Weather really hot and tough on the feet. Met a local lady hanging out her washing. She said, "Conistan by six." I thought four. She was right. Met another lady on the trail, (day walker) who said Tracy looked like a 'seasoned walker' but she didn't see her at the end! Went wrong near the end as always and added another half a mile to the day. Campsite packed! (Cumbria in summer.) Tracy made me walk another mile into town to get supplies coz she couldn't be bothered to walk to the pub.

With regard to the four fellas, we had quite a few meetings with them over the time of the Cumbria Way. They were northern lads from Yorkshire, but they got on alright with us soft southerners! We had some laughs between us and two of the guys were called John, and I know that one of the other two was called Mick because I wrote it in the diary, the other guys name I do not remember. So at the time of writing this I just called them the two Johns, Mick and the other bloke.

However, it was nice to sit in the pub and have a meal with these chaps from up the north of England and get some of their views and opinions about things in general. I found it very interesting as to the opinions about things from people from different parts of the country, and I think that all people who take on a long trail have some sort of bond between them, no matter where they come from. Well I already knew that from walking the North Downs Way, Pennine Way, Coast to Coast and the West Highland Way!

Diary. Day two. Conistan to Dungeon Ghyll. Eleven miles.
Started off at 9.00 not 8.00 as planned. Pretty uneventful morning, but scenery very pretty. Typical Lakeland stuff. Stopped at Colwith force for cooked pasta lunch. (Woman fell on her face.) lots of tourists around @ Skelwith bridge and Elterwater. Wife had a sense of humour failure about a mile from the campsite,

but o.k. now. Campsite is really nice and free showers! Walked up to Old Dungeon Ghyll Hotel and met the boys from Yorkshire. Had a Cumberland sausage and chilli. (*Free campsite!! Got in too late to pay and left too early.*)

What can I say about this section of my diary? Well the last bit in italics had been scribbled in by my then wife Tracy, which I had not know until later when I read it at the time of writing this book. With regard to the woman falling on her face, well I have no idea about what happened there.

Diary. Day three. Dungeon Ghyll to Keswick. Fifteen and a half miles.
Got a fairly early start at 7.10. Campsite was as midgy as hell so we got out quick! Got up the road and Tracy had water pissing out of the bottom of her pack, she hadn't tightened up her platypus bottle enough. Made our way up Langdale quickly and got to the climb up Stake Gill at 8.23. Saw the Yorkshire boys on their way up. Caught them up at the top. Crossed over Stake Pass to Langstrath. Passed the boys and moved on to Rosthwaite. Stopped in Borrowdale and had sarnies. Mick (Yorkshire boys.) took the bus to Keswick. Last couple of miles we went about a mile an hour and got to the campsite at 6.00 p.m. I went to Booths supermarket and got barbee and beers. Great campsite at the head of Derwentwater. Tracy picked up a tick somewhere which I removed.

Tracy at the top of Stake Pass.

221

To clarify some of points for the reader here. A Platypus bottle is a plastic bag with a tap on the bottom, and the bag shrinks as you drink the water from the bottle. When I went to the supermarket to get supplies I brought some food and a throw away barbecue that we could cook the food on. For those who are unaware a 'tick' is a large blood-sucking mite of the order Acarina. They usually infest the fur of sheep that live on the hills, but sometimes will latch onto a passing unaware walker while he or she in this case, is walking through the heather. As you can imagine Poor Tracy was pretty horrified when she found out the tick that had a liking to her! I removed it by burning it off.

Diary. Day Four. Keswick to Caldbeck. Fourteen miles.
Woke up to rain hitting the tent, but that soon stopped and also the Yorkshire boys snoring. Packed up and hit the road by 7.15. Stiff climb up through the woods to the car park at the ascent to Skiddaw. Made a long traverse through a lovely valley to the hostel at Skiddaw House. Then a long drag down the valley to the start of the ascent up Grainsgill Beck. Got passed by the two Yorkshire Johns earlier. We got John's number to find out about campsites at Caldbeck. Stopped at the rescue hut before High Pike (Highest point on the way.) to put on more gear. Tracy was a bit of a mish mash! Ascended High Pike but could not see Solway Firth due to mist. We made an easy descent into Caldbeck. Tried to ring John's number but no signal! There are no campsites in Caldbeck so we took B and B. We decided to call it a day as the rest of the trail is just a drag into Carlisle and time and money is short. So we will get the bus tomorrow and be home a day early. Tracy done well today. All in all a good trail with excellent scenery and even better weather.

In hindsight I wish that we had pressed on to Carlisle so that I could say that I had completed the trail, but there you go. The decision was made on the day and so I have to live with that. I really enjoyed walking the Cumbria Way and would recommend it to anyone who was thinking of walking a mountain trial, but never done one before, because I think that it would be a good introduction to long distance mountain trail walking.

It was about this time that I had the beloved 2cv re-vamped by a Keith that worked at the garage at the back of the top of our English country (but in Wales) rear garden. Keith used to do a lot of spraying work for people who owned sporting cars and he knew what he was doing. So I approached Keith and asked him if we could work together and re-vamp my old 2cv. With some negotiation we agreed a price. I would provide the body panels and the labour, and he would provide the spraying skill to get the job done.

With some investigation I found out that there was a place not far away from Knighton that I could get some more body panels for the 2cv that we could re-spray and make the little car that I loved look really good. I went to the place at Cleobury Mortimer in the Berlingo with Tracy and we got the panels required. It was a shame what they did there, they would get old 2cv's and pull them apart because all they were after was the chassis, which they then used as a base to make a kit car. All the rest of the 2cv was scrapped. Criminal! Well, at least they provided us with the body panels that we were after. It was then that Keith and I set to work.

I drove my little car around to his workshop and we stripped off all the body panels and dumped the ones that where damaged. He then told me to take the car away as it would get in the way in the workshop. This I did and drove the car (what was left of it!) down the road to put in our garage.

Tracy took this picture from up on the bank by the workshop.

Keith spent some time bashing the panels for the car into shape and I do remember him complaining about how bad the bonnet was. But he got the job done. Then it came to the paint work. What did I want for colours? I decided that I would break the mould and go for an all white 2cv with a black roof and silver trimmings.

Keith mixed up the correct amount of paint accordingly and the spray job started. While Keith was doing this, I got on the internet, and ordered a new roof for the car and it was delivered as promised. Keith had done an excellent spray job on the panels and after they were done and ready to go back on the car, I drove the stripped 2cv back up to the workshop and we re-assembled it. I then drove my refurbished car back to the house and later took some photographs.

Does she look great or what?

Eventually I decided that I would need some professional landscapers in to sort out the rear garden. It was beyond the capacity of my skill and time to do it myself. First of all they built a retaining wall at the side out of steel girders hammered deep into the ground and then slotted railway sleepers between them and it formed a good strong wall. Then they levelled off the pile of dirt that I had managed to create. And lastly they built a nice split level patio.

The overall effect was very pleasing and Tracy and I were very happy with the job. We should have done that in the first place! I worked on the garden and laid some turfs for a fine lawn and for my birthday present Tracy brought me a good cylinder lawn mower. Thanks for that, it was a good choice of birthday present. Which at the time of writing this I still possess the cylinder mower. All I wanted to do in the garden was to have a striped lawn like they do in all English country gardens! And that is what I achieved in the end. 'How many flowers are there that grow in an English country garden'. (In Wales.)

We did lots of work in the rear garden of Rosehill in the spring and it soon started to shape up really well. Eventually after all our work and effort we finally got the back garden of Rosehill looking great! In the summer the garden looked fantastic, with the walls and split level patio built, the flower beds all planted and the lawn with the nice stripes provided by my cylinder mower.

It was about now in January 2005 that I had my first fit. I was at work doing a presentation to a group of old ladies at the blind college. It was not that the ladies were blind it was just that the blind college sometimes hire out their lecture rooms to outside groups when they are not needed. This would be to generate some further income for the college. Standing up in front of a group of people and talking about the physics of combustion, and how fire can be avoided is something that does not normally worry me. I gave my normal spiel and presentation and then about halfway through I forgot what I should be saying. What should I be saying? It was very odd.

The woman in charge took me out in the corridor and spoke to me thinking that I was just nervous about things. She tried to calm me down. I was not worried about having to talk to a few old ducks. I don't think she understood what was happening. Anyway, I went back in and had another go, but my mind was in total confusion!

I couldn't remember all the things that I was supposed to be saying and it was very unnerving! I tried to put over my pitch, standing in front of them and then suddenly I fainted. I just went down like a roman candle, I had collapsed.

225

They obviously called an ambulance for me as when I regained consciousness I realised I was in hospital. At the hospital they did some tests on me and the result was that there were no results really! There was no conclusive evidence as to why this had occurred.

I was well aware that something 'serious' had happened there, but I didn't know what? I had some time off work and then when I felt somewhat better I was returned to duty.

I carried on with the Community Fire Safety work for some time after this, but the organisation decided that I would be better occupied doing the Legislative side of Fire Safety and that the role of Community Fire Safety could filled by a none uniformed person. Consequently I was moved from West District Headquarters at Hereford to South District Headquarters at Malvern at the foot of the Malvern Hills. So I started my new role in South District on the 1st of February 2006.

It would be later in this year that the new fire legislation would come in to place in the U.K. This would replace the legislation 'The Fire Precautions Act' which had been in place for 35 years in the U.K. This was replaced with the 'Regulatory Reform (Fire Safety) Order.' This came into force on 1st October 2006. This made a huge impact on the way that the Fire Service operated in a Fire Safety office and how the inspecting Officers would work.

Previously the Fire Safety Officer would only inspect certain premises that would be covered by 'The Fire Precautions Act'. This piece of legislation didn't cover every type of business. However, the new legislation applied to every business premises throughout the country. Any building that was not a private domestic home would be covered by the Order. Each business would have to do a Fire Risk Assessment and if they felt that they were not capable of doing this, they would have to get an independent advisor (Fire Risk Assessor.) in to do the job.

It was not the job of the Officers of the Fire Safety Department to go and do the Fire Risk Assessment for them. The role of the Fire Safety Officer was to go to the business premises and rather than 'Inspect' them as it was referred to under the old legislation they would do an 'Audit' to see if they were in compliance. The Audit involved looking at the Fire Risk Assessment they had done. During which he would see if it was suitable and sufficient, and to make sure that they had taken the correct Fire Precautions in relation to their business.

So, this was quite a huge change in legislation for the Fire Service and for people who were running a business. When in the premises a Fire Officer would have a look at what was going on at the business in relation to fire issues during the Audit. He would conduct the Audit very much on his opinion at that time of how he thought the management was addressing the issue. For instance, if on arrival and asking to see the Fire Risk Assessment, and it was immediately 'whipped' out of a drawer and on reading it seemed suitable and sufficient, he may probe a little more and if everything seemed 'Hunky Dory' he would leave them alone and go away.

If however on asking to see the Fire Risk Assessment, he was asked "What is one of those?" He would certainly dig deeper and check out other things that they were not doing to comply with the Order. Things such as look at the records they had of any fire drills that had taken place. Check to see that the fire alarms where tested on a regular basis. Look to see if a suitably qualified engineer had done and annual test on the fire alarm and emergency lighting systems. And so on and so on.

Following the Audit of the business if the auditing Fire Safety Officer felt that things at the business had some short comings then he would issue an 'Improvement Notice' and they would have to achieve the items mentioned in the improvement notice, in the time allocated to do so.

If he thought it was more serious, he would issue an 'Enforcement Notice'. Or if he thought that it was such a risk to life in his professional opinion, as an ex-operational Fireman, that the business, or sections of the business should be shut down, because he fairly sure that a fire in the premises was imminent, and that if there were a fire in the building people would almost definitely get killed, he would issue a 'Prohibition Notice'. This would prevent the use of that part of the business or all of the business entirely.

So, that is how we worked as auditing Fire Safety Officers. This would ensure that all the businesses were in compliance with the current new legislation.

Unfortunately for me things from there went a little downhill again because I was in the photo copying room at the office and I went down like a Roman candle again! I had had another fit and collapsed in the middle of August 2006. What the bloody hell is going on here? I was somewhat baffled as to WHAT THE HELL WAS GOING ON? I am just getting into the job that I loved and feeling in full flow and then Bosh! Down I would go. As you can imagine, this was somewhat worrying and frustrating! Grrrrrrrr!

It was about this time during my time in my Fire Service career the Queen also gave me a Long Service and Good Conduct Medal for being in the Fire Service for so many years. There is nothing that I possess, and that I treasure more than my medals from the Queen of England. If someone were to break into my home and steal something from me, take my wallet, take my car keys. Even take my beloved 2cv, TAKE ANYTHING! But please, don't take my medals. Not my medals. Because that would break my heart! They are really not worth anything of financial value anyway.

So anyway on my return to work again things went well for a while and I loved it being at the Fire Safety Office with Jan and Ness and the other Fire Safety Officers. I felt at that stage that I really was saving lives! Not by going out and fighting fires, but by helping people to understand the new legislation and guiding them in the way that they needed to go. Pro-active as opposed to post-active fire-fighting I called it.

It was sometime around then that unfortunately, that my wife Tracy and I fell out after all the number of years of living at Rosehill. These things happen with people and something that I regret to this day! Perhaps she didn't like her husband keep falling down! We had no children during our married life so it was not the end of the world. So, we had to sell on Rosehill and go our different ways. Such a shame, but as they say in the Fire Service, "shit happens and then you die."

I hold it true, whate'er befall;
I feel it, when I sorrow most;
'Tis better to have loved and lost.
Than never to have loved at all.

Success is the ability to go from failure to failure without losing your enthusiasm!

We managed to get a good price on the sale of the house which we had done up since we brought it. We had put a lot of effort in improving the property and we made a good profit on Rosehill, which we split straight down the middle. At the time I thought that it was only fair for Tracy and me to divide the money we had made on the property as we had both worked on it over the years.

After shopping around a little I brought a house in a place called Bromyard, where I am living when writing this book. It was another house that needed some fixing up, I don't know what it is with me? I seem to be obsessed with buying houses that need to be worked upon? Perhaps that is just another way of how I made some additional income outside of the Service.

When Tracy and I went our separate ways, she made a decision that she thought that the two dogs Poppy and Tom should not be split up because they had lived together for so long and were fond of each other that the right thing to do was to keep them together. I agreed with her and so after all the years that Tom had been her dog she would have to let him go, to come and live with me, Poppy and Scorcher at Bromyard.

Tracy and I had sold our beloved Rosehill and in June of 2007 we went our separate ways, how sad. Tracy went off to live with a friend for a short while before she brought a house in Hereford and I moved into my new house in Bromyard. So now another stage of my life was to begin.

CHAPTER TWENTY TWO

FIRS ORCHARD

The house that I had brought in Bromyard is called 4 Firs Orchard and is a semi-detached place with a small garden at the rear but a very large garden on the side. There is a garage for a car that is part of the property, in which I keep the beloved 2cv, and also a space at the front of the property to park my second car yet another Citroen, a Citroen Berlingo.

The strange thing about Firs Orchard is that there is no house that is number two? How can that be? I think that somehow in the past when the houses were built the plan was to eventually build a number 2 Firs Orchard, but it never happened. So the piece of land was allocated to number four in which I live. Of course when I brought the property I was happy about this because the land had just been left and was completely overgrown. I could make another really nice garden there.

It was in December 2007 when I was living at Bromyard that poor old Tom, Tracy's old dog had to be put down. He had had a fit (Hey, I know about these things!) and was obviously not himself. He was clocking on in years and that's what happens to pets! I called Tracy who then was living not far away in Hereford because she was still working at Kingspan. She came over and had a look at Tom and we took him to the vet.

The vet took a look at him and shook his head. The time had come. Tom was put down and I have to admit there were a few tears that day. The vet asked me if I would like him cremated and that I could then have the ashes. I said that

I would and that is what happened. It was nice of them to do that. The ashes even came back in a nice little wooden box and had a brass plate on it with his name on. I have to say that having a pet can be such a good time and also such an emotional experience!

Things went well for a while until in February 2008 I did another of my Roman candle impressions at work, and was again carted off to hospital. This was starting to become a regular occurrence! After leaving hospital I had a visit to my General Practitioner Doctor or my G.P. She put me on some tablets designed to prevent this from happening. This was alright for a period and things carried on as normal.

Then later in the year when I was sitting at my desk at work I could feel my back itching. It felt like I had got a bit of sun on my back which was possible as I had been working in my garden at the weekend with my shirt off. I was wrong about this, it was not sunburn at all it was a bad reaction to the medication the Doctor had put me on. It was a rash and this rash spread all over my body, head to toe! Jesus Christ! If it wasn't one thing it was another!

Obviously I had to take some MORE time off work and paid another visit to the doctor. The doctor made it plain that I would have to come off that drug as I was having an allergic reaction to the medication. So that was that.

It was not long after this that I did yet another Roman candle impression and yet another trip to the hospital. Golly I was getting somewhat fed up with this now and I knew that my employers where starting to seriously think about having to let me go. After going to the hospital I went to see my G.P. again and she put on another drug different from the other one that I had the reaction to.

It was at this time that Ma had paid some professional fence builders to come and put a good strong ship lapped fence around my garden and make a good gate to provide me with the privacy that I wanted. I chiselled in some of my own money into the pot to get them to bring in the digger to heave out all the trees and bushes that were there in the potential garden. Why did I do this? Well after my experiences with the mini digger in the garden at Rosehill, I thought that this would be the best and safest way of doing it!

The garden was not as large as the previous one I owned at Rosehill, but of a fair size and I wanted to create a lawn, and a vegetable patch. I wanted to make the cleared garden into two split levels with the lawn slightly higher than the vegetable patch. I knew that my Ma's friend Tony was by profession a dry stone waller and I had seen some of his work previously. AMAZING STUFF! The man was a natural, so I thought hmmm, if I invite them over they may help me achieve this.

It's a bloody good fence and they done a great job, so thanks for that Ma. Anyway, what happened was that I had a girlfriend at that time called Janie. She lived in the small town of Bromyard as did I. I had been going out with her for a while and we had been to my lovely Niece Amanda's wedding not so long back.

We were getting on alright and so she said. "Well, as you only have the two bedrooms available in your house. Why don't we let your Mother, Tony and Con come and stay at my house?" She had a four bedroom house in another part of the town. I thought that was a blinding idea! That would give them some nice free accommodation and they could help me with the wall.

So, that is what happened. Conrad, Ma and Tony came to visit me in Herefordshire, and help me build the wall in the garden. This was in the spring of 2009. There was plenty of natural stone that I had piled up near to where I wanted the wall built.

Prior to their visit I followed the instructions from Tony which he gave to me over the telephone. I dug out all the footings and then mixing the concrete up on a board, I made the footings for the wall below ground level.

Once Ma, Tony and Con arrived late on the Saturday morning after driving up from Oxfordshire, we got on with the job. Ma supervised, Tony and Con laid the stone and I was the 'muck' man. When the wall was being built Tony laid most of the stone, dry stone walled, but occasionally he would put in a bit of cement that had been mixed up by me for additional strength when required. The mixed up cement was what was referred to as the 'muck'. As the building of the wall continued Tony would shout out to me "MORE MUCK REQUIRED!" and I would have to go off and knock up some more 'muck'.

The wall gradually took shape and form and by the end of the day it was starting to look good. On the Sunday morning we made and early start and cracked on with it. "MORE MUCK REQUIRED!" By the time I had knocked up that lot (Knocked up meaning mixed together.) Tony would be calling "MORE MUCK REQUIRED!"

As they had to go home later that day unfortunately we didn't get to finish the wall completely. I said that I would finish it later, time permitting.

Unfortunately, the wall is still not finished at the time of writing this, because I had planted up my garden and was growing all my vegetables at the time and they got in the way of finishing the 'wall'. Then I started writing, using my typing skills taught to me by Nick, and created this book. However, I do intend to get that done in the spring before I plant up the vegetable patch. So it will be another case of "MORE MUCK REQUIRED!"

Well eventually it happened. The Fire Service had been giving my case some scrutiny for some time and the management had to make a discussion, the upshot of it was that I would have to leave the Fire Service. I had been given early retirement. I had not long to go before my official retirement date anyway.

They had no choice really and I don't hold that against anyone. I loved my time in the Service, but to keep a man on who cannot be put back on operational duties if required is not on and that is fair enough. If I were absolutely fit and healthy, I would not want to enter a burning building with a man that I had serious reservations and concerns about. You need to completely trust your buddy in those situations. You need to know that he can 'Cut the mustard' if required. And he is not going to go down like the Roman candle just when you need to get someone out in a hurry. You just cannot take that gamble. So that was that!

When I left the Fire Service I was at a loss of what to do for a while. Well the house certainly needed looking at, as so far I had only got as far as rewiring the house, putting in a central heating system and decorating the living room. The rest of the house still needs decorating. Obviously there had been major work done on the gardens so they were fine. Did I want to seek out another job?

After pottering about for about a month I had the idea. I was thinking to myself, well I can type. I have some interesting stories to tell. So what about writing a book?

I loved my job in the Fire Service, and I was very sorry to leave the Service. It was said by David Henry Thoreau, that love must be as much a light as it is a flame. How true is that!

As I have never written a book before it was a totally new experience for me. As a mere ex-Soldier and ex-Fireman how would I go about writing a book?

Well begin at the beginning I suppose! So that is exactly what I did. The whole experience was a real emotional roller coaster ride.

Most of the things that I have put in this book, are in my opinion, things I think that people would find interesting or amusing. I have only written this book telling the truth and the things that I feel the reader would want know about.

Sometimes I would be typing away and have tears of laughter rolling down my cheeks while laughing my head off. Then half an hour later I would be typing away, with tears of pure completely 'bottled up' emotion.

Then another half an hour later I would be typing and laughing my head off again. In places I was laughing so much I had tears of laughter that obscured my vision and I couldn't type as I couldn't see the computer screen! As I said, a new experience, but mostly it has been tears of laughter and not tears of sorrow or released emotion I am glad to say.

So I had to have a think. What am I going to do now? Well I have a few ideas that I have been toying with even at the time of writing this book. I think that I know now that I would like to be an author, but to be an author you need to have material to write about. In the back of my mind there is a growing idea that could evolve into something that could be my next book. We will have to wait and see about that though.

Well that's it then, thank you for reading my book, and I hope you have enjoyed reading it as much as I did in writing it.

Lightning Source UK Ltd.
Milton Keynes UK
11 December 2010

164239UK00001B/29/P